Let Every Soul
Be Jesus' Guest

Let Every Soul Be Jesus' Guest

A THEOLOGY OF THE OPEN TABLE

Mark W. Stamm

Abingdon Press
Nashville

LET EVERY SOUL BE JESUS' GUEST
A THEOLOGY OF THE OPEN TABLE

Copyright © 2006 by Abingdon Press

This book is printed on acid-free paper.

Library of Congress Cataloging-in-Publication Data

Stamm, Mark Wesley.
  Let every soul be Jesus' guest : a theology of the open table / Mark W. Stamm.
    p. cm.
  ISBN 0-687-49383-8 (binding: pbk. : alk. paper)
  1. Close and open communion. 2. Intercommunion. 3. United Methodist Church (U.S.)—Doctrines. 4. Methodist Church—Doctrines. I. Title.

  BV825.7.S73 2006
  234'.163—dc22

                                                            2005028554

06 07 08 09 10 11 12 13 14 15 — 10 9 8 7 6 5 4 3 2 1

MANUFACTURED IN THE UNITED STATES OF AMERICA

Contents

Acknowledgments

In my experience, a book like this one emerges from the midst of many conversations, and much help is needed throughout the process. I will try to name some of my conversation partners and helpers, and beg forgiveness of anyone whom I may have overlooked.

I am grateful for the encouragement of William Lawrence, my dean at Perkins School Theology, Southern Methodist University, and that of my former dean, Robin Lovin. Provision of a semester's leave and a faculty research grant were invaluable. I was able to present various portions of these materials at gatherings of the Perkins faculty, and I received spirited feedback on every occasion; I treasure the insights and diligent attention of my colleagues. In particular, I thank Marjorie Procter-Smith for reading and commenting on portions of the manuscript, and Michael Hawn for his response at the Faculty Symposium and his general encouragement of the project.

Presentations made to the following groups also helped form my thinking: The Christian Initiation Seminar of the North American Academy of Liturgy, the Sacramental Study Group of the Presbyterian Church, (USA), and the 2004 Convocation of the Order of Saint Luke. I also spent a morning in helpful conversation with members of the California-Pacific chapter of the Order of Saint Luke. Students in the "Word and Worship" course at Perkins asked many perceptive questions, as did students in my upper level seminars, particularly those in the "Agápe to Eucharist" course. Time and prudence will not allow the naming of the various United Methodist Sunday School classes, participants at Perkins continuing education events, and the clergy and laity who became conversation partners in various ways. I am continually impressed by your passion for the open table; in a sense, you forced me to pay attention.

Tom Miles, my research assistant, read the manuscript and checked the footnotes. In the process, he saved me from errors and provided a number of useful insights, as did Marcia Pounders, who also read the manuscript. Joyce Ann Zimmerman, C.PP.S., editor of the North

American Academy of Liturgy Proceedings, and Hendrik Pieterse of Quarterly Review gave permission to use and expand upon materials first published in their respective journals. Thanks to each of these and also to my editors at Abingdon Press.

Most of all, I am grateful for the support of my wife, Margaret, and son, Timothy, who have supported and understood me both when I wanted to talk incessantly about my research and when I wanted to close the door and do nothing but write. They tolerate my eccentricities and continue to welcome me into their lives.

Introduction

The very heart of Methodist identity is expressed in its invitations. All people are invited to hear the gospel, to believe it; to participate in what hymn writer Charles Wesley called "the Gospel Feast." The movement itself was designed to facilitate such invitations, and many of its heroes have been those most committed to offering them. This hymn text by Wesley, first published in 1747, expresses important Methodist heart language:

> Come, sinners, to the Gospel feast;
> Let every soul be Jesu's guest;
> Ye need not one be left behind,
> For God hath bidden all mankind.
>
> Sent by my Lord, on you I call;
> The invitation is to all:
> Come all the world; come, sinner, thou!
> All things in Christ are ready now.
>
> Come, all ye souls by sin oppressed,
> Ye restless wanderers after rest;
> Ye poor, and maimed, and halt, and blind,
> In Christ a hearty welcome find.
>
> Come, and partake the gospel feast,
> Be saved from sin, in Jesus rest;
> O taste the goodness of your God,
> And eat his flesh, and drink his blood.[1]

Wesley insisted that all Christians are the guests of Jesus, that none deserve their place at the Gospel Feast. As guests at that feast, Methodists believe that they speak for Jesus as they invite all people to join them.[2] That conviction is expressed in the impassioned communion invitations offered by many clergy. For example:

"We practice an open table. . . . That's why I love the United Methodist Church, because all are welcome—the abled and the disabled, the law breakers and the law makers . . . All are welcome. That's how we beat swords into ploughshares."[3]

Here open table means an invitation without restrictions, as in "all are welcome." One cannot find such invitations printed in the official ritual texts of the church, but it seems that they are written on the hearts of the faithful.

One can expect a similar passionate response if such an open invitation is not offered. Not long after I completed my graduate work in liturgical studies, I placed the following statement in the advertisement for my congregation's Christmas Eucharist: "All baptized Christians are invited to receive Holy Communion." Most of my liturgical studies colleagues and mentors would have approved of that statement, but several of my members were sharply critical. Why? They were critical because they heard my statement as restrictive, in spite of my gracious intentions. Members of the United Methodist Holy Communion Study Committee received similar criticism when they attempted to express the historic linkage between baptism and first communion. Few, if any, unbaptized persons are present at any particular celebration of the Eucharist. Nevertheless, many United Methodists find it deeply important to announce that such persons may come if they are moved to do so. That conviction is clearly expressed in *This Holy Mystery: A United Methodist Understanding of Holy Communion* when it states, "All who respond in faith are to be welcomed." That statement is followed immediately by its corollary, "Holy Baptism normally precedes Holy Communion."[4] In spite of that important qualifier, it is clear that United Methodists will not, as a whole, tolerate any notion of the lack of baptism as barrier to the Table.

In this book, I will explore the meaning of this deeply held conviction. How does it function within the church? How can United Methodists explain it to their ecumenical partners, much less defend it to them? As background to this investigation, in the first chapter I will cite some ancient sources that illustrate the historic linkage between baptism and the Eucharist, and I will note some of the important values embodied in that classic *ordo*. Then, I will compare the ancient *ordo* to a contemporary account of the open table. In the second chapter, I will introduce the concept of the liturgical and sacramental "exception" as a category for examining and understanding practices that diverge from the classic patterns. In chapters three through five, I will defend the United Methodist practice of the open table, using Scripture, tradition, and experience. Specifically, I will draw upon the New Testament and Wesleyan sources. I will also cite the experience of Methodists from the nineteenth century along with that of contemporary church members. As I have done in my previous work, I will assume that congregations are usually correct in their most basic, positive convictions. For instance, the assertion that Holy Communion should be "special" should not be dismissed out of hand, but rather it should be clarified, explored, and affirmed, where possible, even though the negative assertion—that it should therefore be held infrequently—might be rejected.[5] Sometimes I make this assumption about positive convictions grudgingly or apprehensively, but if liturgy is truly the work of the people, as we assert it is, then we must treat the piety and practices of the faithful as serious text for theological reflection. Sound liturgical theology must attend to the experience of the people. After making a theological defense of the open table, in chapters six through eight, I will challenge the practice of the open table, raising hard questions based on those same biblical and Wesleyan sources. As with my defense of the practice, I will also raise challenges that draw upon the experience of the people.

Throughout the book I will be asking whether this United Methodist practice of the open table is well-founded. Is it defensible? To that end, let us make some preliminary observations about "Come Sinners to the Gospel Feast," the hymn text from Charles Wesley quoted earlier. "Come Sinners . . ." has been a particularly important hymn for Methodists. Indeed, John Wesley placed it second in his *A Collection of Hymns for the Use of the People Called Methodists* (1780). Only "O for a Thousand Tongues to Sing" was placed before it.[6] It remained in a prominent position (second or third) in editions printed throughout the first half of the nineteenth century,[7] and has been included in the four major hymnals of the twentieth century.[8] The text has changed somewhat, most notably the move from "mankind" to "humankind" in the first stanza, but it remains part of the mainstream Methodist repertoire.

The story has been told about early American circuit rider Jesse Lee, who used it when he preached his first sermon in Boston (1790). His biographer William Henry Meredith relates the story:

> At the appointed time, with only a few people standing by to see what the stranger would do, he gave out the hymn beginning:
> Come sinner, to the gospel feast:
> Let every soul be Jesus' guest;

There need not one be left behind,
For God hath bidden all mankind.

Then, himself starting the tune, he made Boston Common vocal with his sonorous voice, as it called the people together by holy song. . . .

The new preacher preached what were to them new doctrines, such as free grace, full salvation, and blessed assurance of it after it is obtained. It is said that, as he was reading the couplet which says,
There need not one be left behind,
For God hath bidden all mankind

A Calvinist present shouted, "That isn't true! It is only for the elect!" or some such utterance. But Jesse Lee and the Methodist Church he represented believed that "whosoever will" are the elect, and whosoever will not, and they alone, are the non-elect.[9]

Granted, Lee used the hymn as a general invitation. Indeed, there was no service of Holy Communion offered that day. Methodists have long used the hymn in that fashion, and the current hymnal commends such a practice by offering one version for communion occasions (*UMH* 616) and a slightly different version for more general occasions (*UMH* 339). In the latter sense, "Gospel Feast" is used as a synonym for the reading and preaching of the Word, much like Vatican II texts use the phrase "more lavish fare at the table of God's Word" to speak of the church's need for a more comprehensive exposure to the Scriptures.[10]

Two emphases in Wesley's hymn are particularly important for our purposes. First, the invitation is universal, intended for all. He draws on imagery from the parable of the Great Banquet (Luke 14:15-24) to insist that all are invited ("Ye need not one be left behind"), especially those in greatest need ("ye poor, and maimed").[11] According to the final stanza of the 1780 version, persons should come immediately, without delay:

This is the time: no more delay!
This is the acceptable day;
Come in, this moment, at his call,
And live for him, who died for all![12]

Second, even though the hymn has been used as a general invitation to receive the Gospel, references to Holy Communion are unmistakably present. The fourth stanza of the 1780 version, stanza three in *The*

United Methodist Hymnal, delivers the following exhortation intended for all humankind:

> Come, and partake the gospel feast,
> Be saved from sin, in Jesus rest;
> O taste the goodness of your God,
> And eat his flesh, and drink his blood.[13]

Taken literally, the hymn insists that sinners should hurry to the Table as soon as they are awakened to their need, whether they have been properly churched or not, whether baptized or not. With good reason one might insist that the Wesley brothers, having been Church of England priests in good standing, never would have considered such a thing. One might insist that the "come . . . and live for him" implies a journey of sacramental formation culminating in the Eucharist, at the least after one has learned the catechetical responses, taken the vows of baptism, and received the water bath administered in the Triune Name. One might even insist that "this is the acceptable day" and "this moment" should be understood as the continuing eschatological moment of Christ's presence, and not "this moment" in the literal sense.

One might also observe that we are, after all, dealing with a poem here, and thus Wesley's phrasing was an exercise in hyperbole. One might argue that such a lyrical invitation should never be understood as a proper sacramental rubric, as a decent and orderly expression of the church's will. Moreover, one might insist that we should not separate this hymn from everything else that the Wesley brothers said about baptism and admission to the Table, even though that teaching is far from systematic.

After all objections are noted, however, "Come, Sinners, to the Gospel Feast" is part of the Wesleyan liturgical witness; it clearly invites all persons to the Table, and it invites them to come without delay. Sentiments and convictions like those expressed in this hymn are a central part of mainstream United Methodist thought and practice, and they reflect important biblical themes. Those values are expressed in the call to the open table. In the remainder of this book, I will seek to articulate a deeper understanding of this practice, both its prospects and its potential problems.

Chapter One

What Is Required for Admission?

STORIES ABOUT THE INVITATION

What is required for admission to Holy Communion? The church's discernment about this issue is rooted in Scripture; but reference to the Bible rarely settles the matter. Which Scripture texts are decisive, and why? The church has often appealed to the so-called Institution Narratives (Matthew 26:26-29, Mark 14:22-25, Luke 22:14-23, 1 Corinthians 11:23-26), but they do not easily resolve the issue. In Matthew's account of that last meal, even the betrayer Judas dips his hand in the bowl with Jesus (Matthew 26:23). Does that witness say anything about which persons we may invite, or is it irrelevant?

The 1 Corinthians text is part of a teaching that addresses meal practices gone awry. In that congregation, the wealthy members were arriving early and charging ahead with their meal, leaving little for their less-fortunate, less-leisured sisters and brothers. Paul called the assembly to "wait for one another," to gather the whole church before beginning the holy meal (1 Corinthians 11:33). No church member should be excluded, says this text, although nothing is said about outsiders.[1]

One finds many other biblical passages that refer to meals and banquets. In the Parable of the Great Banquet (Luke 14:12-24) Jesus says,

> When you give a luncheon or a dinner, do not invite your friends or your brothers or your relatives or rich neighbors, in case they may invite you

in return, and you would be repaid. But when you give a banquet, invite the poor, the crippled, the lame, and the blind." . . . Go out into the roads and lanes, and compel people to come in, so that my house may be filled. (Luke 14:12b-13, 23)

Does this parable reflect an early Christian invitation to communion? In the Parable of the Wise and Foolish Maidens, those who prepared themselves are welcomed to the wedding banquet and those who did not prepare are denied entrance; "and the door was shut" (Matthew 25:10). Does this passage reflect an early Christian understanding about admission to the Table, albeit a different one? Scholars will differ regarding the extent to which these banquet stories reflect the Eucharistic practices of ancient Christians. They do, however, belong to the contemporary church, and Christians are free to hear them in dialogue with their communion practices. Nevertheless, they do not provide us with direct rubrics and complete ritual texts.

The development of appropriate ritual practices is left to the churches, and that discernment process continues today. The churches shape their ritual practices in dialogue with (1) Scripture, (2) Christians of other times and places, and (3) their congregations and cultures. Persons within churches must decide how to administer their sacramental rites, and it is altogether likely that different groups of Christians will come to differing conclusions. Liturgical diversity has existed throughout the history of the church, and it persists today.[2]

Churches have answered our question in a variety of ways. An early second-century document, *The Didache*, said, "You must not let anyone eat or drink of your Eucharist except those baptized in the Lord's name. For in reference to this the Lord said, 'Do not give what is sacred to dogs.'"[3] Another second-century document, *The First Apology of Justin Martyr*, includes the expectation that all baptized Christians receive communion every Lord's Day, yet none but the baptized were admitted.[4] In contrast, during many late medieval masses the priest alone received communion while the laity usually received but once a year, on Easter.[5] The English Reformers of the sixteenth century insisted that clergy and laity commune together, but theirs was not a simple return to the ancient baptismal norm. Learning the short catechism and confirmation were required, so young children were kept away.[6] Others could be warned away as well. Priests were also instructed to exclude unrepentant sinners and persons who were estranged from one another.[7]

Contemporary Catholic doctrine insists that only Catholics receive communion; that is, those in full communion with the Bishop of Rome. In contrast, most United Methodists have practiced an "open table," allowing all Christians to receive, and many will defend their right to welcome even nonbaptized seekers. To varying degrees, all of these practices draw upon biblical models and insights from Christian tradition.

As witnessed in *This Holy Mystery*, two of these patterns are given serious consideration by United Methodists: (1) the early church baptismal norm as witnessed in *First Apology* and (2) the open table.[8] In this chapter, I will review Justin Martyr and then a contemporary witness to the open table. Having done that analysis, I will offer several short vignettes that raise questions about the meaning of the ancient norm as it is actually practiced in contemporary churches.

JUSTIN MARTYR, FIRST APOLOGY: WITNESS TO AN EARLY CHURCH NORM

First Apology (circa 150 C.E.) offers a defense of Christianity in the face of Roman imperial power. It was a hostile environment, where martyrdom was always a possibility.[9] Indeed, Justin himself was martyred, thus gaining his title.

This treatise pursues a difficult agenda. On the one hand, Justin insisted that Christians were loyal, tax-paying citizens, believers and not atheists, and thus no danger to the empire.[10] On the other hand, Justin argued that Christians were different, set apart for a morality and religious practice superior to that followed by the pagans, whose myths and rites were little more than demonic imitations of the Christian sacraments.[11] Within this context, he described their practice of baptism and admission to communion.

As many as are persuaded and believe that what we teach and say is true, and undertake to be able to live accordingly, are instructed to pray and to entreat God with fasting, for the remission of their sins that are past, we praying and fasting with them. Then they are brought by us where there is water, and are regenerated in the same manner in which we were ourselves regenerated. For, in the name of God, the Father and Lord of the universe, and of our Saviour Jesus Christ, and of the Holy Spirit, they then receive the washing with water. For Christ also said, "Except ye be born again, ye shall not enter into the kingdom of heaven."

And for this [rite] we have learned from the apostles this reason. Since at our birth we were born without our own knowledge or choice, by our parents coming together, and were brought up in bad habits and wicked training; in order that we may not remain the children of necessity and of ignorance, but may become the children of choice and knowledge, and

may obtain in the water the remission of sins formerly committed, there
is pronounced over him who chooses to be born again, and has repented
of his sins, the name of God the Father and Lord of the universe....[12]

But we, after we have thus washed him who has been convinced
and has assented to our teaching, bring him to the place where
those who are called brethren are assembled, in order that we may
offer hearty prayers in common for ourselves and for the baptized
[illuminated] person, and for all others in every place, that we may
be counted worthy, now that we have learned the truth, by our
works also to be found good citizens and keepers of the commandments.... Having ended the prayers, we salute one another
with a kiss. There is then brought to the president of the brethren
bread and a cup of wine mixed with water; and he taking them,
gives praise and glory to the Father of the universe, through the
name of the Son and of the Holy Ghost, and offers thanks at considerable length for our being counted worthy to receive these
things at His hands. And when he has concluded the prayers and
thanksgivings, all the people present express their assent by saying
Amen. This word Amen answers in the Hebrew language to
genoito [so be it]. And when the president has given thanks, and
all the people have expressed their assent, those who are called by
us deacons give to each of those present to partake of the bread
and wine mixed with water over which the thanksgiving was pronounced, and to those who are absent they carry away a portion.[13]

And this food is called among us *Eucheristra* [the Eucharist], of which no
one is allowed to partake but the man who believes that the things which
we teach are true, and who has been washed with the washing that is for
the remission of sins, and unto regeneration, and who is so living as
Christ has enjoined. For not as common bread and common drink we
receive these; but in like manner as Jesus Christ our Saviour, having been
made flesh by the Word of God, had both flesh and blood for our salvation, so likewise have we been taught that the food which is blessed by
the prayer of His word, and from which our blood and flesh by transmutation are nourished, is the flesh and blood of that Jesus who was
made flesh. For the apostles, in the memoirs composed by them, which
are called Gospels, have thus delivered unto us what was enjoined upon
them; that Jesus took bread, and when He had given thanks, said, "This
do ye in remembrance of Me, this is My body;" and that, after the same
manner, having taken the cup and given thanks, He said, "This is my
blood;" and gave it to them alone. Which the wicked devils have imitated
in the mysteries of Mithras....[14]

And we afterwards continually remind each other of these things. And the wealthy among us help the needy; and we always keep together; and for all things wherewith we are supplied, we bless the Maker of all through His Son Jesus Christ, and through the Holy Ghost. ... [15]

In *First Apology*, the eating and drinking of the Eucharist stands at the center of a complex matrix of relationships, doctrinal understandings, and ethical obligations. I will discuss these, and their relationship to the question of admission to the Table, under two broad headings. First, the church is the community that says "Amen" to the Gospel, both by words and actions. Second, the church is a family born of the Spirit, a fellowship of mutual support and obligation.

THE COMMUNITY THAT SAYS "AMEN" TO THE GOSPEL

The "Amen" is the primary liturgical response of the gathered congregation. After receiving the offerings of bread and wine and mixing the contents of the chalice, the president would offer a long prayer of thanksgiving. Perhaps the president would give thanks for Creation and for God's work in calling, delivering, and forming the Hebrew people. In all likelihood, he would give thanks for the life and teachings of Jesus, for his Passion, Death, Resurrection, for his continuing presence in the community, and his coming again in glory. Perhaps he would ask that the Spirit make Christ's presence effective in and through the sacramental body and blood, and through their bodies offered as a living sacrifice. As Justin witnessed, when he finished his prayers and thanksgivings, "all the people present express their assent by saying Amen."[16] By their "Amen," the people publicly professed their assent to the prayer offered by the president, that it expressed their faith.

Such assent was deeply rooted in the life and self-understanding of Justin's church community. His description of Christian Initiation (the process of spiritual formation and ritual acts by which one becomes a member of the church) came after he had gone to great lengths to indicate the many ways in which Christians were different from the rest of Roman society. As noted earlier, the church had a different sacred narrative, a different understanding of God, and a different ethic.[17] They were not trying to be like their culture—quite the opposite, in fact. Candidates to enter the church were those who "are persuaded and believe that what we teach and say is true, and undertake to live accordingly."[18] Through prayer and fasting they separated from the old ways. These candidates had decided to enter this new life. There was no entrance without their assent. Nevertheless, just as they were brought into this world through natural birth, so they were brought into the church by the new birth of baptism. God had washed them, illuminated their minds in the way of the Gospel, and made them part of the church.[19]

> Only after baptism were they admitted to the Eucharist, and not before.

> And this food is called among us **Eucaristia** [the Eucharist], of which no one is allowed to partake but the man who believes that the things which we teach are true, and who has been washed with the washing that is for the remission of sins . . .[20]

Justin continued,

> For not as common bread and common drink do we receive these; but in like manner as Jesus Christ our Saviour . . .[21]

Thus the Eucharist is food, but not "common" food. It is the offering of the elements by the people, the thanksgiving by the president, and the "amen" of the people. Through baptism, one is admitted to the community of people who can say this "Amen," even in the face of great opposition.

OBLIGATIONS FOR THE FAMILY BORN OF THE SPIRIT

While the Eucharist involves the eating and drinking of the people, it also includes sending the elements to those who are absent along with a continuing obligation to live as the people of God. According to the logic described in *First Apology*, one cannot simply eat and drink and then walk away with no further obligation.

The church is a new family born from above, by water and the Spirit. The baptized become as one's brothers and sisters, and the Eucharist becomes a family meal. Manifestations of these dynamics are present throughout Justin's description. The sisters and brothers exchange the kiss of peace before they make their offering and share communion. Thus they maintain reconciled relationships within the church family; and through their prayers, they show their desire to live in peace with all persons everywhere.

They were obliged to care for all members of the family and especially for the weaker members. Thus the wealthy were expected to make offerings for the needy members, perhaps for persons without the support of nuclear families. Deacons took communion to those who could not be present, thereby embodying Jesus' call to care for sick persons, prisoners, and others who could not be present (see Matthew 25:31-46).[22] Indeed, theirs was a family meal, and obligation to these relationships was not an optional part of the Eucharistic service. Once one was a member of the church family, the family had a continuing responsibility to that person. An outsider could hardly be entrusted with such obligations—how could they know what to do? Nor, for that matter, would it be fair to impose them on an outsider.

The understanding of initiation and admission to the Eucharist expressed in *First Apology* is both coherent and compelling. It is consistent with the Gospel and makes sense according to its cultural context. It makes sense in a post-Christian culture in which many once again equate Christianity with committed discipleship. This ancient norm is not, of course, the only compelling, ethically coherent vision rooted in the values of the Gospel, as we will see in the next description.

A CONTEMPORARY WITNESS TO THE OPEN TABLE

Our second invitation story is a contemporary account from First United Methodist Church in Chambersburg, Pennsylvania.[23] Every Thursday evening, the church hosts a dinner for residents of their neighborhood. Participants are invited to a worship service, which follows the meal. The following newsletter article, written by their current pastor, John J. Dromazos, describes a communion service that he and Dianne B. Salter, their Minister of Evangelism and a Deacon in full connection, led during October 2002.

On Thursday, October 10th, it was my privilege to celebrate the Eucharist with the Thursday night supper crowd. I did not think much about it when Dianne asked me to be the one to consecrate the bread and cup, but I did feel "my heart strangely warmed" as we formed a circle and passed the bread and cup to all those in Fellowship Hall. It mattered not whether they were card carrying United Methodists or baptized Christians for that matter. As I began, a silence fell upon the room. If any of you have helped on Thursday evenings, you know that silence is not very often present. But here we were, receiving Christ's body and blood, and I felt the very presence of the living Christ in that room. We all received Christ's gifts. Some made the sign of the cross. Others bowed in prayer as if being touched by Christ himself. It didn't matter how we did it. Dianne gave a brief homily, and I asked them to meditate after a prayer of confession while I sang a very ancient version of "Lord Have Mercy." What mattered was that a profound unity of mind and spirit took place, and I knew the Unseen Guest was present to all.

John Wesley once remarked that the Sacrament of Holy Communion is a converting Sacrament. I don't know if anyone became a disciple of Jesus Christ that night, and I most likely will never know. I pray that some life was touched and transformed and yes, converted to give up alcohol and drug abuse, and whatever addiction and demon that is keeping them from becoming fully human. Then, their prayer requests were prayed over. Here were the most heart wrenching requests, but also there were numerous statements of gratitude for the food and those who prepared it. My heart was warmed again. If any doubt the effectiveness of providing this Thursday night meal, I invite you to come and witness for yourself the impact of this ministry. You too may find your "hearts strangely warmed."

Yours, John.[24]

Like its second-century counterpart, in this contemporary witness the eating and drinking of the Eucharist stands at the center of a complex matrix of relationships, doctrinal understandings, and ethical obligations. I will discuss two primary values expressed in this description, each of which relates to the question of admission to the Eucharist: (1) Experience as a source of theological insight, and (2) Compassion and conversion as more important than strict obedience to church rubrics and traditions.

EXPERIENCE AS A SOURCE OF THEOLOGICAL INSIGHT

As one can see in the two references to "hearts strangely warmed," Pastor Dromazos appeals to his experience as justification for this open invitation.[25] The phrase "hearts strangely warmed," of course, comes from John Wesley's Journal for May 24, 1738. In that passage, Wesley describes his experience in a Moravian society meeting on Aldersgate Street, London.

> In the evening I went very unwillingly to a society in Aldersgate Street, where one was reading Luther's Preface to the Epistle to the Romans. About a quarter before nine, while he was describing the change which God works in the heart through faith in Christ, I felt my heart strangely warmed. I felt I did trust in Christ, Christ alone for salvation, and an assurance was given me that he had taken away *my* sins, even *mine*, and saved *me* from the law of sin and death.[26]

American Methodists commonly refer to this event as John Wesley's "conversion experience." Recent scholarship has questioned the importance of this particular event in Wesley's theology and personal history;

nevertheless, one cannot doubt its importance in the eyes of American Methodists.[27] To speak of the "heart strangely warmed" is a shorthand way of appealing to the importance of experience for Methodist theological reflection.

To what am I referring when I use the word "experience?" Is appeal to experience simply a convenient way to justify any practice or belief? It may indeed work that way on occasion—just as persons have used Scripture and Tradition to justify all manner of unfortunate practices—but that is not how I am referring to experience in this particular case. Pastor Dromazos' appeal to experience reflects a deep sense of discernment manifested in compassion and theological insight. It speaks to biblical, theological, and spiritual insight that is *felt* more than *verbalized*. The insight arises out of a deep sense of the biblical story, a deep sense of relationship with the God made known in Jesus Christ. His particular insight was crystallized—"the heart strangely warmed"—as he stood in the immediate presence of persons in need, and it might not have been realized apart from them. Again, responding in the face of human need is part of the Jesus tradition (see, for instance, Mark 6:30-44, 7:24-30). Such appeals to experience are most authentic when expressed by persons who are well formed in the Scriptures and the Tradition of the church. In any event, it is a mistake to insist that an insight is theologically valid only if it has been properly verbalized, because feeling and thinking are not separated in human experience.

COMPASSION AND CONVERSION MORE IMPORTANT THAN RUBRICS

In this description of the Thursday night Eucharist, compassion and conversion are more important than obedience to ecclesiastical rubrics and traditions. These categories are not, of course, mutually exclusive. One finds many traditional elements witnessed and affirmed in this description. After all, the church leaders described here did choose *Holy Communion* as a means for serving their guests when they might have assisted them in any number of other ways: through family counseling, through literacy training, medical care, and even political advocacy. Any of those methods could have been a justifiable form of ministry. On the occasion described, however, the church offered the Eucharist. A homily was preached and intercessions made. The pastor took bread and cup, over which he offered a prayer of consecration. He referred to the consecrated elements as "Christ's body and blood," that is, in deeply traditional language. He led the people in a prayer of confession and sang a *kyrie eleison*. He expressed his belief that the Risen Christ ("the Unseen Guest") was present in the gathering. Pastor Dromazos was referring to recognizable Christian practices and he was describing them in traditional terms; yet he made an equally clear decision to ignore traditional rubrics about admission to the Table.

Why make such a decision? In the context of a room filled with people in need, perhaps it simply did not make sense to mention those rubrics about baptism and church membership, much less enforce them. To have spoken Justin Martyr's statement that "no one is allowed to partake but the [one] who believes that the things which we teach are true"[28] might have seemed callous, against the spirit of Jesus. Thus the pastor's testimony that "It mattered not whether they were card carrying United Methodists or baptized Christians for that matter." One must be careful not to make too much of his statement. To say "it mattered not ..." is not to say that baptism and membership do not matter at all, that they are not important considerations for this congregation and the church at large. It is to say, rather, that if United Methodists are forced to choose between ecclesiastical rectitude and compassion, compassion usually will be deemed more important. In that case, the people will be fed, regardless of their credentials for admission.

A similar logic is at work in his discussion of conversion. Methodists link conversion and compassion, for they believe that God's compassion is moving people toward conversion, that is, toward a redemptive *telos* or "goal." Depending on their theological and spiritual perspective, United Methodists will speak of that goal in a variety of ways. Pastor Dromazos spoke of "transformation," liberation from addictions, and "becoming fully human." Holy Communion is rightly part of discussions about conversion, for in classical Methodist understanding, the Lord's Supper is one of the "means of grace," one of the chosen ways by which God brings forgiveness, freedom, and holiness into the lives of broken people.[29] It is a "converting sacrament" (or "converting ordinance," to use Wesley's term) that can help transform the lives of persons in deep need. Methodists believe in the redemptive power of God's grace, and that they are called to share it with all people. Such belief is an integral part of their identity.

For these reasons, if Methodists perceive a need to choose between ecclesiastical traditions and offering the means of grace, ministry in service of conversion usually will be deemed more important. That is not to say that there is an integral conflict between church order and conversion; indeed, many of the classic rubrics for fencing the Table were intended to serve the process of conversion. Rather, the point is primarily one of perception—if the rubrics are *perceived* to impede the free movement of God's grace, then those rubrics may be ignored. Such is the case especially when leaders are faced with a case of immediate human need.

FIRST CHURCH AND FIRST APOLOGY: COMPARING THE TWO INVITATIONS

The two patterns of communion invitation reviewed above emerged from quite different contexts. Not the least consideration is the fact that the second occurred over eighteen hundred years after the first, but there are other important differences, as well. In the situation addressed by Justin Martyr, the church was a minority movement within a hostile political and religious environment. They were subject to intense persecution. In order for them to survive, much less protect their spiritual integrity, they had to develop clear, well-marked ecclesiastical boundaries, and they had to work hard at caring for their weaker members. Without clear boundaries, the church was even more vulnerable to its political enemies and it was difficult to avoid falling into the non-Christian spiritual practices that surrounded them.

The situation encountered at First Church Chambersburg is considerably different. Generally speaking, in the American context persons do not expect to become martyrs. The government may be indifferent toward the churches, and even suspicious of them, but it is rarely openly hostile toward them.[30] At First Church, the church building itself is located in an old downtown neighborhood, used both for residential and commercial purposes. In that neighborhood, one finds some single-family dwellings along with a significant number of apartments and other rental properties. Some of their members live in the immediate neighborhood of the church building, but the majority commute to church from other, more affluent parts of the community. In their context, they do not need to erect boundaries nearly as much as they need to guard against constructing them. An open table gives ritual shape to that insight.

Sacramental practice is important to each of the churches described here. Each, in its own way, witnesses to the presence of Christ in the Eucharist: Justin Martyr speaks of the "transmutation" of "the food which is blessed by the prayer of His word," by which it becomes "the flesh and blood of...Jesus."[31] Pastor Dromazos witnessed that he and others "felt the very presence of the living Christ," like a touch from "the Unseen Guest."[32] There is no arid memorialism at work here—

each witnesses to the Eucharist as a vital life-changing encounter. Arguably, baptism is important in both places. In the case of Justin Martyr's church, baptism was a decisive, radical step, signaling a complete change of culture and family. In that culture, baptism put one at immediate risk. The typical First Church member would not consider baptism a life and death matter, but the rite is practiced and believed nonetheless. Most of their children are presented for baptism at an early age, according to the prevailing practice of United Methodism. Baptism holds a prominent place in many Sunday services. Their active Sunday School and Neighborhood Ministry programs are important expressions of their fidelity to the baptismal covenant.[33] Pastor Dromazos' comment that it did not matter if the communicants were "card carrying United Methodists or baptized Christians..." must not be taken to imply that baptism does not matter to him or his congregation. It means, rather, that he was willing to make an exception to the norm, for the sake of addressing the immediate need of those who were standing before him.

A major difference, then, between the two descriptions is the actual presence of people in the First Church description. People are discussed in *First Apology*, but in a general, theoretical manner. Pastor Dromazos, however, describes an encounter with specific people. That difference is critically significant, although, quite surprisingly, it is not always given its due consideration in discussions of liturgical theology and practice. Discussions about admission to the communion table can be notably abstract in character, even legalistic; yet churches seem oddly reluctant actually to enforce such rubrics, to enact what they claim to believe. Many times, when persons deemed technically unqualified according to the rubrics present themselves for communion, the clergy and other communion servers give them the sacrament anyway, in spite of the rules. They do not ask to see their baptismal certificate, nor do they check the membership rolls. Certainly there are no deacons guarding the church doors, as some ancient sources tell us they once did.[34] If a norm exists, it appears that it is but sporadically enforced. What, then, is the meaning of the norm?

Liturgical theologians often do their work according to the canon *lex orandi lex credendi*, which translated means "the law of praying is the law of believing." In other words, beliefs are revealed in practice. Indeed, much of the prayer and praise of the people, along with their sacramental practices, occurs at a pre-reflective stage. That is, the people sing their praises, make their prayers, and break bread together first, and only later do they begin to analyze, clarify, and categorize the meaning of what they have done. Beliefs exist, however, long before they have been expressed in formal analysis. Rather than calling the theological work of liturgical assemblies "pre-reflective," it may be more accurate to call it a "supra-reflective" reality, an advanced stage of reflection. Liturgical patterns and styles of worship manifest a spiritual formation deeply ingrained and felt. The Spirit given in baptism, nurtured through reflection on scripture and previous sacramental liturgies, expresses itself in deep feelings about what is appropriate in a particular moment. Such feelings are not merely subjective or capricious, for many times they are quite deeply rooted in the biblical narrative and its spirit. Thus one must take the worship of the people—including what they actually do when they invite persons to the Table—as a clear indication of their faith.

HOLY COMMUNION AND FENCES WITH HOLES: WHAT DOES THE CHURCH BELIEVE ABOUT ADMISSION TO THE TABLE?

I will now offer four short anecdotes that illustrate the gap that exists between official norms and the practice of congregations. Many readers will be able to provide similar stories of their own. Are these stories theologically significant? In the face of this evidence, anecdotal though it may be, one might question what the church actually believes about admission to communion. At the least, it appears that the various chancel fences may contain a significant number of holes.

A Visit to a Monastery

In February 1993, I attended a weekend retreat at a Catholic retreat house in Massachusetts. A friend in the Episcopal Church had attended retreats there previously and had recommended that I go. Although he assured me that I would be able to receive communion there, I decided to ask permission from the priest who would be leading the services. I told him, first of all, that I was a United Methodist elder and that I intended to remain in that office. Second, I told him that I was a regular communicant in my church, and as such, I hoped to receive communion at the retreat liturgies. Would he permit me to do so? He paused for a moment, and then he asked me, "What do you believe about the Eucharist?" I said, "I believe Jesus Christ is present there." Mine was an honest answer in the tradition of Charles Wesley who wrote thus about the sacrament: "Sure and real is the grace, the manner be unknown; only meet us in thy ways and perfect us in one."[35]

The priest assured me that I would be welcome at the Table. Thus it was that I communed at both the Saturday night and Sunday morning services, even though that retreat house was subject to the rules and discipline of the Catholic Church, which say that I was ineligible. It is possible that I would not have been admitted to the Eucharist had I been asked to subscribe to a strict definition of transubstantiation, but he did not ask that of me. One can hardly, of course, imagine asking a guest such a question. The only somewhat unusual aspect of my story is my intentional request of the priest and our subsequent conversation about the meaning of the sacrament. The fact that I was welcomed at the Table in a Catholic setting, in spite of the rules, is not particularly unusual.

A THEOLOGICAL ARGUMENT WITH AN "EXCEPTIONAL" TWIST

The second vignette comes from a faculty symposium in which I detailed some of my early thinking on the subject of open communion in the United Methodist Church. I argued that the widespread practice of the open table reflected a United Methodist "sense of the faithful" and that we could regard this practice as an exception to the ancient baptismal norm.[36] The response to my paper was pointed and challenging, as is typical of such gatherings. Some affirmed the concept of the exception, but insisted that I was overstepping in using the term "sense of the faithful." Some insisted that the American practice of the open table was not theologically motivated at all, as I was claiming. Rather, they said, it emerged from a desire to avoid giving offense that functioned along with an assertion of rugged individualism, as in "Who are *you* to tell *me* that I can't come to communion?" The critique was sharp, stimulating, and clarifying.

One critique was particularly revealing. One respondent made a strong and effective argument in favor of maintaining the ancient baptismal norm described earlier in this chapter. Having made the argument, however, he then told a story from his pastoral practice. He had done some evangelistic work in the former Soviet Union, with a newly forming Methodist church. In that congregation, the majority of persons were recent converts to Christianity. In the course of his work with these new believers, he and some colleagues were preparing to lead a communion service when it came to their attention that one of the prospective communicants had not yet been baptized. It seems that this congregation administered most of its baptisms in a local stream, by immersion, and the summer sun had not yet warmed the water to a tolerable level. The new convert desired communion, but he was not yet baptized. What would they do? According to my colleague's testimony, they decided to include him in communion anyway, without benefit of baptism.

Thus my colleague opposed the open table on normative grounds, but then he related a story in which an exception to that rule was allowed for pastoral reasons. The life of the church is filled with such statements about normative practice followed by stories about exceptions to those norms. Nevertheless, if those who lead the Eucharist set aside the norm when confronted by such pastoral circumstances, as well they might, then what is the meaning of the norm and how does it really function?

SOME BUDDHIST MONKS AND SOME ESTRANGED CHRISTIANS

A third anecdote comes from the book *Good Fences, the Boundaries of Hospitality* by Caroline Westerhoff. A group of Buddhist monks visited her Episcopal congregation. Printed in the service bulletin was a statement often used in Episcopal parishes: "All baptized persons are invited to receive Holy Communion at this altar." According to the author, when the ushers came to their pew the monks rose, came to the altar and knelt, then put forth their hands and were given communion. No one, it seems, gave them any indication that they were not to come, nor do the spoken rubrics in *The Book of Common Prayer* say as much.

Westerhoff reports that her parishioners engaged in spirited discussion about this event in the days following the visit of the monks, a discussion about the propriety of giving them communion, a discussion about the boundaries of the church. She noted that an exception had been made, but that the boundary was not broken for all time. If the monks were to return, they would need to engage them in conversation about the Eucharist and its relationship to baptism and commitment to the Christian faith. Note, however, that no one raised that question within the liturgical assembly itself.

The conversation within the parish took an interesting turn. Another person, reported the author, widened the discussion by observing that a number of persons were served communion that day even though they were not properly reconciled with their neighbors. The traditional rubric of the church says,

Ye who do truly and earnestly repent you of your sins, and are in love and charity with your neighbors, and intend to lead a new life, following the commandments of God, and walking from henceforth in his holy ways: Draw near with faith, and make your humble confession to Almighty God, devoutly kneeling.[37]

Thus those who were not reconciled with each other had no business coming, either![38]

THE POLICY OF THE CHURCH, THE PRACTICE OF THE CHURCH, AND A CONFERENCE FIELD TRIP

A final set of anecdotes comes from a recent ecumenical gathering of liturgical scholars. In a seminar discussion about the relationship of baptism and admission to Holy Communion, one United Methodist participant mentioned a well-known Catholic abbey, which commonly allows its ecumenical visitors to receive communion. Commenting on the practice of the abbey, a Catholic specialist in liturgy and canon law with some background in that community noted, "The policy of the abbey is the policy of the church." By that she meant that Catholics in full communion were the only proper recipients of communion. Having said that, however, she added, "But we don't believe we should turn away a person who presents herself." I am not at this point questioning the Roman Catholic Church's right to define access to the Table according to their discernment. What, however, is the meaning of a policy (or norm) that this congregation and many others like it decline to enforce? If all those who present themselves at the chancel are served, then is not "presentation" the norm for admission, regardless of what the canons may claim?

At that same ecumenical conference, the primary worship option for Sunday involved an invitation to participate in the regularly scheduled liturgy of the local Catholic Cathedral. As a relatively new member of the gathering, I wondered to myself, "Would I be able to receive communion?" I decided to sit in the back of the nave and watch what the other United Methodists did. Many of these Methodists were prominent scholars, whose denominational backgrounds were quite well known by the Catholic colleague who was presiding at the Table. They could not possibly present themselves incognito. When I saw them approach the Table, along with Catholics and persons of various other denominational backgrounds, then I decided that it was acceptable for me to go forward, as well. As is often the case, I was instructed by the actions of the assembly. Official ecclesiastical rubrics notwithstanding, in that particular setting non-participation would have seemed oddly disruptive, against the spirit of the assembly.

PRELIMINARY CONCLUSIONS

The stories told here are not uncommon or unusual, but represent other stories much like them. What do such occasions say about the ancient baptismal norm for admission to communion? Like a good jury member, the reader will have to decide the significance of the testimony. I will offer some preliminary conclusions.

While the anecdotes relate fairly common pastoral scenarios, they do not necessarily suggest a revision of the classically stated norm and standards for admission to Holy Communion. The cases involving Catholics and members of other denominations speak to a growing ecumenical consensus, albeit an informal one, that baptism (and only baptism) is the proper requirement for admission to the Table. In these cases the ancient norm is affirmed and attempts at stating a stricter norm are ignored. In each instance, even the cases of the not-yet-baptized convert and the nonbaptized Buddhist monks, the baptismal norm is acknowledged even though temporarily set aside.

It seems important to note that the baptismal norm, although assumed by many liturgical theologians, is not directly stated in many contemporary liturgical texts, especially those of the Protestant communions. No one issues communion tickets, as Methodists once did. The dismissal of the catechumens (that is, nonbaptized seekers) is practiced in many Catholic parishes, but it is not required.[39] Even there, no one guards the doors. We can hardly expect to claim the norm if it is not given more explicit liturgical shape, both in words and actions. For a variety of reasons, we may lack the will to do so.

There appears, however, to be something more occurring in these stories than simply a temporary setting aside of the norm for admission to the Table. It is not as if these congregations waited while an ecclesiastical court convened to weigh the evidence in a cool and dispassionate manner, eventually rendering a decision in favor of admission. Rather, in each case we have stories about committed Christians faced with the needs of people standing directly in front of them. It is difficult for persons formed in the stories of Jesus to turn away people in need, especially when they are looking those very people in the eye. For now, then, let us conclude that the church knows the wisdom of the ancient baptismal norm as well as it knows the necessity of occasionally setting it aside. I have called such decisions sacramental and liturgical exceptions. In the next chapter, I will describe the dynamic at work in these exceptions.

C h a p t e r   T w o

Sacramental and Liturgical Exceptions

DEFINITION AND APPLICATIONS

DEFINING THE CATEGORY

I will define the open table as a Methodist exception to the classical order for Christian initiation (see chapter 1). What do I mean by exception? An exception is a conscious departure from an ecclesiastical norm, yet not for disobedience or lack of faith. Sacramental and liturgical exceptions are prophetic in nature. They seek a deeper fidelity to the Gospel, a higher embodiment of Christian faith.[1] An exception will highlight meanings of the Eucharist that may be obscured by the normative pattern itself. For example, the Society of Friends does not celebrate the Lord's Supper in the ritualized sense practiced by most Christians. Some members of the Society might challenge us, however, were we to accuse them of setting aside Jesus' commandment "Do this in remembrance of me" (1 Corinthians 11:24). According to John Wesley, the only way to obey this commandment is to practice "constant communion," to receive communion at every available opportunity.[2] George Fox, founder of the Society of Friends (Quakers), shows us a different possibility. He insisted that every meal shared by Christians is the Lord's Table, an *agápe*, and an occasion for *koinonía*. Fox rejected the idea of sacraments, but he also wrote, "The bread that the saints break is the body of Christ and the cup that they drink is the blood of Jesus Christ, this I witness."[3]

What did Fox mean? With this sacramental exception, Fox and early members of the Society reminded the church that first-generation Christians knew no sharp distinction between *agápe* meals and the Lord's Supper. Their witness reminds contemporary Christians to seek a closer connection between Holy Communion and the rest of our eating and drinking. Fox's exception follows a longstanding prophetic tradition that criticizes ritual practice, and even rejects it, as a means of breaking open its deepest, most essential meanings. That the Society has experienced some difficulty maintaining Fox's understanding of the Lord's Table is a problem that we will take up toward the end of this chapter. For now, we will look at three biblical examples that illustrate the dynamics at work in sacramental and liturgical exceptions.

BIBLICAL EXAMPLES OF THE LITURGICAL EXCEPTION

"I hate, I despise your festivals" (Amos 5:21-24)

Scripture includes texts that legitimize established worship traditions as well as others that denounce them. Of the latter category, one of the best-known examples is the following from Amos, written in the mid-eighth century B.C.E.:

> I hate, I despise your festivals,
>   and I take no delight in your
>   solemn assemblies.
> Even though you offer me your
>   burnt offerings and grain
>   offerings,
>   I will not accept them;
> and the offerings of well-being of
>   your fatted animals
>   I will not look upon.
> Take away from me the noise of
>   your songs;
>   I will not listen to the melody of
>   your harps.
> But let justice roll down like
>   waters,
>   and righteousness like an
>   ever-flowing stream. (Amos 5:21-24)

God demands justice. Strict obedience to sacred calendars and sacrificial rites will not excuse injustice and oppression. When Israel did not practice such justice, Amos warned them that they would face exile and their place of worship would be destroyed. According to this text, cultic practices are not indispensable, exceptions can be made, and refusal to participate can be a faithful way to affirm a liturgy's primary values. Quite clearly, Amos believed that *God* had decided to skip the proceedings.

Dr. Martin Luther King Jr., quoted this passage in his famous "I Have a Dream" speech: "But let justice roll down like waters and righteousness like an ever-flowing stream." When he said that phrase, he was criticizing American culture while calling it to its highest values, to that day when the "liturgy" of American society would be celebrated with integrity, "with liberty and justice for all." At the very least, this passage insists that liturgical traditions are not ends in themselves; rather, they are means to the goal of justice and love. Traditions that appear to obstruct that goal may be criticized and altered. Worship that ignores it is false worship, no matter how well performed.

"Is not this the fast that I choose?" (Isaiah 58)

Isaiah chapter 58, written during the Babylonian captivity of the sixth century B.C.E., criticizes fasting rituals.[4] The people could not understand what God was doing. The trumpet had sounded calling a fast, and they had responded. They refrained from eating food, from drinking water, from sexual relations. They dressed in sackcloth, put ashes on their heads, and prostrated themselves. They said their prayers and sang Psalms. They performed the ritual correctly, so they thought, but God did not respond as they expected.[5] Even though they enacted the ritual, their captivity and their oppression did not end. The text states their obvious questions to God: "Why do we fast, but you do not see? Why humble ourselves, but you do not notice?" (Isaiah 58:3a). "Why isn't the ritual working?"

According to the prophet, their problem had little to do with their ability to follow the rubrics:

> Look, you serve your own interest
> on your fast day,
> and oppress all your workers.
> Look, you fast only to quarrel and
> to fight.

and to strike with a wicked fist.
Such fasting as you do today
    will not make your voice heard
        on high.
Is such the fast that I choose,
    a day to humble oneself?
Is it to bow down the head like a
        bulrush,
    and to lie in sackcloth and ashes?
Will you call this a fast,
    a day acceptable to the LORD? (Isaiah 58:3b-5)

Theirs was a ritual without repentance. Such a rite, no matter how meticulously performed, could not make God act on their behalf, much less could it excuse their violence. Prophetic logic—the severe logic of monotheism—insists that no ritual can compel God to act. Ritual employed as a cover for injustice is repugnant.

In response to their confusion and rebellion, the prophet redefined their fasting ritual. He offered them a liturgical exception, a ritual that was no ritual at all:

Is not this the fast that I choose:
    to loose the bonds of injustice,
    to undo the thongs of the yoke,
to let the oppressed go free,
    and to break every yoke?
Is it not to share your bread with
        the hungry,
    and bring the homeless poor into
        your house;
when you see the naked, to
        cover them,
    and not to hide yourself from
        your own kin? (Isaiah 58:6-7)

In a sense, justice becomes the new ritual, and the liturgy of justice is never performed incorrectly. The prophet insists that God will respond.

Then your light shall break forth
    like the dawn,
and your healing shall spring
    up quickly;

> your vindicator shall go
> > before you,
> > the glory of the LORD shall be
> > your rear guard.
> Then you shall call, and the LORD
> > will answer;
> > you shall cry for help, and he
> > will say, Here I am. (Isaiah 58:8-9)

How should one respond to this passage? Readers can receive this prophetic critique in either of two different, yet related, ways. One response involves returning to the ritual with a renewed appreciation of its deeper meaning, with a renewed commitment to justice and compassion. In this case, one fasts as a means to an end, as a committed participation in the suffering of others, including God. This participation then continues beyond the formal end of the cultic action. In a variant on this first response, one keeps a basic liturgical structure and makes amendments to it.

In a second response, faithful listeners might discard the ritual entirely or otherwise refuse to practice it. In choosing this more radical option, they are deciding that abuse and misrepresentation of a ritual's *telos* (or "goal") render it unredeemable. One does works of compassion in place of the old ritual. Those who reject one ritual may develop a new one in its place, beginning the process anew.

The making of sacramental and liturgical exceptions reflects the prophetic dynamics described above. One finds similar dynamics at work in the New Testament, as the following example demonstrates.

The Shift in New Testament Sacrificial Language as a Liturgical Exception

The New Testament retains the language of sacrifice, but the shape of the sacrificial cult is radically changed, along with the meaning of the language. This process is clearly expressed in the Letter to the Hebrews:

Now even the first covenant had regulations for worship and an earthly sanctuary.... But when Christ came as a high priest of the good things that have come, then through the greater and perfect tent (not made with hands, that is, not of this creation), he entered once for all into the Holy Place, not with the blood of goats and calves, but with his own blood, thus obtaining eternal redemption. For if the blood of goats and bulls, with the sprinkling of the ashes of a heifer, sanctifies those who have been defiled so that their flesh is purified, how much more will the blood of Christ, who through the eternal Spirit offered himself without blemish to God, purify our conscience from dead works to worship the living God! (Hebrews 9:1,11-14).

According to this redefinition of the sacrificial system, Jesus is the high priest as well as the one sacrifice "offered for all time" (Hebrews 10:12). He is the sacrifice that ends sacrifice.

Indeed, the author is redefining a ritual tradition. On the one hand, the worship of the Temple is rejected along with its priests and sacrifices: the gifts and sacrifices of the "first tent... cannot perfect the conscience of the worshiper" (Hebrews 9:6, 9). Christ's death is itself a sacrifice, but unlike the previous sacrifices, which were offered frequently, he makes the complete and perfect atonement for sin, making further sacrifices unnecessary (Hebrews 9:26). The old ritual system is fulfilled and abandoned. Quoting Psalm 40, the author denounces the former worship with language in the best prophetic tradition:

> Sacrifices and offerings you have
>   not desired,
>   but a body you have prepared
>   for me;
> in burnt offerings and sin offerings
>   you have taken no pleasure. (Hebrews 10:5b-6; see Psalm 40:6)

But then he takes up the very language that he has denounced and uses it as an exhortation to faithful discipleship:

> Therefore, my friends, since we have confidence to enter the sanctuary by the blood of Jesus, by the new and living way that he opened for us through the curtain (that is, through his flesh), and since we have a great priest over the house of God, let us approach with a true heart in full assurance of faith, with our hearts sprinkled clean from an evil conscience and our bodies washed with pure water. Let us hold fast to the confession of our hope without wavering, for he who has promised is faithful. And let us consider how to provoke one another to love and good deeds, not neglecting to meet together, as is the habit of some, but encouraging one another, and all the more as you see the Day approaching. (Hebrews 10:19-25)

The author has constructed a liturgical exception. The metaphors and spiritual dynamics of the sacrificial system remain, but they exist now on a higher, newly defined level.

This dynamic persists throughout the New Testament. In the Letter to the Romans, Paul used the same language of the temple cult, now redefined, to exhort the Romans to faithful discipleship:

> I appeal to you therefore, brothers and sisters, by the mercies of God, to present your bodies as a living sacrifice, holy and acceptable to God, which is your spiritual worship. (Romans 12:1)

In like manner, the author of First Peter borrows language about priesthood to describe the entire church:

> But you are a chosen race, a royal priesthood, a holy nation, God's own people, in order that you may proclaim the mighty acts of him who called you out of darkness into his marvelous light (1 Peter 2:9).

A danger exists, however, in maintaining the old language and concepts, as a type of ritual-linguistic inertia seems to pull the redefined language back toward its original meaning. Even with this renewed understanding of sacrifice, Eucharistic practice in the church drifted back toward the assumptions of the temple, to the point where the late medieval mass was understood as an efficacious sacrifice for sins offered on behalf of souls in purgatory. In that case, the dynamics of this sacrificial exception asserted themselves once again, as evidenced in the eucharistic language of *The Book of Common Prayer* in which the priest asked God to accept "this our sacrifice of praise and thanksgiving."[6] Taking its lead from Hebrews, the language of sacrifice was employed, but with a radically different meaning.

In each of the biblical cases described above, a principle, concept, or language category is maintained while its liturgical form is altered, sometimes radically. Such is the dynamic of the liturgical and sacramental exception as well as its biblical foundation. Liturgical and sacramental exceptions are practiced in all reforming movements, as ritual patterns are received, yet under a hermeneutic of suspicion.

WHY DOES THE CHURCH NEED THIS "EXCEPTION" CATEGORY?

At their best, Christian ritual patterns will embrace both traditional and prophetic dynamics, holding them in creative tension. The church's ritual should be conservative, maintaining biblical norms and hard-won spiritual insights. At the same time, it should be prophetic, embodying God's call to justice and liberation. Such a potentially creative tension is rooted at the very center of the church's life, in the person of Jesus Christ.

Traditional Dynamics, Rooted in Jesus Christ

The church conserves its ritual patterns because it believes that they are rooted in the life and ministry of Jesus Christ. When it gathers for the Eucharist, the church proclaims a Great Thanksgiving that recounts key events from his life and ministry. In particular, we remember his institution of the Eucharist:

> On the night in which he gave himself up for us,
>   he took bread, gave thanks to you, broke the bread,
>   gave it to his disciples, and said:
> "Take, eat; this is my body which is given for you.
> Do this in remembrance of me."
>
> When the supper was over, he took the cup,
>   gave thanks to you, gave it to his disciples, and said:
> "Drink from this, all of you;
>   this is my blood of the new covenant,
>   poured out for you and for many
>   for the forgiveness of sins.
> Do this, as often as you drink it,
>   in remembrance of me."[7]

Commonly called "The Words of Institution," this text functions as a biblical warrant for the Eucharist; that is, as biblical justification for it. In praying the Great Thanksgiving, we remind worshipers that Jesus gave this sacrament to the church, that we are stewards of a tradition.[8] The church does not take that stewardship lightly. We take bread and wine, we give thanks, and we share them because Jesus did those things, and we believe he commanded us to continue doing them. Of course, the narrative of Jesus builds upon the biblical narrative that he inherited as a Jew. Thus the Exodus becomes part of the church's story and we are called to live within its dynamics as well.

While the Scriptures provide the foundation for the various Eucharistic traditions, it remained for the churches to develop them, under the guidance of the Holy Spirit. Discerning the proper shape of the liturgy is a complex process that continues even today. The various churches have discerned who presides at their celebrations and how they are chosen. They have decided when they will celebrate the Eucharist, how they will prepare for it, and how they will conduct the liturgy itself. They have decided how one becomes a communicant, and how one can become ineligible for communion. The churches have discerned what matter may be used in the sacrament; that is, what constitutes proper bread and wine. They have decided how to reach out to persons who cannot attend the liturgy. There have been a variety of responses to each of these challenges and varied responses continue to emerge, all of them in dialogue with the narrative of Jesus and with culture.

In the main, the churches do not make decisions about the Eucharist lightly. Because they believe that the Holy Spirit has been at work in previous generations, they tend to respect the wisdom of their forebears and they are not quick to make major changes in the patterns they have received. Indeed, they usually defend these patterns; after all, they have been means of grace. Nevertheless, the biblical narrative that the church conserves includes the prophetic witness. Thus the church nurtures the seeds of its own liturgical critique.

Prophetic Dynamics Rooted in Jesus Christ

Continuity is commendable, generally speaking. It can also become a barrier to liberation. For instance, traditions about Eucharistic presidency developed as a safeguard against schismatic tendencies, as a way of making the members of the church "wait for one another" before beginning the Eucharist (First Corinthians 11:17-34, especially v. 33). Approximately half a century later, St. Ignatius witnessed to a similar dynamic:

> You should regard that Eucharist as valid which is celebrated either by the bishop or by someone he authorizes. Where the bishop is present, there let the congregation gather, just as where Jesus Christ is, there is the Catholic Church. Without the bishop's supervision, no baptisms or love feasts are permitted.... He who acts without the bishop's knowledge is in the devil's service.[9]

Such divisions of labor have often served the church well, but this pattern that developed for the sake of unity can become divisive and hierarchical, dividing the clergy from the laity. When presidency is restricted to one gender, the church is divided in another way. When the granting of clergy status is tied too closely to a political regime, as it was in the Church of England of John Wesley's day, patterns for choosing clergy can hinder the church's work of mission and evangelism, a problem Wesley's movement tried to address.

When such a gap develops between God's holiness and human attempts at faithfulness (however well-intentioned), believers may hear a different voice of continuity, the voice of the prophetic tradition. It, too, is rooted in the life and work of Jesus Christ. For the sake of those in need, Jesus disregarded Sabbath regulations (Mark 2:23-28, Matthew 12:1-14) and he broke purity laws (Mark 2:15-17, 7:1-23). He enacted a prophetic sign when he drove the moneychangers out of the Temple (John 2:13-22). He drew upon the prophetic tradition when he proclaimed:

> "The Spirit of the Lord is upon
>   me,
>   because he has anointed me
>   to bring good news to the
>   poor.
> He has sent me to proclaim release
>   to the captives
>   and recovery of sight to the
>   blind,
>   to let the oppressed go free,
> to proclaim the year of the Lord's
>   favor." (Luke 4:18-19, see also Isaiah 61:1-2)

The prophetic spirit speaks the truth of the God who sets captives free, the God who will allow no other gods. Because Jesus walked in this spirit, the church must nurture the voice of prophecy that calls it to deeper faithfulness, to the core values of the liturgy.

This category of the liturgical and sacramental exception allows the church to affirm the values of continuity—that is, of establishing norms—while also discerning the prophetic impulse of the Spirit. From its beginnings, the Methodist movement has discerned a particular call to stand at the nexus of tradition and the prophetic witness. Thus Methodist ecclesiology is characterized by the making of exceptions.

METHODISM: AN ECCLESIOLOGY CHARACTERIZED BY THE MAKING OF EXCEPTIONS

As John Wesley described it, the Methodist movement was an "extraordinary" movement within the Church of England.[10] What did he mean by this phrase? "Extraordinary" should be defined over against its corollary term, "ordinary." Wesley defined the phrase "ordinary channels" in his sermon "The Means of Grace."[11]

> By "means of grace" I understand outward signs, words, or actions ordained of God, and appointed for this end—to be the *ordinary* channels whereby he might convey to men preventing, justifying, or sanctifying grace . . .
>
> The chief of these means are prayer, whether in secret or with the great congregation; searching the Scriptures (which implies reading, hearing, and meditating thereon) and receiving the Lord's Supper, eating bread and drinking wine in remembrance of him; and these we believe to be ordained of God as the ordinary channels of conveying his grace to the souls of men.[12]

This treatise emerged out of his controversy with Moravian Quietists of the early 1740s, who taught that one should not use the means of grace prior to justification; to do so was to seek salvation by works. Wesley disagreed, insisting that the faithful seeker waits for God in and through these ordinary means.[13] While the means are vitally important, Wesley taught that they must be understood in relation to the proper end of life in Christ, love.[14] When speaking on this point, Wesley's language echoes that of the prophetic texts described earlier.

> But we allow that the whole value of the means depends on their actual subservience to the end of religion; that consequently all these means, when separate from the end, are less than nothing, and vanity; that if they do not actually conduce to the knowledge and love of God they are not acceptable in his sight; yea, rather, they are an abomination before him; a stink in his nostrils; he is weary to bear them . . .[15]

His discussion about the proper "end of religion" makes sacramental and liturgical exceptions possible, if not necessary. In a Wesleyan understanding, the means of grace are not an absolute value, not an end in themselves. If the practice of the appointed means is not tending toward "the end of religion," then the church must question its *praxis*, if not alter it. As we shall see later in this chapter, Wesley employed such logic at key points in the development of the Methodist movement, arguing that various practices should be understood as extraordinary measures.

What was at stake in these assertions about the extraordinary character of Methodism and its practices? On the one hand, they preserve a conservative respect for the church and its ordinary means of grace. Extraordinary measures exist in dialogue with ordinary means, as Methodism existed in dialogue with its Anglican context. Methodism, Wesley believed, was not like other movements that emerged within the established church, such as the Presbyterians, the Independents, the Anabaptists, and the Friends.[16] Wesley went to great lengths to assert that Methodism was not a schismatic or independent movement; quite the opposite, he claimed: "Methodism, so called, is the old religion, the religion of the Bible, the religion of the primitive church, the religion of the Church of England."[17] In spite of this commitment to the church, when Wesley's ministry was rejected in congregations of the established church, he preached in other places, even in the open air. He wrote, "Not daring to be silent, after a short struggle between honour and conscience I made a virtue of necessity, and preached in the middle of Moorfields."[18] Such decisions about using extraordinary means were not made lightly, but they were made nonetheless. One sees here a dual commitment. On the one hand, he was trying to maintain commitment to the traditions of the church. On the other hand, he claimed the prophetic freedom to innovate within those traditions as necessary. There remains some question as to whether Wesley's dual commitment was little more than a legal fiction.[19] What matters most of all, however, is that Wesley believed in the dual commitment and held it as a workable ideal. His was the beginnings of an ecclesiology based on the making of exceptions, one that Methodists continue to hold as an ideal even when they fall short of actually practicing it. Methodists are committed to maintaining historic ecclesiastical norms. They are equally committed to their calling to set them aside when necessary.

Does Methodism present a weak, confusing ecclesiology? It may seem so if one insists on defining it solely in terms of Catholic and Anglican norms, but Wesley did more than that. It may appear deficient if one is disheartened by the seemingly endless contention about the meaning of ministry and sacramental practices, not to mention the continuing discussions about the place of gays and lesbians in the church. It may be, however, that a church living at the nexus of tradition and prophetic freedom will never be done discussing the meaning and shape of its ecclesial vocation. Its processes will always seem a bit messy. As Scott Jones wrote,

One of the least well-defined areas of United Methodist doctrine is its ecclesiology. United Methodists view themselves as a church.... Yet, the tensions between the Catholic and Protestant parts of its heritage, between its Anglican doctrinal roots and experience as a missional society, and between its concern for correct doctrine and the pragmatic focus on results all lead to a mixture of views in tension with each other.[20]

The church and its leaders may decide that living within these tensions is a potential strength, as Wesley did. Let us look at some of the ways he applied this dual commitment.

Examples from the Practice of John Wesley

The Use of Lay Preachers, Including Women

Wesley's understanding of the Gospel led him to become an itinerant preacher. As the movement expanded, he sought the assistance of other Church of England clergy. When he was unable to recruit a sufficient number of them, he turned to gifted laypersons. He gave them an important yet carefully circumscribed role—he sent them to preach but they were not to administer the sacraments. He justified this practice as an extraordinary call of God. This company of lay preachers expanded over time and eventually included some women. Giving regular preaching responsibility to lay preachers moved beyond the canons of the church, and the decision to employ women in this role was an especially radical step. He believed these women preachers also had an extraordinary call. In his notes on First Corinthians 14:34, a text that instructs women to be silent in church, Wesley wrote,

> *Let your women be silent in the churches*—Unless they are under an extraordinary impulse of the Spirit. *For,* in other cases, *it is not permitted them to speak*—By way of teaching in public assemblies. *But to be in subjection*—To the man whose proper office it is to lead and to instruct the congregation.[21]

Here he has outlined the possibility of an exception, clearly upholding the (perceived) norm of an all-male teaching office while allowing that women might teach under extraordinary circumstances, should the Spirit decide to override the norm.

Wesley employed this insight in a 1771 letter to Mary Bosanquet, one of his lay preachers.

I think the strength of the cause rests there—on your having an *extraordinary* call. So I am persuaded has every one of our lay preachers; otherwise I could not countenance his preaching at all. It is plain to me that the whole work of God termed Methodism is an extraordinary dispensation of His providence. Therefore I do not wonder if several things occur therein which do not fall under the ordinary rules of discipline. St. Paul's ordinary rule was "I permit not a woman to speak in the congregation." Yet in extraordinary cases he made a few exceptions; at Corinth in particular.[22]

Wesley's commentary and subsequent letter beg several questions. Since many lay preachers held their office on a semi-permanent basis, are we to assume that the so-called extraordinary impulse (or calling) of the Spirit was believed to continue unabated? The charismatic language of the extraordinary call may be overextended. Be that as it may, Wesley's logic is demonstrated in his explanation of the preaching office. He justified a radical move in traditional, even conservative terms. Can the church sustain such a logic that contains such tensions? A similar logic supported Wesley's decision to ordain clergy for the American church.

The Ordinations for America

For Methodists in America, their tenuous relationship to the Church of England ended with the close of the Revolutionary War. How would Wesley provide leadership for these Methodists, and especially for their sacramental needs? He could hardly send them to the local Anglican parish. Citing the extraordinary situation he faced—he called it "a very uncommon train of providences"[23]—he claimed an exception to the ordination traditions of his Church. As was his habit, he defended that exception on traditional grounds. Citing scholarly arguments "that Bishops and Presbyters are of the same order," he claimed that he had long believed in his right to ordain, even though he had not exercised it until that time. He had deferred to the canons of his church that insisted that valid ordination came only through the agency of bishops ordained within the historic apostolic succession.[24]

While he was able to construct this historical rationale for the ordinations, his primary motivation was pastoral and missional. He wrote,

Here there are Bishops who have a legal jurisdiction. In America there are none, neither any parish ministers. So that for some hundred miles together there is none either to baptize or to administer the Lord's supper. Here therefore my scruples are at an end: and I conceive myself at full liberty, as I violate no order and invade no man's right, by appointing and sending labourers into the harvest.[25]

Following that rationale, he ordained Thomas Coke and Francis Asbury as "joint Superintendents" for North America and he also ordained Richard Whatcoat and Thomas Vasey to serve as elders with them. In this manner sacramental authority was established for American Methodists along with two important yet potentially conflicting commitments. On one side, the new church would retain a visible form of continuity with apostolic tradition, even though the rest of the church, particularly the Anglican Communion, might be reluctant to recognize it.[26] On the other side, the church would insist that the sacramental needs of specific persons are more important than strict adherence to the apostolic norm. The Methodist Episcopal Church was born in a unique convergence of these commitments. It was born, if you will, as an exception to the apostolic norm.

Given the circumstances of this birth, it is not surprising that Methodists have continued this practice of making exceptions for the sake of their mission.

Exceptions in Later Methodism

The Use of Grape Juice at Communion

The normative matter for the celebration of Holy Communion is bread and wine, even though maintaining this norm is a continuing challenge. Can the church use rice or some other staple in those cultural contexts where wheat bread is uncommon or unknown? Celiac disease, a debilitating allergic reaction to wheat products, can be controlled only by complete abstention. Are gluten-free wafers acceptable?[27] How far can the church vary its use of sacramental matter and still retain continuity with apostolic practice? Methodists face this question regarding their use of grape juice for communion.[28]

John Wesley used wine for Holy Communion and at common meals, although he instructed Methodists to avoid use of distilled liquors.[29] Methodists in the nineteenth century discerned a calling to abstain from all use of alcoholic beverages, including wine and beer. As a manifestation of this concern, Methodist physician and dentist Thomas Bramwell Welch developed "Dr. Welch's Unfermented Grape Wine," a process he completed in 1869. He began marketing his new product to the church.[30] That invention, coupled with the Temperance Movement, brought a crisis of conscience to Methodists. They could hardly use alcoholic wine at the Lord's Table if it was unfit for use in other contexts, so the church began making a sacramental exception in favor of grape juice. They sacrificed some degree of continuity with the apostolic norm that they might establish a Eucharistic practice that was consistent with their ethical ideals.

The church has been criticized for making this exception, both by its own members and by other Christians. Nevertheless, the vast majority of congregations maintain the exception, primarily as a means to avoid excluding alcoholics and children. After practicing it for more than a century, this sacramental exception has gained a certain traditional weight of its own, becoming something of a new norm. The first three Methodist hymnals of the twentieth century (1905, 1935, and 1966) included a rubric that said, "The pure, unfermented juice of the grape shall be used."[31] When a similar rubric was not included in *The United Methodist Hymnal* (1989), a correcting resolution was passed by the 1996 General Conference restoring the phrase to the official ritual.[32] Even the rare United Methodist congregation that offers wine at communion usually feels constrained to offer grape juice as well, for purposes of Methodist continuity and as a concession to children and alcoholic members.

The Continuing Use of Lay Preachers

The appointment of non-ordained persons as the leaders of congregations did not end with Wesley's ordinations of 1784. Although Wesley did not allow lay preachers to preside at the sacraments, at various times in American Methodist history, including the present, *The Book of Discipline* has allowed licensed or "commissioned" lay persons to exercise such leadership.[33] Why? Perhaps the church is simply confused about the meaning of ordination. One can, however, suggest a more positive rationale for the practice.

After all, the church does maintain a practice of ordaining clergy. This commitment to ordination and the attendant formation processes that lead to it, like requiring completion of a seminary degree and the subsequent three-year probationary period before ordination, witness to the church's desire for continuity with the best theological and ecclesiastical traditions. Wesley was an Oxford graduate and tutor, deeply formed in the best academic and spiritual disciplines. His witness will always rebuke anti-intellectual tendencies along with shallow spirituality. Even if it is not possible for all Methodist leaders to have such a background, the church desires it for a significant core of its leaders. Through an ordained clergy, the church maintains a vital connection to apostolic tradition, yet churches that appeal to apostolic precedent must remember the meaning of apostle—"to send." It is a word that refers to missionary practice. Methodists will remember that their first Bishop, Francis Asbury, spent most of his life traveling for the sake of the Gospel. His saddle was his *cathedra*, his episcopal throne. Thus Methodists will remind themselves that apostolic traditions of ordination do not exist for their own sake, but for the sake of spreading the Gospel. In Methodist understanding, the spread of the Gospel is the weightier consideration, so we appoint some persons to lead congregations prior to ordination.

When it employs such persons as the leaders of local churches the church affirms what ordination does—it provides sacramental leadership for congregations—without allowing the preparatory process to hinder its ability to respond. As Catholic theologian Edward Schillebeeckx has argued, the church's *praxis* of ordination should serve its missional and congregational needs. If the church at large is committed to the existence of a congregation, then it is obligated to find sacramental leadership for it. If formational processes take too long— or if they somehow express a built-in class bias—then they should be altered in a way that provides congregations with the leadership they need.[34] United Methodist exceptions to the ordination norm retain commitment to venerable and fruitful formational processes while also giving the church maximum flexibility for mission. Such is the ideal. Ordination is not renounced nor is it an absolute ideal. The balance between these values can be a tenuous one, with the church often leaning toward pragmatism. Congregations that are little more than family chapels may receive unwarranted leadership resources that may not be justifiable. Sometimes we seem to think that any warm body will do as a leader of a congregation. In spite of the obvious problems, Methodists continue living with this tension felt by Wesley and embodied in their use of lay pastors—the simultaneous pull of tradition and the call to missionary evangelism—and they continue to seek a workable balance between them.

PROBLEMS AND LIMITATIONS WITH THE CATEGORY OF EXCEPTION

The Ordination of Women: From Exception to Norm

In some cases claiming an exception does not make a strong enough statement. As we witnessed in the original Wesleyan understanding of female preachers, describing the phenomenon as an extraordinary measure allowed important gifts to emerge. In time, however, the church realized that the exception category provided an inadequate description of these gifts. The church could no longer adequately justify the old norm of an all-male clergy, and thus it moved toward a new norm, one that embodied its intention to receive the spiritual gifts of all people, regardless of gender. The movement was completed when the General Conference of 1956 granted women the right to seek ordination. The church continues to defend this norm as witnessed in their official response to the 1982 *Baptism, Eucharist, and Ministry* document.[35] The United Methodist bishops said, "Just as the Roman Catholic and Orthodox churches have allowed no concession on ordaining women, we Wesleyans allow no refusal to do so."[36]

Many believed that the Holy Spirit led the church to change its understanding of the norm,[37] but their assessment was not unanimous. Order of Saint Luke correspondent Lawrence Guderian called the decision to ordain women "an unfortunate issue . . . (a departure) from historic practice." One should remember, he argued, "that Jesus chose twelve men."[38] Members of other churches have made similar arguments against the ordination of women, generally focusing on the fact that the twelve apostles were men.[39] These dissenters remind us that many Christians still view the ordination of women at best as an exception, and at worst, as an egregious departure from the apostolic norm.

Given such entrenched opposition, in some cases the establishment of a new norm requires something like a revolution. This more radical dynamic was demonstrated in the Episcopal Church of the early 1970s, when eleven women deacons sought ordination as priests. They had fulfilled all the requirements for priestly ordination, but were denied simply because they were not men. When the General Convention refused to change its canons, they and three sympathetic bishops disobeyed the rules of the church and the women were ordained at the Church of the Advocate, Philadelphia, Pennsylvania on July 29, 1974.[40] Carter Heyward, one of the ordinands, described the thought process that led to that occasion:

> I take great comfort, and find inspiration, in the fact that Jesus did not hate or leave his religious tradition, but rather loved it and worked to restore it to its soul—its awareness of God's active presence. Where it was errant, Jesus challenged it, often harshly. Where it made ungodly, compromising demands upon him, Jesus ignored it and went about his business, together with his disciples.[41]

Some moderate Episcopalians called the ordinations "irregular." That is, although the ordinations did not conform to the normative practice of the church, they could accept them as valid without changing that norm. In other words, they viewed the ordinations as a liturgical exception. There can be little doubt, however, that Heyward and her colleagues intended to overturn the old norm and create a new one. In such cases, the essentially conservative exception category is not adequate.[42]

The process of moving from exception to new norm raises questions about the open table. If the church decides to understand the open table as a sacramental exception, will it eventually become a new norm? Exceptions, by their very nature, must stand in prophetic tension with the norms that they critique. In the case of ordination, the normative status of an all-male clergy could not, ultimately, be defended, and the old norm gave way to the new. Will the same thing happen with the open table? Has the shift occurred already?

Sacramental Exceptions Can Be Difficult to Maintain: An Example from the Friends

Sacramental exceptions can be difficult to maintain, including those that are fully defensible. As we have established, sacramental and liturgical exceptions exist in creative tension with the norms of the church. However, prophetic fervor cools, the creative tension dissipates, and liturgical exceptions can become new norms, sometimes in unfortunate ways. The Society of Friends provides a case in point.

In a sense, the entire Friends' movement was a sacramental and liturgical exception. Its positive principle was the conviction that the "Light of Christ" is present in every person,[43] which led to their iconoclasm, not to mention their impressive ethical commitment. Friends were expected to follow that Light in truth and integrity. They were called to non-violence, to respect all persons equally. Because the Light was within them, they rejected the forms and rituals of the established churches. As George Fox wrote, "My desire after the Lord grew stronger, and zeal in the pure knowledge of God, and of Christ alone, without the help of any man, book, or writing."[44] Having experienced this Light, it was not uncommon for them to repair to nearby congregations to confront clergy and people with the truth that they had discovered. As they understood it, these confrontations took place not in churches but in "steeple-houses," and the leaders of those gatherings were not pastors, but they were "priests," hirelings of the worst kind.[45]

Fox believed that he was called to lead such people from vain forms to truth:

> I was to bring them off from all the world's fellowships, and prayings, and singings, which stood in forms without power; that their fellowship might be in the Holy Ghost, and in the Eternal Spirit of God; that they might pray in the Holy Ghost, and sing in the Spirit and with the grace that comes by Jesus....[46]

Fox's was a faith that began in disillusionment with the visible churches—both the Anglicans and the Dissenters—and it was defined over against their forms. The Society of Friends was a church for those who were disillusioned with forms, who believed that such forms had lost their power and integrity. It was a church of the exception.

This exceptional dynamic is still at work within the movement, as demonstrated in this testimony by Friends theologian Patrick Nugent, a former Roman Catholic:

> Sacraments are a failure when the outward performance distracts attention from the real presence of Christ...I am a Quaker precisely because I am a disappointed Catholic. I was brought up to believe in the Real Presence in the Eucharist but never experienced it inwardly through the sacraments.[47]

Such an exceptional spirituality seems to work best in the first generation, in persons like Nugent who have become disillusioned with the old ritual. In a sense, the old ritual remains as a conversation partner. Such spirituality does not work as well in subsequent generations. For instance, in the early days of their movement, Quakers experienced "a sacramental universe," one full of God's presence.[48] They remained in conversation with the Eucharist, believing that every meal shared by Christians fulfilled Jesus' commandment to "do this in remembrance of me" (1 Corinthians 11:24). The Love Feast embodied this belief.

Unfortunately, their ritual iconoclasm led them to drop the love feast, to become more clearly nonsacramental.[49] The Friends were no longer a group living in creative tension with disappointing ritual practice; rather, they were a non-ritual tradition. The difference is subtle but significant. Nugent comments on this problem as it manifests itself in the contemporary movement:

> Friends are accustomed to answer questions about the sacraments . . . with a short and dismissive rejection of "ritual." Yet there are good rea-

sons for arguing that certain kinds of Quaker practice are in fact deeply sacramental.[50]

He complains, however, that many Quakers do not grasp this sacramental principle. They are unable to explain why they would follow Christ's command to love the enemy and pray for the persecutor, yet not celebrate the Eucharist, also seemingly commanded by Jesus. In his words, there must be a better answer than "Quakers just don't do that."[51] It seems that the exception to the Eucharistic norm made its best sense when the Friends movement was newly separated from the old practice, and it makes renewed sense when Christians disillusioned with their ritual traditions join the movement. It is not for us to solve the problem identified by Nugent. It is, however, our concern to apply this insight to the discussion of the open table.

OPEN TABLE AS A SACRAMENTAL EXCEPTION

For this Methodist exception to make its deepest sense, it must exist in creative tension with a regular *praxis* of the church's baptismal norm. Indeed, the church's official teaching on baptism, "By Water and the Spirit," allows a sacramental exception but not a new norm: "Because the table at which we gather belongs to the Lord, it should be open to all who respond to Christ's love, regardless of age or church membership."[52] Nonbaptized persons may present themselves for the sacrament, and the church will not turn them away; yet that is not the last word. The document also says that "Unbaptized persons who receive communion should be counseled and nurtured toward baptism as soon as possible."[53] An open communion is permitted but the ancient baptismal norm is maintained. The norm and the exception exist in creative tension and the church can learn the wisdom of each.

I am not, therefore, advocating a position like that articulated by Richard Fabian, rector of Saint Gregory of Nyssa Episcopal Church, San Francisco. Fr. Fabian argues that the open table should become the normal way for the church to welcome seekers.

As they move from table to font, newcomers who have known Christ's banquet welcome and his presence before they could prepare or manage it, now undertake to share his work with us, carrying the good news wherever they go, and serving the world as Jesus and his followers have done. Unqualified sinners summoned to Jesus' Eucharistic table can respond like Zacchaeus by a change of life through baptism....[54]

My proposal is more cautious. Rather than proposing a new norm for Christian Initiation, I am affirming the ancient norm while defending the unusual—yet passionately believed—open table practices of United Methodist Christians. Theirs is a sacramental exception to the norm. In the next three chapters, I will defend that practice, beginning in chapter 3 with the biblical argument.

Chapter Three

The Meals of Jesus

JUSTIFYING AN OPEN TABLE
ON BIBLICAL GROUNDS

A Methodist exception to the normative pattern for Christian Initiation calls the church to look beyond the so-called "Institution Narratives" (Matthew 26:26-29; Mark 14:22-25; Luke 22:14-23; 1 Corinthians 11:23-26) to the wider context of Jesus' eating and drinking and also to stories about first-century churches. All of the New Testament stories about meals reflect the insights of first-century churches—that is, of active Eucharistic communities—and we can assume that their telling is shaped by the experience of eating and drinking in the Eucharist.

WITNESS FROM THE GOSPELS AND ACTS

The Gospels present numerous stories about the meals of Jesus along with other stories and parables about meals. He would eat with disreputable people and this habit troubled his more scrupulous opponents, as the following passage suggests:

And as he sat at dinner in Levi's house, many tax collectors and sinners were also sitting with Jesus and his disciples—for there were many who followed him. When the scribes of the Pharisees saw that he was eating with sinners and tax collectors, they said to his disciples, "Why does he eat with tax collectors and sinners?" (Mark 2:15-16)

Jesus offended them when he did not fast (Mark 2:18-20) and when his disciples picked grain and ate it on the Sabbath (Mark 2:23-26). Jesus sought out the rich tax collector Zacchaeus, a notorious sinner who had cheated many, and he demanded an invitation from him. His opponents were dismayed: "All who saw it began to grumble and said, 'He has gone to be the guest of one who is a sinner'" (Luke 19:7). Yet Zacchaeus was saved by this meal, and he resolved to do justice both to the poor and to those he had cheated (Luke 19:8-10). It seems that Jesus would eat with anyone and especially with those who needed him the most. These stories shape the imagination of Christians.

Jesus taught the crowds who came to him in the wilderness, and when it was time to eat he became their host, even when his disciples did not think he had sufficient means. "You give them something to eat," said Jesus (Mark 6:37); and he ignored the disciples' protests about their limitations (Mark 6:37-38). The church told this story and they did so in a Eucharistic shape. Note the same four-fold action that we see at the Last Supper, the taking, blessing, dividing, and giving:

> Taking the five loaves and the two fish, he looked up to heaven, and blessed and broke the loaves, and gave them to his disciples to set before the people; and he divided the two fish among them all. And all ate and were filled . . . Those who had eaten the loaves numbered five thousand men (Mark 6:41-42, 44, cf. Mark 14:22-25).

In the wilderness banquet, all were seated and Jesus fed them all. We may assume that the story reflects something of the writer's on-going experience of the Lord's Table.

In Luke, Jesus teaches that the banquets of disciples should operate outside the *quid pro quo* assumptions of their culture. In the ancient world, banquets and invitations helped set boundaries, they defined one's place in a social group and solidified one's relationships within it;[1] but Jesus called his followers to a different kind of table fellowship. They should not seek the reward or repayment that close friends and business associates offer.

> "But when you give a banquet, invite the poor, the crippled, the lame, and the blind. And you will be blessed, because they cannot repay you, for you will be repaid at the resurrection of the righteous."
>
> (Luke 14:13-14)

To illustrate, Jesus told the Parable of the Great Banquet: "Someone gave a great dinner and invited many" (Luke 14:16).[2] When the first invitations were refused, "the owner of the house became angry" and the invitation list was changed:

> (He) said to his slave, "Go out at once into the streets and lanes of the town and bring in the poor, the crippled, the blind, and the lame." And the slave said, "Sir, what you ordered has been done, and there is still room." Then the master said to the slave, "Go out into the roads and lanes, and compel people to come in, so that my house may be filled. For I tell you, none of those who were invited will taste my dinner"
> (Luke 14:21b-24).

The parable does contain a boundary—between those who refused the first invitation and those who came to the banquet—but it is self-imposed. This parable is more than a story about an unusually generous host; it is also a judgment story about the people who *refused* the invitation, a judgment on the whole pattern of inviting guests. The host not only makes an invitation, but he aggressively gathers a table full of guests, none of whom seems to belong. When such a parable becomes embedded in the church's imagination, it weighs against excluding persons from the Eucharist.

Another banquet story, the Parable of the Prodigal Son, occurs in the fifteenth chapter of Luke. It is the third in a set of parables about lost things—a lost sheep (Luke 15:3-7), a lost coin (Luke 3:8-10), and a lost son (Luke 15:11-32). They appear as response to the scandal of Jesus' eating with sinners:

> Now all the tax collectors and sinners were coming near to listen to him. And the Pharisees and the scribes were grumbling and saying, "This fellow welcomes sinners and eats with them." (Luke 15:1-2)

Indeed, the parable of the Prodigal Son is a judgment on that complaint as well as an offer of grace. Let us hear it again in terms of our investigation. The young man claimed his inheritance while his father was still alive—in essence saying "I wish you were dead"—and he went to "a distant country" (a Gentile place) where he squandered his wealth (Luke 15:12-14).[3] He had effectively excommunicated himself. He ended up living among the swine, who ate better than he did. In Jewish terms, he had reached rock bottom. In his poverty, "he came to himself" and decided to return to his father's household as a servant, confident that he might receive room and board. He went home as a penitent (Luke 15:17-18), yet what a surprise he found. There would be no penitential discipline. The father ran out to welcome him and, not only that, he announced a banquet of celebration:

"Quickly, bring out a robe—the best one—and put it on him; put a ring on his finger and sandals on his feet. And get the fatted calf and kill it, and let us eat and celebrate; for this son of mine was dead and is alive again; he was lost and is found!" (Luke 15:22-24)

How does this parable shape the church's thinking about invitations to the Lord's Table? One can argue that it does not imply an open table nor rule out the possibility of pre-baptismal disciplines. Indeed, the son was part of the father's household before he took the money and went away and thus we should view him as a penitent and not as a proselyte or catechumen. The problem with such logic is that the parable is theological poetry and not a church order filled with rubrics. Besides, when Luke was written, there were no church orders. Nevertheless, the poignant imagery of this parable will at least raise questions about chancel rails, about long catechumenal and penitential disciplines. Churches may discern the need to keep such disciplines and they may build a fence around the Table—indeed, they have done so—but the images of this parable will raise continuing questions about such things. Are they always necessary? Churches formed in the dynamics of this parable will feel its weight when confronted by persons in spiritual need. More often than not, they will respond with the compassion of the father who receives the son unconditionally, holding the banquet in his honor. Their songs will reflect the spirit of the parable, as one hears in the following eighteenth-century hymn:

Come, ye sinners, poor and needy,
    weak and wounded, sick and sore;
Jesus ready stands to save you,
    full of pity, love, and power.

I will arise and go to Jesus;
    he will embrace me with his arms;
In the arms of my dear Savior,
    O there are ten thousand charms.[4]

Another Lucan text, the story of Paul's voyage to Malta (Acts 27), bears intriguing witness to an open fellowship. Paul, a prisoner en route to Rome, warned the ship's owner not to set sail from Crete; but he was ignored and the journey began (Acts 27:9-13). Before they traveled far, the ship was beset by a storm and they were in danger of death. Over the next few days, they threw most of their stores, their cargo, and equipment overboard (Acts 27:18-19). They feared for their lives.

Having received a reassuring message from an angel, Paul announced that no one would die but that they would run aground and lose the ship. On the fourteenth day of the storm Paul told them that the final crisis was imminent; they should eat a little. Note that the story of the meal is told in a four-fold Eucharistic shape, not unlike the story about feeding the crowd in the wilderness (Mark 10:30-44; cf. Luke 9:10-17):

> "Today is the fourteenth day that you have been in suspense and remaining without food, having eaten nothing. Therefore I urge you to take some food, for it will help you survive; for none of you will lose a hair from your heads." After he had said this, he took bread; and giving thanks [eucharisteo] to God in the presence of all, he broke it and began to eat. Then all of them were encouraged and took food for themselves. (We were in all two hundred and seventy-six persons in the ship.) (Acts 27:33b-37)

One cannot, of course, prove that Paul celebrated the Eucharist on a ship full of non-Christians. Open communion, indeed! One cannot escape, however, the Eucharistic shape of the story with its four-fold action of taking, blessing, breaking, and giving food. At the least, it is another story of Eucharistic hospitality in the wilderness.[5] This text cannot be used as some sort of proof text for the open table, nor does it negate the wisdom of catechumenal rites and disciplines. It is, however, part of the church's storehouse of narrative images, and a striking one at that. It lends a certain plausibility to an occasional, exceptional practice of an open table. In the midst of persons facing spiritual storms, would a church formed by this story fence the Table against the supposedly unqualified?

WITNESS FROM PAUL'S LETTER TO THE GALATIANS

In the second chapter of Galatians we find another window on meal practices in the early church. Paul and other first-century Christians were forced to wrestle with the meaning of the circumcision norm and its relationship to God's covenant-making activity. Circumcision was, after all, established as a biblical norm. God had given the commandment to Abraham:

> This is my covenant, which you shall keep, between me and you and your offspring after you: Every male among you shall be circumcised . . . Throughout your generations every male among you shall be circumcised when he is eight days old, including the slave born in your

house and the one bought with your money from any foreigner who is not of your offspring . . . Any uncircumcised male who is not circumcised in the flesh of his foreskin shall be cut off from his people; he has broken my covenant. (Genesis 17:10, 12, 14)

Because the commandment was so clearly established in Scripture, many believed that followers of the Way should continue submitting to this rite, including Gentile converts. After all, Jesus had been circumcised (Luke 1:59). But there were significant cultural differences between Jews and Gentiles, to the point that many seekers would have remained outside the church had circumcision been required, just as the God-fearers had remained outside of the synagogue (see Acts 10). Thus, the church faced a major theological crisis: How should they interpret the call to circumcision? The church decided, quite wisely, that it would not require its Gentile converts to undergo circumcision, but would receive them through baptism alone (Acts 15:1-35, cf. Acts 10). In spite of the overly optimistic report offered in Acts 15, there was significant friction over the decision. Proponents of circumcision believed that Pauline Christians were teaching against the tradition of the fathers, yet Paul believed that freedom from the circumcision norm was absolutely essential to the proclamation of Jesus Christ; to do otherwise was turning to "a different Gospel" (Galatians 1:6). The circumcision debate manifested itself at several points, including Table fellowship. Those who believed in maintaining the circumcision norm followed the logic of purity to its obvious conclusion; the non-circumcised were unclean, outside the covenant, and thus they could not eat with them.

Paul recounted the story of his meeting in Jerusalem with "James and Cephas (Peter) and John, who were acknowledged pillars" of the church (Galatians 2:9). These leaders validated Paul's vocation, that he "had been entrusted with the gospel for the uncircumcised, just as Peter had been entrusted with the gospel for the circumcised" (Galatians 2:7). They did not ask him to circumcise the Gentile converts, but only "that (he and his churches) remember the poor" (Galatians 2:10); yet their agreement did not hold. "When Cephas came to Antioch, I opposed him to his face, because he stood self-condemned" (Galatians 2:11). What happened? Before he came under pressure from the Jerusalem conservatives, Cephas (Peter) had eaten with the Gentiles.

But after they came, he drew back and kept himself separate for fear of the circumcision faction. And the other Jews joined him in this hypocrisy so that even Barnabas was led astray by their hypocrisy. (Galatians 2:12-13)

This division of table fellowship was a threat to the Gospel; thus Paul publicly accused Cephas of hypocrisy:

> "If you, though a Jew, live like a Gentile and not like a Jew, how can you compel the Gentiles to live like Jews?" We ourselves are Jews by birth and not Gentile sinners, yet we know that a person is justified not by the works of the law but through faith in Jesus Christ. (Galatians 2:14b-16a)

In this context, justification by faith means one table in the church, not two.

When Paul referred to this divided table fellowship, was he referring to a divided communion service? There is no way to make such a determination. We know that all meals in the ancient Mediterranean world were to some extent ritual occasions, that our concern for distinctions among types of meal fellowship (e.g., Lord's Supper and *agápe*) were not theirs. In that sense, this rebuke of a divided table in the ancient church informs contemporary practice of table fellowship, including the Eucharist. It thereby adds significant weight to arguments against fencing of the Table for denominational, racial, or cultural reasons. If the divided table in Galatia was a denial of justification in Christ, then contemporary divisions of the Table may be a similar denial. At the very least, this passage is cause for raising questions about access to the Table. Which is worse—to admit someone who does not belong at the Table or to exclude someone who should be admitted?

Although this Galatians narrative witnesses against a divided table within the church, it does not preclude the possibility of boundaries between the church and the world. Paul knew the importance of such boundaries as we can see in this dialogue from First Corinthians:[6]

> Do you not know that wrongdoers will not inherit the kingdom of God? Do not be deceived! Fornicators, idolaters, adulterers, male prostitutes, sodomites, thieves, the greedy, drunkards, revilers, robbers—none of these will inherit the kingdom of God. And this is what some of you used to be. But you were washed . . . (1 Corinthians 6:9-11a)

Of course, the Galatians 2 narrative tells the story of a miserably failed attempt at boundary making. Again, the example of the circumcision party does not preclude the constructing of justifiable Christian boundaries. Arguably, the well-known Galatians teaching on baptism provides such a boundary:

For in Christ Jesus you are all children of God through faith. As many of you as were baptized into Christ have clothed yourselves with Christ. There is no longer Jew or Greek, there is no longer slave or free, there is no longer male and female; for all of you are one in Christ Jesus. And if you belong to Christ, then you are Abraham's offspring, heirs according to the promise. (Galatians 3:26-29)

The text suggests that the boundary between church and world is baptism, but the primary focus of the argument is *against boundaries*, against the unjustified boundaries that Christians construct among the baptized. Thus the primary dynamic at work in Galatians is an inclusive one, one that seeks to include more and more people in the covenant rather than less and less. There is nothing here to support something like a rigorous Christian purity system.

The force of the principal theological and spiritual arguments in the New Testament moves the church toward including more and more people; they move the church toward "Samaria and the ends of the earth" rather than away from them (Acts 1:6-8). Therefore, even when the church constructs necessary boundaries—as, for instance, in the baptismal boundary between the church and the rest of the world—the church should regard those boundaries with a certain degree of suspicion. The temptation to construct a new purity system always lurks inside the baptismal doors. Perhaps the church's boundaries should not work too well.

The Scriptures we have discussed in this section provide witness against boundaries that work too well. In the next section, we will discuss some ways that the church has appropriated this witness and how it may understand its continuing dialogue with it.

"He ate with sinners": Appropriating Insights from the Meal Ministry of Jesus

Toward a More Biblical Great Thanksgiving

As we have noted, when it hears the Words of Institution the church is remembering but one part of the meal ministry of Jesus. The church remembers the wider context of that final meal when it speaks this sentence in its The Great Thanksgiving: "He healed the sick, fed the hungry, and ate with sinners."[7] That sentence is part of a longer summary of the Gospel narrative:

Holy are you, and blessed is your Son Jesus Christ.
Your Spirit anointed him
   to preach good news to the poor,
   to proclaim release to the captives
     and recovering of sight to the blind,
   to set at liberty those who are oppressed,
   and to announce that the time had come
     when you would save your people.
He healed the sick, fed the hungry, and ate with sinners.
By the baptism of his suffering, death, and resurrection
   you gave birth to your church,
   delivered us from slavery to sin and death,
   and made with us a new covenant
     by water and the Spirit.
When the Lord Jesus ascended,
   he promised to be with us always,
   in the power of your Word and Holy Spirit.[8]

The prayer continues with the Words of Institution, the Memorial Acclamation ("Christ has died. . . . etc.") and the Epiclesis, that is, the petition "Pour out your Holy Spirit on us . . . "[9] This summary represents an attempt to include more of the Gospel narrative in the Great Thanksgiving.[10] Embodying this commitment, the most recent revisions of Eucharistic prayers composed by the United Methodist Church and other denominations recall not only the death and resurrection of Jesus and the Words of Institution, but also his life and ministry.[11] Thus United Methodists remember Jesus' eating with sinners and by doing so, they insist on a connection between those meals and the Eucharist. Almost inevitably, such anamnesis will shape their *praxis* of inviting people to the holy meal.

At this point, a review of the process that brought this phrase "ate with sinners" into the United Methodist Great Thanksgiving is enlightening. On a broader scale, the movement toward remembering more of the biblical narrative is based on the study of ancient Eucharistic prayers, many of which drew upon the Bible in fuller measure than the prayers Methodists inherited from the English Reformers. For example, *The Apostolic Tradition* by Hippolytus includes a strong reference to the Incarnation:

We render thanks to you, O God, through your beloved child Jesus Christ, whom in the last times you sent to us as a savior and redeemer and angel of your will; who is your inseparable Word, through whom you made all things, and in whom you were well pleased. You sent him from heaven into a virgin's womb; and conceived in the womb, he was made flesh and was manifested as your Son, being born of the Holy Spirit and the Virgin.[12]

The Liturgy of Saint Mark includes extended reference to the Hebrew Bible:

> When [man] transgressed, you did not despise him or abandon him, for you are good, but you called him back through the law, you taught him through the prophets, you reformed and renewed him through this awesome and life-giving and heavenly mystery.[13]

Over against such texts, the Eucharistic prayer in the 1966 *Book of Hymns* (essentially the 1662 *Book of Common Prayer* rite) seemed overly penitential and its range of biblical imagery too restricted.[14] With but minimal exceptions the focus was on the passion and death of Christ:

> Almighty God, our heavenly Father, who of thy tender mercy didst give thine only Son Jesus Christ to suffer death upon the cross for our redemption; who made there, by the one offering of himself, a full, perfect, and sufficient sacrifice for the sins of the whole world; and did institute, and in his holy Gospel command us to continue, a perpetual memory of his precious death until his coming again:

> Hear us, O merciful Father, we most humbly beseech thee, and grant that we, receiving these thy creatures of bread and wine, according to thy Son our Savior Jesus Christ's holy institution, in remembrance of his passion, death, and resurrection, may be partakers of the divine nature through him:

> Who in the same night that he was betrayed, took bread . . .[15]

In a process instituted by James F. White and Hoyt L. Hickman, the church has expanded the repertoire of themes that it uses at the Eucharist. Biblical themes and texts covered in the church's twenty-four official versions of the Great Thanksgiving[16] include the birth of Jesus,[17] his baptism,[18] the Magnificat,[19] the visit of the magi,[20] the forty-day fast in the wilderness,[21] and the Great Commission,[22] to name but several. Besides the phrase in "Word and Table I," reference to Christ eating with sinners occurs in three other versions of the Great Thanksgiving.[23] This work of expanding the images prayed at the Lord's Table did not end with the publication of *The United Methodist*

Book of Worship but it continues to this day, as the church tries to draw more and more of the biblical narrative into the Eucharistic liturgy.[24]

While the mainline churches have expanded upon their Eucharistic prayers by drawing upon the same Bible and ancient sources, it remained for United Methodists to add the phrase about Jesus eating with sinners. It appeared for the first time in the 1972 version of the prayer, the first published recension of the text.[25] White, who at that time was serving as Professor of Worship at Perkins School of Theology, tells the story of its inclusion. He heard a seminary chapel sermon delivered by New Testament scholar William Farmer in which Dr. Farmer reflected upon Jesus' scandalous practice of eating with sinners. He noted the wide scholarly consensus supporting the historicity of that claim. Convinced by the presentation, White added the phrase "ate with sinners" to the proposed text.[26] Indeed, the Perkins community had a unique opportunity to influence the shape of this service. As White tells the story, eight variants of the Word and Table text were tried in Perkins Chapel.[27] Professor Fred Gealy wrote the final version of The Prayer for Illumination and also the confession.[28] Old Testament faculty members were consulted on the wording of the Preface.[29] Professor Grady Hardin wrote the original version of the prayer after communion and statement of pardon.[30] Professor Virgil Howard added the spoken rubric for introducing the Lord's Prayer, "And now, with the confidence of children of God, let us pray."[31] Professor Albert Outler reputedly expressed his disappointment at the decision to move beyond the Cranmerian patterns that the Methodists had used since the beginning of their movement.[32] Given this ongoing dialogue, it is altogether possible that Dr. Farmer preached his sermon intending to influence the shape of the Word and Table service; but the scholarship he cited was readily available in the wider scholarly community. Be that as it may, Methodists were the first to include such a phrase in their Great Thanksgiving. We may assume that the ethos of a United Methodist theological school helped Professors Farmer and White hear this part of the biblical narrative with particular clarity. The claim that Jesus ate with sinners is deeply biblical. That the message resonates with Methodist piety is readily apparent in the writings of the Wesleys and their followers. Given that background, it is not at all surprising that a Methodist community was responsible for introducing this phrase to the ecumenical church's *praxis* of the Eucharistic prayer.[33] This image of Jesus eating with sinners is the key biblical image supporting a *praxis* of the open table. For more than thirty years now, United Methodists have been reminded of it every time they have used

"A Service of Word and Table I" and its predecessor rites. We can assume that such usage has shaped the piety of the church.

We will now review some of the scholarly discussion related to the claim that Jesus ate with sinners.

The Scholarly Issues Relating to the Open Commensality of Jesus

The insight preached by Farmer is based on the research of New Testament scholar Norman Perrin.[34] Perrin's insights have been expanded and developed by other scholars such as John Dominic Crossan[35] and Marcus Borg.[36] These have insisted that table fellowship without regard to purity laws was central to the *praxis* of the historical Jesus. Crossan has coined the phrase "open commensality" to describe this practice.[37] Working backward from the cross, Perrin insisted that a historical understanding of the life and ministry of Jesus "must make sense of the fact that that ministry ended on the cross."[38] How did Jesus offend and threaten the religious authorities so deeply? Open commensality provides a plausible motivation. According to Perrin, observant Jews believed that the best way to resist foreign occupation was to close ranks and magnify their religious identity over against the Romans and other Gentiles. If they remained faithful and separate, they believed that God would eventually deliver them and establish the kingdom. Open table fellowship was a rejection of that religious world-view. As Perrin wrote,

> Jesus welcomed these outcasts into table-fellowship with himself in the name of the Kingdom of God, in the name of the Jews' ultimate hope, and so both prostituted that hope and also shattered the closed ranks of the community against their enemy. It is hard to imagine anything more offensive to Jewish sensibilities.[39]

His rejection of their purity system gained him the insult preserved in Matthew 11:16-19, a passage comparing Jesus and John the Baptist.[40]

> "But to what will I compare this generation? It is like children sitting in the marketplaces and calling to one another, 'We played the flute for you, and you did not dance; we wailed and you did not mourn.' For John came neither eating nor drinking, and they say, 'He has a demon'; the Son of Man came eating and drinking, and they say, *'Look, a glutton and a drunkard, a friend of tax collectors and sinners!'* Yet wisdom is vindicated by her deeds." (italics mine)

As the insult suggests, the meals of Jesus were not solemn affairs, but were parties in the spirit of the Lost Son parable. The guest lists were indiscriminate, in the spirit of the Great Banquet parable.[41] Perrin concluded that "this table fellowship [was] the central feature of the ministry of Jesus; an anticipatory sitting at table in the Kingdom of God and a very real celebration of present joy and challenge."[42] He insisted that the best explanation for the meal practices of the early church is to see them as the continuation of the pattern established by Jesus and his disciples.[43] Understood in this way, stories about the meals of Jesus witness against a sacramental *praxis* that functions like a renewed purity system. If the Eucharist is rooted in the meals of Jesus, as these scholars insist, then that insight should affect our practice,[44] although it remains for the church to determine exactly how that will happen. Before moving to that speculation, we must acknowledge a dissenting voice.

New Testament scholar Dennis Smith argues that the pericopes about Jesus eating with sinners are not necessarily historical.

> The representations of meals of Jesus in the Gospel tradition function as idealizations of Jesus as hero . . . in the period after Jesus' death, early Christian preachers told stories about him in the context of the fledgling Christian communities. The banquet emerged as a useful motif for defining aspects of the hero, Jesus. During this period early Christian communities were also centering many of their communal religious activities on meals, which gave special meaning to stories of Jesus at table. At this point in the tradition, the typification of Jesus as a table companion of "tax collectors and sinners" became a symbol of early Christian groups.[45]

His assertion is based on his understanding of banquet practices within ancient Mediterranean culture. According to Smith's analysis, the Seder meal, the Eucharist, and other religious meals developed from a common traditional form, the Greco-Roman banquet with a common set of conventions and practices.[46] Among these are the following:

- Persons were specifically invited to attend.
- Upon arrival, servants would wash the feet of the diners.
- The guests reclined to eat.
- In many cases, their place at the banquet was assigned according to their status.
- Two courses were served, the deipnon (dinner) and the symposium (essentially the drinking party with entertainment).

- The symposiarch (essentially a presider) would regulate the drinking and direct the discussion. He or she worked to maintain the harmony of the gathering.
- The meal itself was a religious celebration, not something that followed the religious observance.[47]

Such banquets, Smith observes, defined boundaries among and between groups of people, between those who were invited and those who were not, between the members of one's social group and the others.[48] Banquet rules, such as rules against arguing or resisting the leadership of the symposiarch, idealized their hope for relationships within the community. Thus the meal defined and shaped relationships beyond the meal.[49] The banquet, Smith insists, was a basic cultural symbol. One could either affirm the institution or critique it, but one could not simply dismiss it.[50]

For example, according to Smith, First Corinthians—and particularly chapters 10–14—can be understood against the background of the banquet tradition. The meal and the whole service took place at table. Their community problems were resolved by eating together:

> [Paul] has identified the question of status as a problem at the communal meal because, in effect, it makes two meals and creates schisms. Such schisms strike at the very nature of the communal meal . . . Thus he constructs an involved argument on the basis of the tradition in order to come to what may appear to be a mundane conclusion: eat together (1 Corinthians 11:33-34). But it is not mundane to Paul; it is essential to the meaning of the meal.[51]

The rules for prophets and speaking in tongues expressed in chapter fourteen reflect symposium rules against speaking out of turn.[52] In Smith's reading of the text, "Paul's concept of a proper worship service is clearly related to the concept of a proper symposium conversation . . ."[53]

Smith insists that the Gospels use the banquet theme just as Paul and many others did. Thus the banquet stories in the Gospel should be analyzed from a literary perspective, as parabolic idealizations of the Kingdom of God and not necessarily as historical accounts.[54] Thus his disagreement with Perrin. In his view, the stories of Jesus eating and drinking with sinners are idealizations presented by the church, stories that call persons to live by their values. They call the church to embody the inclusive kingdom that they portray.[55]

Smith's reading of the data will challenge a *praxis* of the open table based on historical considerations alone. As biblical scholars continually remind the church, it is not possible to write a definitive history of Jesus. The Jesus portrayed in the Gospels combines aspects of the historical Jesus and the Christ of faith and thus is something of an idealized portrait. That is not to say, however, that the portrait is a distortion, or worse, a lie. The Gospels provide an historical witness to the memory and discernment of early Christian communities. The Jesus of the Gospels is rooted in history, yet the stories also reflect the early church's understanding of his presence and continuing work. The Jesus they experienced and proclaimed "healed the sick, fed the hungry, and ate with sinners."[56] It is difficult to imagine such a portrait radically *contradicting* the historical Jesus as they and others had known him; the gospels that contradicted their memories were not, ultimately, received by the churches, nor were the editors allowed to suppress the more difficult aspects of the narrative. Early Christians did, of course, expand upon what they knew of Jesus, as the church continues to do.[57]

What, then, do we make of this scholarly debate? Most likely, the stories about Jesus feeding the hungry, healing the sick, and eating with sinners are rooted in the practice of the historical Jesus and they also reflect the experience of first-century Christians. In the end of the day, however, the stories cannot be proven as historical matters of fact, yet the biblical texts remain. The church has decided to receive them and read them within the community of the church. It is absolutely certain that the images of Jesus feeding the crowds and eating with sinners remain part of our worldview.

Indeed, when one enters the church, one enters a worldview, a cultural-linguistic milieu that shapes what we believe about Jesus and our experience of him. According to theologian George Lindbeck, Christianity functions something like a grammatical system in which becoming a Christian is akin to learning how to speak the language.[58] Our cultural-linguistic worldview is formed by the practices of the church: ritual practices, stories about heroes and villains, doctrinal statements, formal and informal theologies, and, of course, the biblical narrative. A Christian grammar includes rites of initiation shaped by generations of reflection on scripture. How does one become a disciple? What shapes that identity? What threatens it? These rites ritualize joining the church and gaining admission to the Eucharist and they teach the church how to speak about and practice its work of conversion; they do not, however, reflect the entirety of the biblical narrative. A Christian grammar also contains those stories that proclaim the open commensality of Jesus. Reflection on those stories will also shape the church's imagination and influence the way it thinks and practices its life together. It will shape the way Christians invite people to their meals. In the first vision, admission to the Eucharist is related to the deep relationships and responsibilities that one assumes there. In the second vision, admission to the Table is a sign of God's radical generosity.

Does the coexistence of these two visions present a contradiction for a Christian grammar of faith, especially for a United Methodist version of it? Not necessarily. As doctrinal statements establish boundaries for acceptable Christian communication, so sacramental rubrics state the norms—the grammatical rules, if you will—by which the church understands its work of Christian initiation. However, experienced speakers of a language know about exceptions to its rules and the necessity of them. Lindbeck wrote,

> Even more than the grammar in grammar books, church doctrine is an inevitably imperfect and often misleading guide to the fundamental interconnections within a religion. In part this is because every formulated rule has more exceptions than the grammarians and the theologians are aware of... The deep grammar of the language may escape detection. It may be impossible to find rules that show why some crucial usages are beautifully right and others dangerously wrong. The experts must on occasion bow to the superior wisdom of the competent speaker who simply knows that such and such is right or wrong even though it violates the rules they have formulated.[59]

Formed by the stories of Jesus eating with sinners, the church will find it difficult to turn away those who present themselves at its Table. The weight of the biblical narrative brought to bear within the ritualized grammar of the faith will not necessarily force the church to abandon the logic of the classic initiatory system, just as the presence of irregular verbs does not require speakers to abandon a standard conjugation of regular verbs. A reasonably coherent practice of the biblical faith can allow the norm and the exception to exist side by side in creative and fruitful tension. Both usages arise from the deep structures of the Christian narrative.

In the next section, we will examine two modern Eucharistic hymns that exemplify the influence of Gospel meal stories and parables on a contemporary grammar of the faith.

BIBLICAL IMAGERY IN MODERN EUCHARISTIC HYMNS

Many of the Eucharistic hymns written during the twentieth century employ banquet and fellowship imagery, sometimes to the exclusion of other images. This is particularly true of those included in *The United Methodist Hymnal*.[60] The Eucharist is a meal that binds Christians together in spiritual fellowship, transforming all of their meals and sending them forth in compassionate service, as "sacraments of [God]."[61] The Eucharist is God's "feast of victory," the present manifestation of the marriage supper of the Lamb and the sign of our deliverance from sin, evil, and death (Revelation 19:1-10, 5:12-13).[62] The Eucharist is a feast prepared, an invitation offered, and a call to proclaim God's Word.[63] It is a holy meal that overcomes all division, even that between the living and the dead, uniting all Christians in one body for the sake of the world.[64] All of these are compelling images drawn from scripture. "I Come with Joy" (*UMH* 617) by British Congregationalist Brian Wren and "You Satisfy the Hungry Heart" (*UMH* 629) by American Catholic Omer Westendorf are particularly good examples of the modern emphases.

In Brian Wren's hymn, the communicant comes to the Table in the joyful spirit reminiscent of the Gospel banquets. He or she comes to meet Christ.

> I come with joy to meet my Lord,
> forgiven, loved and free,
> in awe and wonder to recall
> his life laid down for me.[65]
>
> (© 1971 Hope Publishing Company. All rights reserved.)

The "I come" is strongly stated; there is no doubt the invitation has been freely received. There is no dwelling on sin and guilt, no protesting one's unworthiness, but rather the strong assurance that one has been forgiven and released from bondage. The communicant comes in "awe and wonder," with something like a deep and holy fascination. There is no mention of holy fear.[66]

Wren continues the invitational themes in the second stanza.

> I come with Christians far and near
> to find, as all are fed,
> the new community of love
> in Christ's communion bread.[67]
>
> (© 1971 Hope Publishing Company. All rights reserved.)

The communicant continues asserting his/her decision to come. This joyful participant comes to the feast as part of a great ecumenical gathering of Christians. There is a boundary implied here—"I come with

Christians"—although it is a much wider boundary than the ecumenical church has normally experienced. Even then, one finds hint of an even greater inclusion; the Eucharist is a meal where "all are fed." The predominant sacramental image is bread, while the potentially more troublesome image of blood is not mentioned.[68] This bread shared is the source of communion and love is its goal.

Eucharistic gathering has a missional purpose, as the fifth stanza asserts. Those who share Christ's bread are sent in the spirit of the gathering:

> Together met, together bound,
>   we'll go our different ways,
> and as his people in the world,
>   we'll live and speak his praise.[69]

They gather in joy and unity and they go forth as witnesses. Sharing the Eucharist commits them to works of love and justice, to care for one another and the world. Such caring is an appropriate extension of the Table.

Similar themes are expressed in Westendorf's hymn, which is organized around its refrain:

> You satisfy the hungry heart
>   with gift of finest wheat.
> Come, give to us, O saving Lord,
>   the bread of life to eat.[70]

This refrain is an affirmation of faith and also a prayer. It speaks of hunger and the exquisite gift that Christ gives in order to meet it. The self-giving Lord is the gift, the bread of life, and its giver.[71] The Lord is addressed directly and intimately, supported by a musical style congruent with such intimacy. While the predominant image is drawn from the John 6 "bread of life" discourse, the hymn text itself does not express the misunderstanding, scandal, and controversy that one finds in that chapter. There, the people misunderstand Christ's multiplication of bread for the hungry and they respond inappropriately, wanting to make Jesus king (John 6:15). While the Jesus portrayed in John's Gospel does promise relief from hunger and thirst, the "bread of life" saying actually rebukes their request for a continuing supply of bread (John 6:34-35). In the biblical text, Jesus' saying is followed by scandal as he pointedly tells his interrogators that the bread he offers is not like the manna given in the wilderness; rather, it is his own flesh and blood and those who would live must receive it (John 6:50-51, 53). Hearing such a difficult and confusing message, many turn away from him. Only the disciples remain, but their response suggests that they stayed only because they had nowhere else to go (John 6: 60-71). These themes are not addressed in Westendorf's hymn, although, in all fairness, a poet can only address so many images in one text.

The first stanza of this hymn evokes another Johannine image, that of the good shepherd who calls the sheep his "family." Hearing him, his children "follow and rejoice" (John 10:1-5),"[72] yet there is no hint of threat from the Johannine "thief" or "wolf" (John 10:10-13). The imagery is that of thanksgiving, unity in Christ, and the mystery of Christ's presence filling human hearts.[73] Since each stanza begins with the refrain, all of these affirmations are rooted in the compelling image of that one who feeds and satisfies hungry hearts. While this hymn witnesses to a generous God who satisfies our hunger, self-indulgence is not the goal of its imagery, as if feeding our personal hunger is all that matters. The final stanza calls the church into a work of self-giving consistent with the gift they have received:

> You give yourself to us, O Lord;
> then selfless let us be,
> to serve each other in your name
> in truth and charity.[74]

Images like those employed by Westendorf emerge from the church's Eucharistic piety and they continue to shape it. Their missional impact is compelling, and yes, potentially controversial. Here, the potential controversy is not rooted in receiving the body of Christ, but rather in becoming it. Hearing this call to feed and serve others makes it difficult for a congregation to fence the communion table; in the face of such imagery any fence will seem incongruous.

The imagery expressed in these modern Eucharistic hymns reflects a wider effort to shift the language that the church uses to celebrate the Eucharist. This dynamic was at work in the revision of United Methodist Eucharistic prayers and their attendant liturgical rites. Hoyt Hickman described it.

> The joyful tone of the new service, emphasizing praise and thanksgiving, contrasts with the heavily penitential tone of the older services. Multiple confessions of sin and unworthiness are shortened to a single

invitation-confession-pardon sequence, which by 1984 is followed by the peace and offering to make a five-step process that leads naturally to thanksgiving and communion. The Lord's Supper is to be *celebrated*.[75]

He commented upon changes in the Great Thanksgiving itself: ". . . joyous celebration of all God's mighty acts of salvation contrasts with the preoccupation with Jesus' death that gave previous communion texts a somber tone."[76] This theme of Eucharist as joyful celebration is typical of Hickman's work and characteristic of the United Methodist revisions. In another place, he wrote, "[The Great Thanksgiving] is a positive, joyous thanksgiving for all God's mighty acts in Jesus Christ, particularly suitable as we commune with the risen Christ, on the Lord's Day or any other day."[77]

Quite clearly, the changes in language were meant to restore the ancient focus on the total scope of Christ's saving work. The changes were also corrective; they reflect an attempt to overcome and replace the older penitential piety. This corrective project is manifested in a variety of ways. One finds an act of confession in the "Word and Table I" order, but the most self-consciously penitential elements have been removed from it. In the new service, we do not "bewail our manifold sins and wickedness." The Prayer of Humble Access, with its striking biblical imagery about "(gathering) up the crumbs under (Christ's) table" (Mark 7:24-30; Matthew 15:21-28) is not appointed for use even though one might argue that Jesus' dialogue with the Syrophoenician woman supports a theology of open access. Nonetheless, the language of unworthiness makes the prayer suspect, so it is not used and neither is the classical *Agnus Dei* ("O Lamb of God," John 1:36).[78] All of these elements remain in "A Service of Word and Table IV,"[79] but it remains as a concession and not as the recommended usage. It was to this older service—its structure, its tone, its language, and its theology—that White and other United Methodist liturgical reformers were referring when they insisted that the Vatican II reforms had made the rites of *The Book of Worship* (1964) obsolete. They were not interested in making a modern language revision of Cranmer's rite.

Indeed Methodism's journey beyond Cranmer's penitential emphasis began with John Wesley himself. Wesley believed that preparation for communion had its rightful place; but he insisted that Christ's call to communion outweighs even the church's counsels on preparation. He wrote,

He commands you to come, and prepare yourself by prayer if you have time; if you have not, however, come. Make not reverence to God's command a pretence for breaking it. Do not rebel against him for fear of offending him. Whatever you do or leave undone besides, be sure to do what God bids you do.[80]

The Book of Common Prayer (1662) included three communion exhortations; two of them counseled against receiving communion unworthily and a third, by Peter Martyr Vermigli, cautioned people against avoiding communion.[81] Wesley's "The Duty of Constant Communion" borrows some of its argument from Vermigli's exhortation. Wesley included none of the exhortations in his 1784 *Sunday Service*—neither the penitential exhortations nor Vermigli's.

Although the Wesleys began the process away from the penitential focus, it was a major project for Hickman, White, and others. They encouraged a substantial revision in Methodist Eucharistic piety by changing the language of the revised services and by introducing the newer hymnody. They persisted in teaching a more celebratory, invitational sacramental theology. References to blood are made, but they are not emphasized. Little is said about atonement, holy fear, and sacrificial discipleship. The language of gift and banquet predominates, along with that of unity and celebration. Indeed, this revision partakes of significant biblical images, portraying a Christ who welcomes the outcast and the unlovable, who sits at banquet with sinners. The church has been emphasizing these images and they are forming Methodist piety and theological imagination. In the midst of this invitational imagery, a fenced table is difficult to justify.

As with most attempts at liturgical and theological corrections, this one is prone to certain weaknesses, especially when the correction is over-emphasized.[82] I will hold detailed analysis of this problem until a later chapter. For now, I will insist that the call to indiscriminate table fellowship and self-giving service implies some obligations, if not a word of caution to those who accept the invitation.

OPEN TABLE, BUT NOT CASUAL EATING

The biblical images we have reviewed in this chapter provide some theological justification for an open communion table. Viewed through the lens of these images, the Eucharist is the hospitable banquet of Jesus where sinners are welcomed along with the poor, the rejected, and the overlooked. They are welcomed first, perhaps even before baptism, and their formation begins with that welcome. Such welcoming before baptism should be understood as an exception to the baptismal norm for admission and not a negation of it.

Images about the hospitable banquet must not be used to justify a casual, non-committed practice of eating and drinking with Jesus. At the very least, those who answer Christ's call to the Table commit themselves to eat with all of the others who come there. There is no private dining in the Lord's banquet hall. Black and white, rich and poor, young and old are welcomed together. Communicants are called to love and serve one another and to live together in peace. Moreover, those who answer the call come to the Lord's Table; thus they are implicated in the mission of Jesus, even to the carrying of the cross. Again, an open table does not justify casual communion.

As Dennis Smith has argued, banquet practices impart an identity to those who eat together;[83] thus celebration of the Eucharist gives the church a particular identity and boundary. The church consists of the people who welcome sinners in the name of Jesus, the people who welcome and care for the unlovable, the people who welcome the needy even when they seem to have few resources. All of these commitments are rooted in the biblical narrative. By committing itself to such values, the church has already created boundaries that mark certain behaviors as acceptable and others as unacceptable. When one sees the embodiment of such Eucharistic values—say, for instance, a commitment to multiculturalism—those who cannot abide such commitments may exclude themselves. They become like the rich young man who heard Jesus' call to give away his possessions and "went away grieving" (Matthew 19:22). Thus Eucharistic communities have boundaries even if they are loath to acknowledge them. Nevertheless, as the people who welcome sinners in the name of Jesus, the church is justified in cultivating a suspicious attitude toward its boundaries. They can become legalistic rule systems. As noted earlier, the church's boundaries should be somewhat porous; but that is different than saying that there are no boundaries at all.

Chapter Four

The Meals of Jesus

JUSTIFYING AN OPEN TABLE
ON WESLEYAN GROUNDS

In this chapter, I will present Wesleyan grounds in support of the open table, although the assumption that the open table is an exceptional practice will remain. The phrase "Wesleyan grounds" must, of course, be defined. I will not claim that John Wesley practiced an open table in the same way that many in the modern church practice it. Nevertheless, I will argue that the modern practice reflects a development of theological trajectories that were clearly present in John Wesley's teaching and practice. In my usage, then, the practice of John Wesley and Wesleyan practice are closely related concepts but they are not synonymous. Such a relationship between founders and their theological heirs is a depth dynamic common to the development of all theological and liturgical traditions.[1]

I will offer a theoretical rationale for understanding this relationship between John Wesley and the *praxis* that emerges from his witness. I will then present two significant examples from the early years of Wesley's ministry that influence contemporary Methodist thinking regarding invitations to the Table. The first of these is a decidedly negative example—Wesley's refusal to serve communion to Sophia Hopkey Williamson in August of 1737. Here we find Wesley as an example to avoid and Wesleyan practice as the embodiment of that avoidance. The second example is his 1740 encounter with the Moravian Quietists of the Fetter Lane Society in London. Those Moravians argued that persons who were seeking Christ should not use the ordinances of God prior to their experience of justification. Wesley vehemently opposed that teaching. He insisted that God had instituted the various means of grace and commanded their use, even among seekers. Here we find Wesley as an example to emulate, with his theology of prevenient grace supporting a generous and frequent use of the Eucharist, even among the unconverted.

As to the development of Wesleyan tradition, of what significance is the fact that most of the seekers Wesley encountered were already baptized? In modern parlance, we might refer to these persons as baptized yet essentially unchurched. Classical Wesleyan piety does not, however, posit much of a difference between the baptized unchurched and those who have not been baptized. Wesley's exhortation to baptized yet unawakened sinners rings in our ears: "baptism is not the new birth: they are not one and the same thing."[2] Whether such a distinction between the baptized and the nonbaptized *should* be made is another consideration altogether.

As a preliminary step in this discussion, I acknowledge a general scholarly consensus that insists that most residents of eighteenth-century England were baptized, even if many were not active participants in the life of the church. Following the long-standing practice of the church catholic, most people had been baptized as infants.[3] Thus when Wesley insisted that those who were seeking Christ not delay in coming to the Table, he was speaking, by and large, to *baptized seekers*. To insist that *most* were baptized is not, however, the same as saying that *all* were baptized. The Society of Friends and various Baptist sects were present in mid-eighteenth century England. Baptists did not baptize children and the Friends did not baptize anyone. The Act of Toleration (1688) protected their right to practice the faith as they understood it. It is important to notice that even before this Act legalized the various dissenting movements, the 1662 version of *The Book of Common Prayer* had included a rite for "The Ministration of Publick Baptism to Such as are of Riper Years," that is, a rite for the baptism of adults. This rite, which had not appeared in previous editions of *The Book of Common Prayer,* implicitly acknowledges the presence of the non-baptized in seventeenth-century England. If one cannot establish *universal* baptism in eighteenth-century England—and it is not possible to do so—then a Methodist exception to the baptismal norm cannot be excluded simply by appealing to the historical circumstances of the eighteenth century. One must evaluate the practice historically and theologically. We will begin that process by discussing the relationship between John Wesley and his Wesleyan heirs.

THE OPEN TABLE AND THE DEVELOPMENT OF WESLEYAN PRACTICES

Christian traditions develop the ideas and practices of their founders in ways that are more or less faithful to their teaching and example. Christians believe that the Holy Spirit guides the churches in this ongoing dialogue with Scripture and Tradition. While claims regarding the faithfulness of particular developments will be debated, such a traditioning process is a normal and recurring part of church life. There are, of course, differing theological understandings of the development process. For instance, church historian Philip Schaff, writing in 1846, insisted that Protestantism was not a new faith but a faithful development of Catholicism. One could not, as it were, turn back the clock to the time of Jesus and the Apostles and pretend that the Catholic Church had never taken shape. A full understanding of God's work in history called for the church to encompass both the Catholic tradition and the Reformation. He wrote,

> Catholicism and Protestantism, do not, separately taken, exhibit the *full* compass of Christian truth; and we look forward accordingly, with earnest longing, to a higher stadium of development...that shall be neither one nor the other.... The realization of this evangelical Catholicity or churchly Protestantism, forms more and more clearly the great problem of the present age.[4]

In Schaff's view, the churches of the Reformation stood in continuity with the Catholic Church but neither represented the end stage in the development process. The telos was yet to be realized. John Henry Newman, another nineteenth-century theologian, also believed in the continuing development of the church, but only within the Church of Rome. In his view, it alone was the true church of Christ.

> No one doubts...that the Roman Catholic communion of this day is the successor and representative of the Medieval Church, or that the Medieval Church is the legitimate heir of the Nicene...[5]

Those who break communion with Rome, Newman believed, inevitably descend into heresy. Rome had not yet reached the end stage of its development, thus in one sense Newman anticipated Vatican II; but he believed that the Protestant developments of the church were illegitimate. One should understand that Newman wrote as a convert from the Church of England and that he had come to believe that the *via media* espoused by the Anglican tradition was an untenable mirage.

John Wesley's view, of course, allowed for the Reformed (and Wesleyan) development of Catholic traditions. In line with that commitment, he believed that the Methodist movement was a faithful development of Anglicanism, standing in continuity with its theology, its liturgy, and its canon law even as it shaped and challenged them with its various exceptional practices (see chapter two). The Anglican tradition of Wesley's understanding—and thereby Methodism—was accountable to the Bible and to the ongoing witness of the church, especially that of the first five centuries. That position, of course, represented fairly standard Anglican theology.[6] While many Anglicans have disputed Wesley's reading of their tradition and his claims of fidelity to it, there can be little doubt that the Methodist movement is a direct development of Anglicanism. Until the revisions of the 1980s, Methodism's sacramental rites were those of *The Book of Common Prayer*. Until American Methodists eliminated ordination as deacon as a transitional step to elder's ordination, its ordering of ministry was essentially the same as The Church of England. With but one exception and some relatively minor editorial changes, the twenty-five Articles of Religion received by Methodists are taken directly from the thirty-nine Articles of the Church of England.[7] Methodist piety and its language of prayer is rooted in the prayer book tradition, although that linkage is fading. Methodists developed new traditions and formularies, like the love feast, and old traditions were altered, as with Francis Asbury's radical revision of the episcopal office, but the roots of the movement are clearly within the Church of England.

As Wesley and his early Methodist colleagues developed the Anglican tradition, so contemporary Methodists continue to interact with and develop Wesley's teachings. It would be a strange practice indeed if the heirs of Wesley, the great innovator, were to freeze such development at the point of his death. As I have argued earlier, innovation for the sake of mission is a fundamental part of the Methodist tradition. To defend the open table on Wesleyan grounds does not mean, therefore, that one must find John Wesley condoning the communion of the non-baptized or actually practicing it himself. Such evidence would not necessarily end the argument. Indeed, Wesley's heirs have argued that various aspects of his practice were mistaken. For instance, we know that Wesley occasionally practiced bibliomancy—that is, opening the Bible in random fashion and receiving that text as if it were a direct message from God.[8] Modern Methodists do not commend this practice. Neither, on our best days, do we commend his overzealous work habits as a good model for our pastors. What, then, constitutes a faithful Wesleyan practice?

One can argue that a practice is Wesleyan if it takes principles established by John Wesley and develops them in ways consistent with his thought, his practice, and his goals. For instance, in an earlier publication, I cited Wesleyan grounds in urging United Methodists to develop a version of the ancient catechumenate for adult baptismal candidates.[9] The catechumenate took various forms in the ancient churches, but its distinguishing characteristic was a long period of formation (as many as three years) preceding baptism. Wesley never practiced such a catechumenate, nor did the Church of England of his day, but his class system was a highly disciplined process for Christian formation.[10] Wesley's process was not related to baptismal preparation; nevertheless, I insisted that the catechumenate was consistent with his thought and practice, and thereby Wesleyan. The ordination of women by contemporary Methodists is another case in point. As we discussed earlier (see chapter 2), Wesley did not ordain women and in fact argued against it, but when he employed women lay preachers he established a trajectory of practice. In a broader sense, his understanding that the presence of spiritual gifts is the clearest evidence of God's call to the preaching ministry made the church's recognition of gifted women more likely. Thus when the 1956 Methodist General Conference passed legislation that allowed women to be ordained elder and gain full membership in the Annual Conference, they believed their decision reflected sound Wesleyan *praxis*. According to their discernment, the trajectory of their founder's thought supported their decision. Theological claims based on such a theology of development will, of course, be subject to arguments and counter-claims.

Such processes of discernment are not unique to Methodism. Christians frequently have made arguments based on theological trajectories, albeit not without disagreement and controversy. The practice of baptizing infants and children provides a classic example. Few, if any, reasonably qualified biblical scholars in the modern era will claim that one can find direct examples of infant baptism in the New Testament, much less a direct commandment for the practice. One might hope, as it were, to peek behind the scenes in the stories about the baptism of households and ask the narrator, "Just how young were the members of Lydia's household?" (Acts 16:15). The jailkeeper of Philippi was baptized, "he and his entire household" (Acts 16:34). Were there, per chance, any babies present? Methodist imagination may want to place some young children in those pictures, but one cannot prove the accuracy of such a portrait; yet even if one could find a full description of the baptismal rites administered by St. Paul on those two occasions, such a text would not freeze the development of the ritual tradition. Since living Christians practice sacramental rites in the midst of their various cultural and community circumstances, ritual traditions continue to evolve, and they do so even in the face of attempts to enforce liturgical uniformity. As a case in point, note that we have much fuller (yet still incomplete) descriptions of the rites Jesus led at the Last Supper. Churches have interpreted that witness in myriad ways and the process continues, as it should. Such is the nature of ritual development. Churches and congregations receive ritual traditions and make them their own, amending and deleting aspects as they see fit.

As we have established, the New Testament does not give us direct evidence about the baptism of children, but along with the Hebrew Scriptures it provides the theological basis for the practice, albeit an arguable one. One begins with covenantal theology, the wide foundation on which the entire biblical narrative is built. When God called Abraham, God made the promise not only to him and Sarah but also to the family and the nation that would descend from them (Genesis 12:1-3). When male children were born, they were circumcised on their eighth day and thereby initiated into the covenant (Genesis 17:1-27). Thus children were part of the first covenant, by promise and by covenantal sign. One can imagine, therefore, the logic of the first Christians: If children born into the first covenant were marked with the sign of that covenant, then surely this new covenant would mark them with its sign. Indeed, the language of covenant and children was present on the day of Pentecost. When Peter called the multitude to repent and be baptized, he said to them, "For the promise is for you, for your children, and for all who are far away, everyone whom the Lord our God calls to him" (Acts 2:39). Yet again, there is no portrait of the baptismal rites conducted that day, and we cannot prove that any children were baptized, nor can one disprove it. *We are free, however, to argue that the theology inherited by Peter and the disciples made the baptism of young children plausible, if not inevitable.*

The baptism of infants is based on other biblical considerations as well, such as the blessing Jesus gave to children. For more than four hundred years, the Anglican and Methodist traditions cited Mark 10:13-16 as their warrant for the baptism of children:

And they were bringing unto him little children, that he should touch them: and the disciples rebuked them. But when Jesus saw it, he was moved with indignation, and said unto them, Suffer the little children to come unto me; forbid them not: for to such belongeth the kingdom of God. Verily I say unto you, Whosoever shall not receive the kingdom of God as a little child, he shall in no wise enter therein. And he took them in his arms, and blessed them, laying his hands upon them.[11]

This pericope is not, of course, from a baptismal scene and thus cannot serve as a proof text for the practice. It has functioned, rather, to bolster the theological case for the baptism of infants. If Jesus received children and said that they belong to the kingdom of God, should they not receive the covenant sign of that reign? So goes the logic. In a much broader sense, finally, the church has based the baptism of children on the doctrine of prevenient grace. The baptism of children embodies our faith in the God who reaches out to us first, before we even knew God or thought to love God. "We love"—and Methodists would say, we baptize our children—"because [God] first loved us" (1 John 4:19).

The church bases its practice of baptizing children on such logic, even though we may understand that the baptism of adults is the normative practice.[12] Another way of expressing the normative status of adult baptism is to say that the goal of all baptism is mature discipleship, regardless of the age at which the candidate receives it.[13] It is possible, of course, to read the biblical and theological data that I have cited in support of infant baptism and come to an entirely different conclusion. These differing conclusions were evident as early as the third century. Two key documents from that time, *The Apostolic Tradition of Hippolytus* and *On Baptism* by Tertullian, acknowledge the church's practice of baptizing children but their conclusions differ significantly. While Hippolytus focused on the formation and baptism of adults, he also provided rubrics for the baptism of children.[14] Tertullian acknowledged the practice of baptizing children and he spoke against it in strong terms.

It follows that deferment of baptism is more profitable, in accordance with each person's character and attitude, and even age: and especially so as regards children. For what need is there, if there really is no need, for even their sponsors to be brought into peril, seeing they may possibly themselves fail of their promises by death. . . . It is true our Lord says, *Forbid them not to come to me.* So let them come, when they are growing up, when they are learning, when they are being taught what they are coming to: let them be made Christians when they have become competent to know Christ. Why should innocent infancy come with haste to the remission of sins?[15]

As we know in our modern experience, Anabaptists and Baptists read the same New Testament as those who baptize young children and yet they come to quite different ritual conclusions. As they understand it, the biblical call to repentance and discipleship provides warrant for baptizing only persons who can make a conscious confession of faith. Challenges to the baptism of children arise from other parts of the church as well. Indeed, twentieth-century Lutheran theologian and martyr Dietrich Bonhoeffer raised serious concerns about the propriety of infant baptism, insisting that such baptisms should occur only "in a living Christian community." To baptize without such community, he insists, "betokens a disgusting frivolity in dealing with the souls of the children themselves. For baptism can never be repeated."[16] In his view, infant baptism is a legitimate practice only within a tightly defined Christian fellowship, and not in the generalized sense often practiced in the mainline churches.

As we see with this case of infant baptism, practices based on theological and liturgical trajectories, like the open table, will be debatable. Indeed, ecumenical honesty demands that such questions be debated, and generally the church benefits from the debate. Even if they represent a minority *praxis*, the Anabaptist witness reminds the rest of the church that mature discipleship is the goal of baptism. My point in this chapter is that theological trajectories established in John Wesley's theology and practice make the sacramental exception of the open table plausible. We will now turn our attention to the narrative of John Wesley's life, to a significant, albeit negative, example that works to discourage fencing of the communion table.

JOHN WESLEY AND SOPHIA HOPKEY: AN EXAMPLE TO AVOID

During his time as a missionary in Georgia, John Wesley developed a romantic interest in Sophia Hopkey, who was a member of his Savannah parish. His relationship with "Miss Sophy" was something of an odd one.[17] Was Wesley her suitor or her pastor? The two spent considerable time together, which Wesley justified in religious terms. They ate breakfast together frequently. They discussed matters of religion, and she often joined him for morning and evening prayers. Wesley even tutored her in French.[18] By all accounts, she was devoted to him and he was equally smitten, even though he found it difficult to admit.[19]

Parishioners wondered, perhaps playfully, what they might be doing in all that time together. While many men would delight in finding an eligible woman of an agreeable and compatible disposition, in Wesley's mind their mutual attraction was a problem. She shook his resolve to remain celibate. He thought marriage would hinder his answering the call to preach to the Native Americans.[20] Clearly, Wesley was attracted to her and that frightened him, as he revealed in the account of a private conversation he held with Miss Sophy at the home of Mr. Thomas Causton, her uncle and guardian.

> Calling at Mr. Causton's, she was there alone. And this was indeed an hour of trial. Her words, her eyes, her air, her every motion and gesture, were full of such a softness and sweetness! I know not what might have been the consequence had I then but touched her hand. And how I avoided it I know not. Surely God is over all![21]

What would he do about her? After praying and fasting with his colleagues, Wesley submitted his decision to the drawing of lots. He prepared three slips of paper: the first said "Marry," the second "Think not of it this year" and the third "Think of it no more." He drew the third, and shortly thereafter told Miss Sophy that he would not marry her.[22] It was, indeed, a strange way to decide a matter of the heart.[23] Likely heart-broken and confused, Hopkey quickly agreed to marry William Williamson, and the wedding was held on March 12, 1737, a mere eight days after Wesley had reported his decision to her.[24] Wesley was deeply hurt.

While Hopkey and Williams were married in a neighboring parish, Wesley remained their pastor, which caused understandable tensions. These came to a head on August 7 of that same year when Wesley refused to admit Miss Sophy to Holy Communion, thus sparking a lawsuit and a series of related complaints that would drive him from the colony by the end of the year. In response to that lawsuit, he explained his decision to exclude her from communion in this letter dated August 11, 1737:

> To Mrs. Sophia Williamson.

> At Mr. Causton's request I write once more. The rules whereby I proceed are these:
> 'So many as intend to be partakers of the Holy Communion shall signify their names to the Curate, at least some time the day before.' This you did not do. 'And if any of these . . . have done any wrong

to his neighbours by word or deed, so that the congregation be thereby offended, the Curate...shall advertise him that in any wise he presume not to come to the Lord's Table until he hath openly declared himself to have truly repented.'

If you offer yourself at the Lord's Table on Sunday I will advertise you (as I have done more than once) wherein you 'have done wrong'. And when you have 'openly declared yourself to have truly repented' I will administer to you the mysteries of God.[25]

The paragraph of the letter beginning with "so many" is drawn from the disciplinary rubrics of the Anglican Service of Holy Communion (*BCP* 1662). Viewed in strictly legal terms, perhaps there were grounds for his action. He was, however, considerably stretching the intent of the second rubric which called for the warning and possible exclusion of a person who had committed serious sins. The full text of the rubric is as follows:

If a Minister be persuaded that any person who presents himself to be a partaker of the holy Communion ought not to be admitted thereunto by reason of malicious and open contention with his neighbours, or other grave and open sin without repentance, he shall give an account of the same to the Ordinary of the place, and therein obey his order and direction, but so as not to refuse the Sacrament to any person until in accordance with such order and direction he shall have called him and advertised him that in any wise he presume not to come to the Lord's Table; Provided that in case of grave and immediate scandal to the Congregation the Minister shall not admit such person, but shall give an account of the same to the Ordinary within seven days after at the latest and therein obey the order and direction given to him by the Ordinary; Provided also that before issuing his order and direction in relation to any such person the Ordinary shall afford him an opportunity for interview.[26]

Miss Sophy's offense, whatever it may have been, hardly seems to qualify as a grave and open sin. Indeed, if one follows the most obvious reading of this rubric, excommunication was to be administered primarily in response to open and public scandal, for sins that would offend an entire congregation. As written, it does not apply to those relatively private struggles with sin that trouble all Christians under normal circumstances.[27] Furthermore, excommunication was not to be effected without consultation with one's ecclesiastical ordinary, normally one's bishop. In this case, where his bishop was not available, an appropriately cautious priest might at least discuss his reading of the case with some other presbyters.

What, in fact, had Miss Sophy done? The nature of her offense is difficult to determine. Against his advice, she had ceased meeting with him for spiritual counsel, which hardly seems surprising given the circumstances.[28] Wesley had mildly reproved Miss Sophy for her "insincerity," specifically that she had spoken well of him until he refused to propose and only after her marriage to Mr. Williamson did she allege that he had behaved himself inappropriately.[29] On July 3rd, he had reproved her about "some things which I thought reprovable in her behaviour," but there is no record of a specific complaint.[30] There is little way to avoid the obvious conclusion. Wesley had taken a rubric meant for extreme circumstances and had used it to his advantage, even vengefully, in a relatively minor personal squabble. His behavior in this case remains an example of exceedingly bad pastoral practice.[31]

The story of Wesley's misadventures in this case presents the archetypal Methodist witness against the fencing of the Table and the overly scrupulous application of sacramental rubrics. Thus we see its relevance to a discussion of the open table. Expelling her from the Table was the worst such offense foisted on the Savannah parish, but it was not the only time during that pastorate that he interpreted the rubrics of the church in a less-than-generous manner. The confrontation with Sophia Hopkey brought similar offenses to light. Wesley insisted on baptizing infants by dipping (i.e., not by sprinkling). The prayer book rubric indicates that babies were to be dipped in the font unless their sponsors certified that they were "weak," in which case pouring was permitted;[32] thus Wesley's reading of the prayer book would have been technically accurate in most cases; yet sprinkling was the prevailing custom. One may well question the pastoral wisdom of fighting that particular battle. The affidavit filed by Mr. Williamson on August 16, 1737 also complained that Wesley had expelled Mr. William Gough from Holy Communion on baptismal grounds. Gough had indeed been baptized, but the officiant was a Presbyterian, a dissenter, and therefore Wesley considered the baptism invalid.[33] In defending himself, Wesley insisted that Mr. Gough had accepted his *de facto* excommunication, remaining in the worshiping congregation but deciding that he would not submit to re-baptism.[34] It is possible that Gough was not offended by the decision, although one wonders since *Wesley* told the story. The charge suggests that Wesley's decision was offensive to some of Gough's fellow parishioners. As a particular matter of interest for our discussion of the open table, the Grand Jurors who investigated the charges insisted that Wesley had on other occasions enforced the rule that required persons to register for communion. Thus Miss Sophy was not the first one excluded on these grounds.[35] What shall we make of this fact? At the least we should note that such practice contradicts the teaching delivered earlier in "The Duty of Constant Communion" (1732). In that text, Wesley insisted that it is good to prepare for communion, yet lack of preparation is not a reason to abstain. He argued the point rather forcefully.

> Indeed every prudent man will, when he has time, examine himself before he receives the Lord's Supper: whether he repents him truly of his former sins; whether he believes the promises of God; whether he fully designs to walk in his ways, and be in charity with all men.... But what is this *to you* who have not time? What excuse is this for not obeying God? He commands you to come, and prepare yourself by prayer if you have time; if you have not, however, come. Make not reverence to God's command a pretence for breaking it. Do not rebel against him for fear of offending him. Whatever you do or leave undone besides, be sure to do what God bids you do. Examining yourself, and using private prayer, especially before the Lord's Supper, is good. But behold! 'To obey is better than' self-examination, 'and to hearken' than the prayer of an angel.[36]

Having read this passage, one might assume that the registration rubric was a good rule in that it encouraged intentional preparation, but that it should not be used against one who presents herself at the last minute, not having time to register.

Be that as it may, in the affidavit we find evidence that Wesley was enforcing some type of Eucharistic fence based on baptism, and a rigid one at that. Indeed, the Wesley of the Georgia narrative appears as the quintessentially ineffective pastor, an uptight and sanctimonious policeman of the altar who provoked the wrath of his community and deserved it. According to a fairly standard version of the entire Wesleyan narrative, the lesson was not wasted and he quickly outgrew such priggish nonsense. The words of nineteenth-century English scholar Luke Tyerman epitomize this reading. Tyerman wrote,

> If we are right in denouncing *ritualism* now, Savannah was right in denouncing *ritualism* then. If the thing is offensive and obnoxious here, it was equally offensive and obnoxious there; and if no other end had been answered by Wesley's mission to America than knocking out of him his high church nonsense, the good effected would have been an ample compensation for two dangerous voyages of six thousand miles...[37]

Tyerman's critique of Wesley's ritualism was shaped by British Methodism's conflict with the Oxford Movement. Nevertheless, this particular reading of Wesley's growth is more accurate than not, although one must be careful not to confuse ritualism with commitment to constant communion and the classical liturgical forms of the church. As Wesley did, one can forsake "ritualism" and a legalistic reading of rubrics without rejecting sacramental and liturgical worship.[38]

In traditional Methodist lore, Wesley's dealings with Miss Sophy and his heavy-handed administration of the rubrics are presented as examples to avoid. Wesley himself looked back on this period of his ministry with evident dismay. In a 1749 *Journal* entry, he reprinted a letter from John Martin Bolzius, in which Bolzius reported on considerable progress of the mission in Georgia. Of Bolzius and his report, Wesley wrote,

> What a truly Christian piety and simplicity breathe in these lines! And yet this very man, when I was at Savannah, did I refuse to admit to the Lord's Table, because he was *not baptized*; that is, not baptized by a minister who had been *episcopally ordained*! Can anyone carry *High Church* zeal higher than this? And how well have I been since beaten with mine own staff![39]

By and large, Methodists have internalized the lesson Wesley learned in Georgia. They are ready, as it were, to beat with verbal staff those who try to fence the Table. I will discuss these dynamics in chapter 5. In the next section I will discuss Wesley's teaching on the means of grace, a positive theological witness frequently used in support of an open table.

JOHN WESLEY AND HIS RESPONSE TO THE STILLNESS CONTROVERSY: AN EXAMPLE TO EMULATE

From a classically orthodox Christian perspective, salvation always begins with God's initiative. John Wesley called this dynamic prevenient grace; that is, the grace that "goes before" human response. This grace enables us to trust God and do works of mercy and justice, and without it we can do nothing. This understanding of grace is deeply rooted in the biblical narrative and particularly in Genesis and Exodus. There we see a realistic picture of humanity. We see disregard for God's commandments (Genesis 2:15-17; 3:1-7), along with deception and selfishness (Genesis 3:8-13). We see forgetfulness and apathy, hatred and violence (Genesis 4:1-25; 6:1-7), and there was little hope for improvement. The best humanity could do was build the Tower of Babel, and that made matters worse (Genesis11:1-9). It is a narrative oft-repeated in human experience. But God did not stand aloof from all of this human rebellion and misery. God acted, calling Abraham, making a covenant with him and his family (Genesis 12:1-3). God blessed and multiplied that family, sometimes in the face of significant opposition and challenge (Genesis 15-22). When famine came to the descendents of Abraham and Sarah, God provided for them (Genesis 37-50). When they were caught in bitter slavery, God set them free (Exodus 1-15). God led them to the Promised Land, and even though they were stubborn and willful (Exodus 17, Numbers 13-14, Joshua), God gave them the land. When they forgot God and fell into idolatry, God refused to turn away from them but sent prophets who bid them to return to the covenant (1 Kings 17ff, Jeremiah 1ff). When they were taken into exile, God promised to bring them home and God acted on that promise (Isaiah 40). In the fullness of time, God sent Jesus. "God so loved the world that he gave his only Son, so that everyone who believes in him may not perish but may have eternal life" (John 3:16). God poured out the Holy Spirit, who enables people to believe the Gospel and embody its way of life (Acts 2). As the Epistle of John insists, "We love because [God] first loved us" (First John 4:19).

In many ways, the Bible is a long story about prevenient grace, about what God did for human beings even before they could respond. Wesley described the continuing dynamic of prevenient grace as follows:

> [It is] all the 'drawings' of 'the Father', the desires after God, which, if we yield to them, increase more and more; all that 'light' wherewith the Son of God 'enlighteneth everyone that cometh into the world', *showing* every man 'to do justly, to love mercy, and to walk humbly with his God'; all the *convictions* which his Spirit from time to time works in every child of man. Although it is true the generality of men stifle them as soon as possible, and after a while forget, or at least deny, that ever they had them at all."[40]

While Christian theologians since St. Augustine had articulated this concept and depended upon it, it was particularly important for Wesley and it was especially so in his disputations with the Calvinists. In its most extreme form, Calvinistic theology insisted that only those chosen by God could come to saving faith and all others were beyond hope.

Calvinistic theology maintained a belief in prevenient grace, as all orthodox Christians must do. Calvinists and Wesleyans shared belief in the total depravity of humanity, that is, in their inability to solve their sinful predicament. They parted company over their understanding of God's work in the face of that depravity. Calvinists believed that God's grace was given only to the elect, and, further, that the elect could not refuse it. Conversely, Wesley insisted that prevenient grace is at work in all people even though many stifle it or ignore it. In Wesley's understanding, one responded to this "drawing" of God and cultivated an openness to it by using the means of grace, particularly prayer and fasting, reading and meditating on the Scriptures, Christian fellowship, and receiving the Lord's Supper.[41] The theological and practical implications of belief in prevenient grace, coupled with this understanding of how one receives it, are profound. For the sake of the world's salvation, Methodists were charged to use the means and to proclaim their availability to all.

Wesley's teaching on the means of grace came to sharp focus in his dispute with the Moravians of the Fetter Lane Society in London, a dispute known as the "stillness" controversy. Wesley spent considerable time with the Fetter Lane Society in the year following his heart-warming experience, but he came into conflict with their teaching. One finds a concentrated description of the dispute in his *Journal* beginning June 5, 1740.[42] These Moravians, whose belief in justification by faith had so impressed Wesley, believed that there is no such thing as a means of grace. As they saw it, there is but one commandment in the New Testament, and that is the commandment to believe.[43] Wesley described that idea and its implications as follows.

> They affirmed also that there is *no commandment* in the New Testament but *to believe;* that no other *duty* lies upon us; and that when a man does believe he is not *bound* or *obliged* to do anything which is commanded there: in particular, that he is not 'subject to ordinances' that is (as they explained it), is not *bound* or *obliged* to pray, to communicate, to read or hear the Scriptures, but may or may not use any of these things (being in *no bondage*) according as he finds *his heart free to it*.[44]

His opponents argued that a seeker should "be still," doing nothing while she or he waits for justifying faith.[45] According to their teaching, an unbeliever who used the means was actually committing sin, presuming upon a privilege that was not his or hers.

It has been inferred that 'Christians are not subject to the ordinances of Christ'; that believers *need not*, and unbelievers *may not*, use them; that these are not *obliged*, and those are not *permitted*, so to do; that these *do not sin* when they abstain from them, but these *do sin* when they do not abstain.[46]

Wesley found their position profoundly unbiblical, if not absurd. It struck at the heart of the Anglican system that had brought him to justifying faith, and he simply could not accept it. Against the Quietists, Wesley argued that the biblical commandments to use the ordinary means of grace must be obeyed by all persons. As he insisted, we perform this obedience to our great benefit.

The sense of it is undeniably found in Scripture. For God hath in Scripture ordained prayer, reading or hearing, and receiving the Lord's Supper, as the ordinary means of conveying his grace to man.[47]

We receive grace that lifts us into right relationship with God and humanity.

As we read Wesley's account of the stillness controversy, it is important for us to remember that he is interpreting both his own position and that of his opponents; thus theirs is presented in the worst possible light. Moreover, we may presume that the position Wesley stated in the midst of this theological battle was somewhat overstated. We should allow for some rhetorical excess. The unmistakable point, however, is that Wesley *believed* that the Fetter Lane Moravians were warning seekers away from the sacraments and he responded decisively.

His *Journal* entry for June 27, 1740, in which he discussed a sermon on the text "Do this in remembrance of me," provides an example. In the sermon, he acknowledges the normative relationship between baptism and the Lord's Supper.

In the ancient church everyone who was baptized communicated daily. So in the Acts we read, they 'all continued daily in the breaking of bread and in prayer.'[48]

The text that he quoted (Acts 2:42b) describes what the early church did in the days following the baptism of the three thousand. We see that Wesley did not challenge the ancient baptismal norm; indeed, he assumed it as historical fact. Nevertheless, he was focused on another more theological agenda. He argued for an ecclesiology that would view the Eucharist as converting ordinance rather than a confirming ordinance, an understanding of Eucharist as means of grace leading to conversion more than sign of unity in Christ. According to Wesley, those early Christians also saw the breaking of bread as converting ordinance.[49] As further evidence for this theology, he pointed to the circumstances of his audience:

> For many now present know, the very beginning of your *conversion* to God . . . was wrought at the Lord's Supper. Now one single instance of this kind overthrows that whole assertion.[50]

In this instance, Wesley clearly presented the sacrament as means of prevenient grace. He pressed the rhetoric one step further, calling his audience to see the disciples in the Upper Room as a gathering of unconverted sinners; and Jesus gave them communion.

> Our Lord commanded those very men who were then *unconverted*, who had *not* yet 'received the Holy Ghost', who (in the full sense of the word) were not *believers*, to 'do this in remembrance of him'. Here the precept is clear. And to these he delivered the elements with his own hands.[51]

Once again, we should remember that Wesley was making a rhetorical flourish in opposition to the Quietist position. Even so, his argument unmistakably supports communing unconverted persons, and such was typical of Wesley in the aftermath of the Georgia debacle. Of course, his heart-warming experience at the Moravian Society meeting on Aldersgate Street in London (May 24, 1738) had occurred less than a year after the unfortunate incident with Sophia Hopkey (August 7, 1737). While some claim that Aldersgate, coupled with Georgia, effectively ended his commitment to high church Anglicanism and its sacramental practices, the assertion is but partially correct.[52] As we noted earlier, Wesley gave up his rigid reading of the prayer book rubrics, but not his commitment to the sacraments. The shift in his understanding of the rubrics, profound in its own way, allowed his deep commitment to Eucharist as converting ordinance. Henceforth, the weight of his argument would fall on receiving the unconverted at the Table. It is not a particularly long leap from defending the communion of the unconverted to defending the communion of the nonbaptized. Although it seems that Wesley himself did not take this leap, given the passion of his rhetoric it is not surprising that some of his theological heirs have taken that subsequent step.

Wesley continued the description of his sermon against the stillness doctrine in his *Journal* entry for June 28. Here we see that the trajectory of his argument clearly moves toward welcoming all who present themselves at the Table. He speaks against preparation, casting it as a potential barrier to the Table. After repeating his assertion that the Eucharist is a means of grace, he wrote,

> I showed at large ... (3) that inasmuch as we come to his table, not to give him anything but to *receive* whatsoever he sees best for us, there is *no previous preparation* indispensably necessary, but *a desire* to receive whatsoever he pleases to give; and (4) that *no fitness* is required at the time of communicating but *a sense of our state*, of our utter sinfulness and helplessness; every one who knows he is *fit for hell* being just *fit to come to Christ*, in this as well as all other ways of his appointment.[53]

His assertion that desire is the only preparation necessary anticipates the language that he would use in the General Rules of the United Societies, published in 1743. In that text he wrote, "There is one only condition previously required in those who desire admission into these societies, 'a desire to flee from the wrath to come, to be saved from their sins.'"[54] Such desire, he insisted, is sufficient to *begin* the journey of faith, although specific Christian formation is necessary for its successful completion. Those who truly desire salvation will bear fruit. They will also "evidence their desire of salvation" by practicing the three General Rules: (1) Doing no harm, (2) Doing good, and (3) Attending upon all the ordinances of God; that is, using the means of grace.[55] No preparation was necessary for using the means except this desire for a right relationship with God. From the beginning of the movement, Wesley believed that the willing seeker would be led to conversion through practicing the virtues and habits of the faith on a regular basis; therefore, there should be few, if any, barriers to the means of grace. Such forceful rhetoric continues to provide a consistent pressure against fencing of the Table.

Perhaps the intensity of this conflict caused Wesley to overstate the case, but his teaching about preparation remained consistent. If, according to Wesley, *preparation* for the Eucharist is not necessary, then it becomes harder to argue, on Wesleyan grounds, that baptism is necessary. One can understand, at least, how committed Wesleyans might find themselves arguing against baptism as a Eucharistic fence. In a Wesleyan perspective, if a person comes to the Table desiring the mercy of God under the sign of the Eucharist, then she or he has met the test for admission. Whether Wesley's case was overstated or not, the theological trajectory established by his rhetoric continues among modern Methodists.

CONCLUDING ASSERTIONS BASED ON WESLEY'S TEACHING

1. In reading John Wesley's discussion of the means of grace, one should understand that his strong rhetoric took shape amid the stillness controversy. Therefore, when he asserts that no preparation for communion is necessary, we should allow for the fact that he was speaking in extreme tones. As the church hears Wesley's statements about preparation, it will be wise to hear them in dialogue with his teachings about discipline and formation. It should also hear those statements in dialogue with the wider church's wisdom about formational disciplines related to admission to the Table.

2. Building upon Wesley's means of grace teaching, one could argue for the absolute necessity of baptism just as much as one could argue for an open table. One could insist that baptism is a necessary embodiment of that desire to "flee from the wrath to come"[56] While Wesley's discussions about the means of grace did not emphasize baptism, one can assert, on Wesleyan grounds, that baptism should be considered the foundational means of grace. Here we remind ourselves that arguing from theological trajectories can lead to quite different conclusions. For our purposes, it is important to note that one can use the means of grace teaching in support of the open table. Of greater importance, one can understand the narrative tradition out of which such assertions are made.

3. The Sophia Hopkey fiasco and the rhetoric expressed within the stillness controversy lend narrative weight to a Methodist practice of the open table. Having read these narratives, opting for an open table practice seems plausible, even if not completely advisable. These two narratives do not, however, offer the final word on the subject of the open table.

4. Even if nonbaptized seekers are received at the Lord's Table based solely on their desire to receive communion, faithful Methodist *praxis* calls for the church to counsel them and bring them to serious formational disciplines as soon as possible. To say that a faithful Wesleyan practice might allow (and even encourage) the

non-prepared to come to the Eucharistic banquet does not imply that they should be left in that state, or that we should somehow expect God to shape disciples without our aid. Wesleyan *praxis* will allow no ultimate separation between sacramental practice and spiritual discipline. Thus for Methodists, an open table must remain a sacramental exception and not the norm.

A Passionate Commitment among Methodists

JUSTIFYING AN OPEN TABLE ON EXPERIENTIAL GROUNDS

$\mathbf{M}$ake no mistake!" said the e-mail posted by a United Methodist clergywoman,

> Those who serve the Eucharist to the not-yet-baptized are in *no* way emulating Christ, who would never have *dreamed* of sitting down to dinner with all comers, or with sinners, or with anyone else who wasn't a part of his sectarian religious group. "Get those sinners the hell out of here," Jesus is known to have said on many an occasion.
>
> And that's what I say too. So what if there are reasonably devout fourth graders in my congregation, who have a living relationship with Christ and wish to have the presence and power of Christ... through the grace of the Eucharist, but whose parents, unfortunately, have an inadequate theology of baptism.... Let the sins of the parents be visited upon their children until they reach the "proper" age for confirmation class! They'll just have to get along without the grace of the Eucharist. Besides, it's only a symbol anyway.

She was responding to an e-mail that had argued that the open table makes a mockery of baptism as the sacrament of Christian Initiation. Mockery indeed! Her sarcastic response provides a vivid example of a passionate commitment to the open table, a commitment shared by many other United Methodists.

What is the theological significance of such passion? Wesley believed that he and the Methodists practiced an "experimental religion," that is, that our faith claims are confirmed in personal and corporate experience. Thus the heart "strangely warmed" confirmed the reality of justification by faith. In a sense it also amplified that doctrine, giving it bodily sensations. One could expect to feel one's freedom from sin. Appeal to experience has been an important part of Wesleyan piety, and Methodists have encouraged a wide range of poetic expression. As Lester Ruth has demonstrated, early Methodists, Wesley included, were not good systematic theologians, but they were excellent poets, able to describe and categorize the various phases and moods of their spiritual experience.[1]

Experience, of course, does not stand by itself. As the current *Book of Discipline* insists, Scripture and experience are not equal sides of a theological quadrilateral.[2] Scripture will always be the primary source for theological reflection; but what does that mean? Scripture itself describes and interprets the experience of the historical Jesus and the early Christians. As I noted in my discussion of Pastor Dromazos and the Thursday night service at First Church Chambersburg (see chapter 1), experience in the Wesleyan paradigm refers to biblical, theological, and spiritual insight that is *felt* more than *verbalized*. Christian insights attributed to experience normally arise from a deep sense of the biblical story as it has been understood and told by the church. Of course, the church and individuals continue their theological work, and thus they will privilege one Scripture over another, even to the point of discerning that certain injunctions no longer apply. For instance, they may argue that St. Paul's assertion about the equality of the baptized (Galatians 3:26-29) is more important than his injunction against women speaking in church (1 Corinthians 14:33-36). That churches and individuals create a hierarchy of texts, even to the point of rejecting some altogether, is not to say that their logic is unbiblical—far from it, in fact. At its best, experience is a felt sense of this evaluative process.

Along these lines, the sarcastic anger expressed in the e-mail is theologically significant, but not in and of itself, as if anger (or heartburn) were a means of grace. It is, rather, an expression of faith rooted deeply in the Gospel and communicated in a form and tone appropriate to the context. It is in this very specific sense that I will speak of the experience of Methodists as a source for liturgical theology. In particular, I will note their passion for the open table and the indignation they often express when access to the Table is closed or otherwise restricted. Throughout, I will insist that such passion is rooted not simply in a desire to be cordial, but in a particular reading of the biblical narrative.

In the first section of this chapter, I will review arguments made by nineteenth century Methodists against the closed communion practices of the Landmark Baptists and other groups with similar principles. In order to set the Methodist argument in context, I will first review the Landmark position and the debate surrounding it, as it existed within some Baptist circles. Having done that, then I will discuss the Methodists. I will note that all parties in these debates tended toward a wooden, literalistic reading of Scripture, as if one could settle the argument with the correct proof text. As one might expect, arguments based on proof texts are not very convincing. As I will demonstrate, the best arguments against closed communion were those made from experience, that is, from a deep sense of the entire biblical narrative. As such persons insisted, it made no sense for Christians to pray together and welcome one another's preachers to the pulpit yet not share communion. I will demonstrate that the open table position is epitomized in the phrase "It is the Lord's Table, not ours," a phrase that one continues to hear in United Methodist communion services.

In the second section of this chapter, I will offer testimony that I gathered through interviews with contemporary United Methodists, both clergy and laity. Many of these persons express a passionate commitment to open communion, along with deep indignation at the very thought of fencing the Lord's Table. As I will suggest, this passion reveals the church's "sense of the faithful," their deeply felt, corporate understanding of the biblical narrative.

NINETEENTH-CENTURY VOICES

Open Table and the Challenge of the Landmark Baptists

As I have demonstrated, fencing of the Lord's Table existed long before Christianity came to America. *The Didache*, a first-century church order, insisted that only the baptized could receive communion; the faithful must not give holy things to the dogs.[3] Other ancient liturgies describe deacons who were appointed to usher the catechumens out of the assembly before the prayers of the faithful and the Eucharist. These deacons would then guard the doors of the assembly against the nonbaptized and the unworthy.[4] As we have noted in earlier chapters,

The Book of Common Prayer and other rites from the Reformation era contain rubrics that fenced the Table for moral reasons.[5]

Fencing of the Table took a different form in the nineteenth-century American context. In the spirit of the great evangelical revivals, Baptists, Presbyterians, Methodists, and others occasionally gathered for joint preaching services. At times they would attend each other's churches and their pastors would preach in each other's pulpits; yet Landmark Baptists would not allow members of other churches to join them for communion. The term "Landmark," by the way, comes from the admonition of Proverbs 22:28, "Remove not the ancient landmark, which thy fathers have set" (KJV).

Why did these Baptists refuse Eucharistic fellowship with others? The Landmark ecclesiology insisted that the local congregation was the only valid expression of the church. Baptism and the Lord's Supper were ordinances for the local congregation only, for that was the only place where appropriate discipline and oversight could be exercised. To share the Lord's Supper on a wider basis was to remove the ancient landmark, that is, to change the standard set in the Scriptures. Not only was intercommunion between Baptists and members of other denominations out of order, but also there could be no communion among members of neighboring Baptist congregations. Landmark Baptists believed that their position had existed in an unbroken Baptist succession extending from the Apostles to the present. All churches existing outside of that succession, including Methodists and Catholics, were not true churches.[6]

John Lightfoot Waller presented the Landmark position in his text *Open Communion Shown to Be Unscriptural and Deleterious,* published in 1859, six years after his death.[7] Waller had been a Baptist pastor in Louisville, Kentucky, and editor of *The Western Baptist Review*. He argued that advocates of open communion were evading the clear teaching of Scripture and were catering to the whim of the masses.[8] Citing St. Paul's discussion of the Lord's Supper in 1 Corinthians 11:17a-34, he wrote:

> The Lord's Supper was celebrated by members of the Church, and all church members, in that age, were baptized disciples. And here we might rest this part of our argument; for, with all true Protestants, who regard the *Bible* alone as their religion, one scriptural precept, or one example of apostolic practice, is enough, and ample to settle every question of the sort under consideration.[9]

When Waller referred to a baptized disciple, he was not using the term as a Methodist would use it. He viewed infant baptism as invalid and thus when he referred to someone who had been baptized as an infant, he referred to them as "unbaptized." This difference in usage must be understood when reading the Baptist commentators, both the Landmark Baptists and their more liberal counterparts. All of them dismissed the baptism of infants as no baptism at all.

Waller believed that the apostles practiced a restricted table and that they were correct in doing so. They were following the teaching of their Lord who taught them (1) to make disciples, (2) to baptize them, and (3) to teach them to observe all of Christ's commandments (see Matthew 28:18-20, also known as "The Great Commission"). Since observance of the Lord's Supper was instituted by the commandment of Jesus, according to this scheme it must come third, after baptism. Notice his claim that the Great Commission implies not only an agenda for the church's mission, but also a strict and invariable *ordo* as well. Although the argument is expressed in wooden fashion, it does retain the historical connection between baptism and discipleship.[10]

Addressing the matter of the communion invitation, Waller wrote, "It is not our business to invite or debar any person. The Lord spread the table, and he alone invites, and he alone has the right to debar from coming. His law is the rule which must govern its approach."[11] Here he reversed the logic that fencing is unauthorized because "the Table is the Lord's." According to Waller, the Table is restricted precisely because it is the Lord's Table and not his. He dismissed Methodists as unintelligent, as unable to read and understand the clear commandment of Jesus. To him, the doctrine of communion as converting ordinance made no sense.

> We are not unapprised of the fact, that a few of the less esteemed Methodist ministers, who have more zeal than knowledge, have, of late years, assumed that the unbaptized, and even the unconverted, may, and in certain cases ought, to partake of the Eucharist. But it would be unjust to notice them, since neither their church nor the intelligent among their brethren lend any countenance to their proceedings.[12]

Waller used strong and compelling language, even the language of law, but to what law was he referring? He used the Great Commission as a proof text, as if it were a rubric. As we shall see, Waller was not alone in his search for proof texts.

In addition to their quarrel with the Methodists and other

pedobaptists (that is, those who baptize infants and children), Waller and other Baptists in the open table debate were in dialogue with Robert Hall (1764–1831), an English Baptist who had argued for a more irenic practice in his book *On Terms of Communion; With a Particular View to the case of the Baptists and Paedobaptists.*[13] Hall based his argument on the assertion that baptism, which is not a condition of salvation, should not, therefore, be required for admission to communion.[14] Hall was not a pedobaptist. He upheld the classic Baptist doctrine, insisting that persons who had been baptized as infants were not really baptized.[15] He believed, however, that one's salvation is based not on baptism but on justification by faith, and therefore all who are justified should be welcomed at the Table, whether or not they have been baptized.

In his view, many pedobaptists are indeed Christians and therefore should be welcomed at the Table. He raised the issue of their cooperative ministries. Many Baptists, he observed, held fellowship with their pedobaptist colleagues and had no objection to their holding communion services of their own. By their approval of such services, they were saying that these colleagues were Christian brothers and sisters.[16] He challenged his Baptist colleagues either to welcome them or reject them completely, withdrawing from all fellowship. They could not have it both ways.

> They (strict communion Baptists) have attempted an incongruous mixture of liberal principles, with a particular act of intolerance; and these, like the iron and clay in the feet of Nebuchadnezzar's image, will not mix.[17]

Hall did insist that churches that baptize infants are in error, but that one should not exclude a sister or brother from the Table because they are mistaken.[18] Of far greater importance is the great "do this" commandment that calls disciples to observe the Lord's Supper (Luke 22:19, 1 Corinthians 11:24-26). On this score, Hall's argument resembles John Wesley's. Hall wrote,

> . . . I must be permitted to believe, that our Lord's express injunction on his followers, 'Do this in remembrance of me,' is a better reason for the celebration of the communion than can be adduced for its neglect.[19]

Although Hall followed Wesley (and others) when he insisted that the Lord's Supper is an ordinance, that is, a commandment to be fulfilled, the rest of his argument conceded far too much. The necessity of baptism for admission to Holy Communion, argued Hall, is based on the idea of baptism as the sacrament of regeneration, and he rejected that belief.[20] Thus the impediment to communion was removed along with belief in sacramental efficacy. For Hall, baptism remained an ordinance to be obeyed, but it was not a means of grace. As he saw it, profession of faith is decisive for salvation, not baptism:

> By orthodox Christians it is uniformly maintained, that union to Christ is formed by faith, and as the Baptists are distinguished by demanding a profession of it at baptism, they, at least, are precluded from asserting that rite to have any concern in effecting the spiritual alliance in question.[21]

Since the "spiritual alliance" is effected by faith alone, baptism was not necessary for admission to the Table. The Lord's Table, it seems, is similarly devoid of sacramental efficacy, thus Hall gave no sense of its being anything like a converting ordinance. While Hall would allow Methodists to receive communion, it appears that he was conceding them little more than an opportunity to obey the commandment of Jesus. He did, however, insist that Christian fellowship should not be alternately extended and withdrawn, a significant theological move by itself.

Samuel Worcester Whitney reflected Hall's position in his book *Open Communion, or, the Principles of Restricted Communion Examined and Proved to be Unscriptural and False, In a Series of Letters to a Friend*.[22] He insisted that all those who profess Jesus Christ are members of the church and thus should be invited to the Table. This emphasis on profession also led to a devaluing of baptism. Listen to his argument:

> It is a favorite idea of some that *baptism* is the door of entrance into the Christian church. But this is overlooking entirely the fact that the church is designed to represent the body of believers in the world. Those whom the Scriptures recognise as its members are the professed people of God. The act that introduces them into this number is obviously the making of a profession of Christianity. Baptism may be the accompaniment of that act, and I believe, as firmly as you, that it should always be. But still it is only an accompaniment...[23]

Methodists normally want to attribute far more meaning to baptism than that. Deficiencies in sacramental theology aside, Whitney made a progressive ecumenical gesture that was well ahead of his time. He was called to assume leadership of a Baptist congregation in Westport, New York, but then they refused to install him when he informed them that he would allow baptized Christians from other congregations to receive communion with them.[24]

Whitney argued that the Table is the Lord's and not that of any particular denomination. Here are several examples:

"Drink *ye all* of it;" not merely the baptized, but all the members of the household of faith who may be present, for it is *the Lord's* table, designed for any who are members of his body.[25]

If this were not the Lord's table, but ours, the case would be different. But as it is, we are not at liberty to adopt any terms of communion not established by the Lord himself.[26]

Why not at once deny the sacramental table to be *the Lord's*, and honestly and avowedly contend for its being a denominational table?[27]

He acknowledged the fact that opponents of open communion can use the same rhetoric.[28] "[Because it is] *the Lord's* table . . . we dare not admit those who have not the prerequisites."[29] For our purposes, however, it is significant to note that the language about the Table belonging to the Lord and not to any particular denomination or congregation is exactly the language one often hears in contemporary United Methodist invitations today. It appears that our language of the open table is continuous with the language that developed in the midst of the nineteenth-century controversies.

A Methodist reviewer saw Whitney's book as a hopeful sign that Baptists were going to abandon closed communion. He wrote, "It will cost [Baptists] many a struggle, but the rapidly increasing light upon the true nature of Christ's kingdom and Christian fellowship will dispel this remnant of sectarian bigotry." Again, note the appeal to the Christian fellowship that many Methodists and closed communion Baptists were already enjoying apart from the Table. He wrote, "Let them hold to immersion, let them hold to Calvinism, but do not let them exclude from the Lord's Supper those whom they concede to be the Lord's people."[30]

Having heard from some typical Baptist writers,[31] we will now examine some texts written by nineteenth-century Methodists. While we will hear these Methodists as they argue for an open table, notice that their logic is not the same as one hears in the modern context.

Their views of sacramental efficacy were different from ours. So was their understanding of the proper scope of the invitation. For them, open table implied a universal invitation given to all Christians, but it did not extend to non-Christians.

Methodist Voices in Support of the Open Table

Leonidas Rosser (1815–1891) was a prolific theological voice within Southern Methodism. He began his pastoral career in New York, but transferred to the Virginia Conference in 1839. Over the years, he served that Conference as a presiding elder in five different districts and on five occasions he was a delegate to the General Conference of the Methodist Episcopal Church, South. He was author of eight books, many of which attempted to define Methodism over against the Baptists. According to one of his reviewers, "[his] industry and talent [were] devoted to the development and support of Methodist views and usages."[32]

For the purposes of this chapter, we will examine his book *Open Communion*.[33] Although he was a significant Methodist voice in support of open communion, his views had more in common with open communion Baptists than they did with John Wesley. *Contra* the Baptists, he praised Methodism as a communion of pedobaptists that showed clear evidence of God's blessing, but he did not argue classic Methodist or Wesleyan themes. Rosser did not mention Wesley's teaching on Eucharist as converting ordinance, although *The Methodist Quarterly Review* tried to insert this theme into the argument, suggesting the following:

> We presume Dr. Rosser is not to be strictly interpreted . . . as he, doubt-less, would admit to the Lord's table any sincere penitent who is seeking to be born again. *We* certainly would.[34]

If this reviewer's assertion about Rosser's position is correct—that he would admit seekers—then he gained that knowledge from some source other than *Open Communion*. Little, if any, of Wesley's theology is present. At one point, he used Charles Wesley's phrase "Christ has bidden all mankind," but he did not cite its source.[35] Perhaps he did not know it. Indeed, Rosser's book is more of an anti-Baptist argument than a pro-Methodist one.

At issue for Rosser was the doctrine of baptismal regeneration, a teaching accepted by John Wesley with some reservations.[36] Rosser rejected the teaching altogether. If baptism is the source of our regeneration, he argued, then requiring baptism for admission to the Lord's Table is understandable and defensible. But, insisted Rosser, that assumption is incorrect.

> It is admitted that many early and modern authorities maintain that baptism is an indispensable prerequisite to sacramental communion. But then, in the first place, these authorities believed in the exploded doctrine of baptismal regeneration; and hence no wonder they fell into the error that baptism is indispensably prerequisite to sacramental communion, since no one has a right to the communion who has not been regenerated.[37]

Since, according to Rosser, regeneration—not baptism—admits one to communion, then Methodists and Baptists were separated over a false issue. Again, Wesley was missing from the discussion, both his belief in the sacramental efficacy of baptism and his understanding of Holy Communion as converting ordinance.

Rosser clearly taught that regeneration, not baptism, admits one to the Table.

> All that should be required by any evangelical church in order to communion is the possession of the substance signified by baptism, no matter by what mode signified, as in the case of pious Pedobaptists, or whether it be conscientiously omitted altogether, as in the case of pious Quakers.[38]

Troubling as that statement may be for those who take the sacraments seriously, it provides an important insight into the state of the discussion at that time, at least as it existed for Rosser. For him, the Lord's Table was not the completely open table practiced by many in the modern church; he defended his *praxis* neither on the basis of the radical hospitality of Jesus nor by an understanding of the Eucharist as a converting ordinance. The Lord's Supper was, rather, a rite for the already converted, for the already regenerate. He exhibited little, if any, understanding of communion as means of grace; indeed, he called the communion of infants and children "a ridiculous absurdity."[39] He was not arguing for completely unfettered access to the Lord's Table, as his title *Open Communion* might suggest to our twenty-first century ears; rather, he was calling for a different understanding of the terms of admission.

> If baptism was instituted for the remission of sins, (as the Campbellites maintain,)—if baptism were necessary to regeneration, (as the Puseyites

and Roman Catholics maintain,)—then there would be strong reason why baptism should have priority in order. But these dogmas both the Baptists and evangelical Pedobaptists reject with abhorrence. But faith is the only condition of remission of sins and regeneration, and there is no reason why the believer should invariably receive one of the sacraments before the other.[40]

It is difficult to determine what he believed the sacraments actually do in the lives of the regenerate. In the end of the day, Rosser made his case for open communion by sacrificing the very idea of sacraments as a means of grace.

While Rosser's theology of the sacraments is disappointing, his understanding of sacramental community was well-developed. Like Hall and Whitney on the Baptist side, he accused practitioners of closed communion of a gross and offensive inconsistency. Christian brothers and sisters worked together in their revivals and in their local congregations, but then they broke fellowship when it was time for the Supper. Note his palpable indignation at such a cavalier discerning of the Body.

> Is this reasonable? It is unreasonable—a shame, a crime—the true reward of which, sooner or later, must come, in this world, or when God arises to judgment.[41]

Methodists, he insisted, would never treat their fellow Christians with such disrespect; they would never exclude from the Table those whom they believe to be God's people.[42] Thus, he called his opponents to account: either rank us with the infidel and the unbeliever or receive us as your sisters and brothers in Christ.[43]

A later Methodist voice, the Reverend Zachariah A. Parker, D.D. (1851–1904), took up the same theme. Parker, an elder in the North Alabama Conference, wrote *The People's Hand-Book on Immersion, Infant Baptism, Close Communion, and Plan of Salvation; or Justification by Water versus Justification by Faith*.[44] Its critics implied that it added little new to the argument against those Christians who were insisting on immersion baptism and close communion.[45] Like many treatments of this topic, his tone was deeply polemical. He called the insistence on baptism by immersion "heresy" and "water regeneration,"[46] a usage that reflects Peter Cartwright's accusation that the Baptists and Campbellites were worshiping a "water god."[47] Not only did he refute the argument that all baptisms in the early church were by immersion, but he also attempted to prove that all baptisms during that age were administered by pouring or affusion.[48] In doing so, he set forth some rather strange exegesis, such as an argument disproving Baptist and Campbellite claims that Naaman the leper, a figure from an Old Testament narrative (2 Kings 5:1-27), had been immersed in the Jordan. Parker attempted to "prove" the opposite. He wrote,

> The prophet told him to go and wash seven times in the Jordan (2 Kings v. 10) Wash what? Why, the affected parts of his body, of course—his hands, or wherever the leprosy had appeared. But the prophet said, Wash "in the Jordan." Is this not immersion? *A thousand times No.*

> If you were to go down to the river this morning and wash your hands or your face, would we understand by that that you plunged your body under the water? By no means...

> Put yourself in Naaman's place. Suppose you had the leprosy in your hands or eyes, and were told to go and wash in a certain stream, would you necessarily go and plunge yourself *head and ears* in order to wash any part of your body? No sensible man would think so.

> Now, we know Naaman's leprosy had not spread all over his body, because in this case he would have long been banished to the lepers' quarter, to die in lingering agony and torture...

> If you want the subject still plainer, read the rites of cleansing a leper in Lev. xiv. 7-9. Here you see in verse 7 that a leper to be cleansed was to be "*sprinkled*" seven times. Then, verse 8, he was to be "washed." The same in verse 9.

> Now the prophet clearly referred to this ceremonial washing, or cleansing, which in the history of all the Church was never done by immersions or plungings, but always by "sprinklings" and "washings"...

> *No immersion here, never was; never will be; never can be.*[49]

The logic is strained. Even though the King James Version text says that Naaman "dipped himself" in the Jordan, Parker insisted that water was poured upon him. He was not immersed. What is happening in such an argument? Parker was trying to answer questions that the biblical writers simply were not asking, questions, for instance, about the proper mode for baptism. Parker insisted that the Bible—even the Old Testament—could answer such questions, and that it must do so. His was not an unusual stance for a Protestant Christian to assume in those days immediately before the flowering of higher critical methods, nevertheless his strange exegesis reminds us that sacramental theology cannot be properly constructed using biblical texts alone.[50]

In his arguments against close communion he finally moved away from proof texts and torturous exegesis toward a more developed theology. Close communion, argued Parker, violated bonds of ecumenical fellowship established through common Christian work. Hear the pain and indignation expressed in the following description:

> I knew, in a union protracted meeting, where two close communion ministers worked for ten days side by side with two brethren of another denomination in love and fellowship, faith and prayer, preaching alternately for the conversion of souls. At the close of ten days the results of the meeting counted seventy converts. A union meeting, mark you, in a union church. By mutual agreement, the immersionists were to have the first Sunday following the meeting as their sacramental occasion. The day came—a beautiful day. A large crowd—immersionists and non-immersionists. The four ministers above referred to were present. The sermon over, they came to celebrate the Lord's Supper. Shall they invite all the brethren who had been working with them in harmony with such faith and zeal for ten days past? Their better religious nature said: "Yes; we have worked together in his kingdom, let us feast together at his table." Said their close communion selfishness: "No; they are good enough to work with us perhaps, but not good enough to eat with us at his table." So the brethren of the "other way" were invited aside to look on and see how religious selfishness, engendered by close communion, could forget all fraternal instinct, and ignore all fraternal feeling.[51]

It is a sharp critique. Parker's appeal to the bonds of Christian fraternity was much deeper than an appeal to American congeniality. He was referring to Christians who had worked together in revivals and other ecumenical settings, and then were forced to divide when it came time for communion. He was protesting the separation of Christian brothers and sisters.

> In the ordinary exercise of religious worship, they manifest considerable pleasure in the presence and cooperation of their brethren of other churches—sometimes even invite their labors—and then on the day of the solemn feast give the outspoken denial to every thing they have said and done before.[52]

Parker did not appeal to biblical accounts of Jesus feeding sinners and the multitudes, nor did this late-nineteenth–century Methodist appeal to John Wesley and his theology of prevenient grace. He did not argue for the communion of seekers but rather he argued against close communion. He made a serious and compelling argument, one that many contemporary ecumenists would affirm.[53]

Observations Based upon these Nineteenth-Century Texts

I make the following observations based on our discussion of these nineteenth-century texts:

1. One finds an overly heavy reliance on biblical proof texts and a grasping for other types of direct biblical warrant, as if locating the correct biblical reference would resolve these complex questions about access to communion. Besides the fact that many Scriptures were thereby taken out of context, this tendency reveals a basic misunderstanding about the relationship of liturgical *praxis* to the Scriptures. One cannot take the church out of the decision-making process. The church—ancient and modern, universal and local—must take the witness of Scripture and the various traditions and then decide what it must do now. Indeed, such decisions are made each time the Christian assembly gathers, even if their decision is simply to do what they did the week before.

2. While there is no explicit biblical commandment connecting baptism with admission to the Eucharist, churches may decide that the shape of the Gospel implies such a linkage. Indeed, most have done so. The church may decide that linking the two sacraments is essential to its integrity. Churches should, however, also entertain the possibility that other Christians might envision another possibility, an alternative embodiment of faithfulness and ritual integrity.

3. These nineteenth-century texts that argue for open communion are largely devoid of the Wesleyan arguments that one finds in modern arguments. They present little discussion of Eucharist as converting ordinance or means of grace. Overwhelmingly, the arguments for open communion found in these texts focus on the Lord's Supper as a manifestation of Christian fellowship. While not the full sacramental theology we might wish to express in our

contemporary contexts, the argument about fellowship is a significant and substantial one (see 1 Corinthians 11:17-34). The fact that these nineteenth-century Christians argued for open communion based on their existent bonds of fellowship does not preclude Christians of later generations from advocating a *praxis* of the open table for other reasons.

4. Unlike what one hears today, there is nothing in these nineteenth-century witnesses that argues for the admission of non-Christians (or emerging Christians) to the Lord's Table. The arguments against closed communion focused their attention on the conditions of salvation, that is, on what makes one a Christian. By and large they insisted that regeneration makes one a Christian. Therefore communicants must be regenerate, but baptism, and particularly immersion baptism, was not required for admission to the Table. Thus these witnesses have called for the communion of the converted, not the communion of the baptized. In this sense, then, the argument one hears in these texts is less forceful than Wesley's argument against the advocates of the Stillness doctrine. In arguing against them, Wesley presented the Eucharist as a means of grace, that is, as a converting ordinance. One does not see that emphasis in the texts reviewed in this section.

5. In the final analysis, therefore, these nineteenth-century texts have not presented the same call to open communion that one finds in some quarters of the contemporary church. Some of the passionate rhetoric that they used, however, persists in modern practice, particularly use of phrases like "This is the Lord's Table, not a Methodist Table." In addition, the indignant tones that nineteenth-century Methodists used in opposing closed communion are echoed in the contemporary discussions. In that sense, the nineteenth-century arguments set a trajectory that continues in the contemporary discussions. In the next section, we will listen to some of those contemporary voices.

Part Two: Contemporary United Methodist Voices

How does one discern the religious identity of congregations and denominations?[54] Positive responses provide important evidence, as in the "aha" sense of the church shopper who finally realizes that she has come home; this after visiting so many places that were clearly *not home*.

What does she experience? Perhaps a style of music, a way of praying, a manner of speaking about God and celebrating the sacraments that seems profoundly right. As we have noted earlier, to treat a feeling response as theologically significant is not to say that the response is merely subjective, as if it were somehow separated from thought about God, the scriptures, and the church. The "aha" is felt, but it arises from thought—distilled thought perhaps, but thought nonetheless.

Conversely, one can discern congregational and denominational identity when its boundaries are transgressed; indeed, such transgressions often yield a sharper picture of religious identity. The lessons learned can be invaluable. Church members may protest, "We never did it that way before," or they may express themselves much more passionately, even angrily. One can meet such anger defensively or as an opportunity to learn. As I interviewed United Methodists about their experience and practice of Holy Communion, I asked each of them to describe the communion invitation given in their congregations. Invariably, I heard reports about invitations to an open table, about pastors who insisted that the Table is the Lord's and not theirs. Having heard that rather predictable response, I would then turn the question and ask the following: "What if the minister were to say something else, like 'All baptized Christians are invited to this table,' or 'This sacrament marks our identity as a people in covenant with Christ and one another. Therefore, all United Methodists in good standing are invited to commune.' What would happen then?"

Passionate (Even Indignant) Responses

My question was clearly hypothetical. Nevertheless, I was struck by the passionate, even indignant responses I received. I asked the question of United Methodists from several different parts of the country. I asked it of Methodists from congregations that commune monthly and congregations that do so on a weekly basis. I asked it of Methodists of differing racial, ethnic, and economic backgrounds, from small and large congregations. I asked it of Methodists associated with the Reconciling Ministries network and of Methodists holding evangelical connections, yet there was a striking similarity to their responses. Almost invariably, they reacted strongly and negatively to the notion of restricting access to the Lord's Table. I am convinced that these responses reveal a key marker of United Methodist identity, a United Methodist "sense of the faithful." The similarity of their responses may suggest a theological basis for the unity that this sometimes-fractious church desires.

Typical among the respondents is Matthew Storey of the Good Samaritan United Methodist Church in Houston.[56] Mr. Storey is a life-long United Methodist who was raised in a pastor's family. When I posed my question about restricting access to the Table, he responded quickly and decisively.

> I would be outraged. That's not my church. That's evil... That is not the Wesleyan tradition. That is exclusive, not inclusive. That is the antithesis of everything I was raised with as a Methodist and everything I believe in this denomination...[57]

Such fencing of the Table, he said, would be "the worst possible sin," a "perversion" of the Gospel. If he were ever to hear such an invitation, he would "call the district superintendent and lodge a protest with him or her. I'd just have to raise a big stink because that's not the church that I want to be in, and that's not the church I was raised in."[58] As a Reconciling Congregation, Good Samaritan is willing to receive all persons into their fellowship, regardless of their sexual orientation. Thus, their membership includes significant numbers of gay, lesbian, bisexual, and transgendered persons. Mr. Storey supports that agenda, yet he seemed willing to exercise patience with respect to the church's negative stance on homosexuality, believing that the church will eventually become more open to its homosexual members. He would, however, openly fight the church if it were to restrict access to communion. Such a position would be immediately intolerable. Constance Allen, a woman from the same congregation, said that a restricted invitation would constitute "fighting words" that would force people to leave the church. If necessary, they would even become unchurched again.[59]

When I posed my hypothetical question to Carlton Sachs, an elderly member of St. Luke's United Methodist Church in Southern California, he was incredulous: "I would think, 'You've lost your marbles, man. That's not what Methodists do!'"[60] Other men in that same church said that they would be "surprised and turned off" or simply "shocked" by such an invitation.[61] A woman in that congregation said, "I would not like that because invitations need to be open." "Why should they be open?" I asked her. She responded that "someone might be searching" and the church should not hinder such seeking.[62]

Martha Cook, for fifty-two years a member of the small Rockwood congregation in rural New Jersey, had a mixed response to my question: "What if, on some Sunday morning, the pastor were to say something different than she normally says . . . something along the lines of 'All

United Methodists in good standing are invited to receive.' How would you respond to that?" She thought for a moment and then said that she would be embarrassed by it, as if the pastor had committed an unthinkably ridiculous faux pas. First, she said, she would check on the well-being of her neighbors: "I think I would look around the church and see who was there." Thus her first concern was relational. Then, if necessary, she would publicly confront this suddenly uncouth pastor. If, by chance, ". . . I felt that these people had been maybe coming for some time but hadn't joined our fellowship yet . . . I might stand up and ask (that pastor) if I could have a word with her."[63] Her response shows typical indignation even though my "what if" clearly indicated that the question was hypothetical. Imagine if someone actually gave such an invitation.

Melody Smith is a young adult member of Fellowship United Methodist Church, a large suburban congregation located near Dallas, Texas. She said that a restricted invitation would simply be "bad form."[64] Does her reference to "bad form" support the claim that open table practices are little more than a low-level expression of cordiality? Taking Ms. Smith's response on the literal level, failure to invite all persons is primarily a breach of etiquette, "bad form" indeed! I am convinced, however, that we should look deeper than the surface meaning of her response and others like it. Granted, the words and categories we choose can restrict theological and spiritual vision. For instance, using categories from the discourse of etiquette can prevent us from hearing the Gospel that sometimes offends and disturbs.[65] Nevertheless, we should understand that persons would use their normal vocabulary. Compassionate listening involves hearing context as well as words, and in Ms. Smith's case, that context reveals a significantly deeper insight. At various points throughout the interview, she discussed a marginally unchurched older brother who comes to hear her sing every Christmas Eve. She hears the communion invitation in relation to him:

> I'm not just hoping that he'll take [communion] just for the sake of taking it, you know, because it does mean something to take it . . . But, I'm hoping, with each year, as I look out there . . . that he'll actually feel moved enough to take it and to mean it and to take it for the right reasons . . . But, like I said, I guess the probability seems a little bit greater on that if there's an invitation . . . [66]

In this deeper context, her "bad form" becomes language that conveys the Gospel. It refers to anything that hinders one's free response to Jesus Christ. Bad form indeed.

Many of the interview subjects claimed that they would leave the church if it began making restricted invitations. Deborah Lucas, a physician who attends Holy Pentecost Church, a multicultural congregation located near Dallas, was raised in an African American church in which persons were strongly urged to examine their hearts before coming forward to receive communion and, if appropriate, to abstain. She cherishes that heritage. Nevertheless, when I asked her my question, "What if the minister were to say something like, 'It's a Table for all Methodists in good standing'; or, 'It's a table for baptized Christians,' how would you respond?" she emphatically said, "I would leave!" When I asked why, she said, "Because Jesus told all to come."[67]

A Sunday school teacher in Fellowship Church joined the United Methodist Church along with his wife, a former Catholic, primarily because it practices the open table. "If they fenced the Table," he said, "I'd have to find somewhere else to go."[68] Members of St. Luke's Church in Southern California had a similar response to my query. Carole Agosto, who emigrated from the Philippines and became a United Methodist when she joined the church in 1991 said, "I would probably be shocked." She would ask herself, "Why am I in this church? …Maybe I should change churches."[69] She had not grown up in a United Methodist context, but she has adopted its ethos. In like manner, Frank Walker, a grandfather who began coming to St. Luke's Church when he was six years old, said that a pastor who made such an invitation would be nothing less than a "false prophet." Even though his congregation has been like a second family to him, "I certainly think my family would leave."[70]

Most people do not leave their congregation in an impulsive manner, especially when one has been a member for many years; but these interviewees threatened to do just that. A church that began making restrictive invitations to the Table would no longer be the church that they had known, loved, and supported. No one expressed this reality more poignantly than the Reverend Mary Theodore, pastor of the Rockview congregation. As a pastor in the church, she believes it her responsibility to maintain its *Discipline*. Were the denomination to legislate usage of a more restrictive invitation—perhaps one that admitted only the baptized—she would not disobey its directive, but she would not keep it, either. She would retire from active ministry.[71]

While all of the responses were to some extent theological, some of the persons responded to my question in overtly doctrinal and theological terms. John Standing, who has been an active part of Fellowship Church for at least seventy years, insisted that inviting only the baptized would not be "the Wesleyan doctrine,"[72] and he spoke that judgment without the slightest hesitation. In his youth, Tom Lightner of the Rockview Church served as an acolyte for an Episcopal congregation in Newark, New Jersey. He filled the same role on the Sunday that I attended the service at Rockview—the first septuagenarian acolyte I have seen in quite some time. In that Episcopal church, Mr. Lightner was not admitted to communion until he was confirmed. Even then, he and the other acolytes could not commune unless they kept the traditional Eucharistic fast before coming to the service. The experience of his youth was far from an open table, but this elderly retiree, now a United Methodist, would have no restrictions placed on the current generation. Children should receive communion. A restricted invitation "would be improper, against Methodist teaching."[73] Lydia Baker, chair of the altar guild at Fellowship Church, responded as if open communion were an irrefutable dogma of the church. Before I could even finish my question, she began shaking her head and saying "No, no." When I asked her why a restricted invitation would be wrong, she said in a rather matter-of-fact way, "It wouldn't be open communion then, would it?"[74] As she sees it, the ritual practice is well established and is self-evidently true. Sarah Johns, a member of St. Luke's Church for about three years, could not specifically say that her pastor had used the language of the open table, but she could recognize the type of statement that he would not use. She said that an invitation open only to the baptized or to church members

> . . . would be contrary to what Christ has taught us and shown us. That's what I think . . . (Our pastor) has been preaching to us . . . nothing except the opposite of that, which is love your enemy, love . . . the people who hate us and things like that. So, I find that hard to believe that he would say it was only open to people who were baptized Christians.[75]

A woman in the Rockview congregation questioned the entire concept of "member in good standing." Who could make such a determination, she wondered? Listen to the teaching of Jesus, she insisted, and "let the judging be up to God."[76]

Perhaps the most interesting theological response of all came from George Thomas of Holy Pentecost Church. Mr. Thomas, a septuagenarian who grew up in an all-white Baptist congregation in a segregated community in rural Tennessee, has been a member of Holy Pentecost, a multi-racial church, for most of his life. I got the feeling that he has found the congregation that he had been seeking for a long time. When I asked him my question about extending the invitation to the baptized alone, he surprised me by saying, "probably that would be correct." Such an invitation would be an improvement over the church of his childhood, which practiced those Landmark doctrines that restricted Eucharistic access to members of the local congregation. As he described it,

> In those days among Baptists, even neighboring Baptist churches could not take the Lord's Supper with us. Even neighboring Baptist churches ... My sister belonged to a conservative Baptist church in Chicago for a long time and there was a discussion whether she and her husband should come and take the Lord's Supper with us there. I thought that was really silly.[77]

While he rejected the Landmark teaching, to some extent he acknowledged the mainstream Baptist teaching that baptism is the norm for admission to the Table. Again, when I asked about inviting only the baptized, he said, "probably that would be correct." His ensuing remark, however, exhibits profound insight into the Gospel and the ways of Jesus. He continued, "But correctness sometimes is not what we need; we need ... love and respect and acceptance."[78] Indeed, Jesus did not set purity laws above the needs of human beings. Mr. Thomas affirmed the baptismal norm for admission to communion but was willing to make an exception in the face of human need. In discerning the difference between law and need, he expressed a key New Testament dynamic. Later on in this chapter, we will speculate more about the foundation of Mr. Thomas' theology of inclusion.

The interview excerpts that I have related to this point demonstrate a deep commitment to the open table. The most passionate responses came when the interviewees' sense of the faithful was transgressed, even hypothetically. The remaining subsections reveal an awareness of two theological convictions that support the practice of the open table: (1) communion as converting ordinance, and (2) communion as an expression of God's hospitality. I will examine each of these in turn.

Witness to Communion as a Converting Ordinance

In chapter 4, I examined the Wesleyan roots of the belief in communion as a converting ordinance. The interviews indicate that many United Methodists believe in this dynamic, even though they do not always use the classic Wesleyan terms for it. Holy Communion is a means of grace that causes profound connections between the people and God. Scripture uses the term *koinonia* or "fellowship" (see 1 John 1:3-7) to describe this reality. Martha Cook said that taking communion can "stir [a] person up and make them . . . want to come back and get more." We "don't have the right" to impede such a process.[79] She uses the language of the civil contract—"rights"—which may trouble some persons. Is this yet another example of the confusion between democracy and discipleship? Before jumping to that conclusion, we should remember the long history of speaking about access to the Table in terms of rights. In medieval England, persons referred to receiving their (annual) communion on Easter as "taking one's rights."[80] As noted earlier, persons have always used the linguistic conventions at their disposal to describe the dynamics of the Gospel. If we can set our linguistic scruples aside, then, we can hear in Ms. Cook's response the testimony of one who hesitates to stand in God's way. Her "we have no right" is not unlike Peter's "can anyone withhold the water for baptizing?" after he saw the Holy Spirit come upon Cornelius (Acts 10:44-48).

What is God doing in Holy Communion? Dr. Lucas testified that she encounters Christ as healing presence but also as judge who convicts her and changes her life. "There are times," she said, "when I encounter Jesus and it's not always comfortable."[81] Constance Allen has witnessed the dynamics of conversation at work in others and also in her life. She sits in the choir loft at Good Samaritan Church where she can watch people as they come for communion.

> I see the ones that come and sit in the pews their first or second time and watch everything else go on and then kind of get up and blend into the crowd . . . on their third visit or something, like they've been there all the time.[82]

God is at work in their lives, converting them from isolation and drawing them into the Body of Christ. She told a personal story of conversion, about how God helped her move into the deeper fellowship demanded by the sacrament.

> One of my more interesting experiences was at the communion rail . . . I was getting accustomed to trans-gendered folk in the church . . . I still was being a bit judgmental about that. One of them served communion on a particular Sunday and it was my first time to take communion from this person. I asked myself, "Are you trying to be a better Christian than she is?" I thought, "No, okay, it's all cool then." That settled it right then and there. I had that encounter happen at the rail . . . not sitting in my seat or

thinking about it at home or talking about it at a meeting. It happened at the rail. That was one of those . . . microconversions where you get another little piece of your heart twitched.[83]

Ms. Allen did not use the term "converting ordinance," but she witnessed to God's converting work in the Eucharist nonetheless. The Wesleyan doctrine lives within her, and such piety drives the practice of the open table.

The Reverend Peter Cornelius, associate pastor at Good Samaritan, used the Wesleyan language quite openly. He agrees with the concept of communion as a "converting ordinance." He said that persons should practice it—they should "do the steps"—and many times a depth of meaning will emerge. Referring to the seekers who attend his congregation, he remarked, "I don't want to say you have to believe in Jesus yet . . . I want to throw the net as far and wide as I can and invite as many people as we can."[84] At Good Samaritan Church, their pattern of approaching the altar is itself an occasion of koinonia, an experience of grace. Cornelius described it:

> People want to crowd into the aisles here, to come to communion. We give the invitation and everyone leaves their pew and starts standing in the aisle . . . There is that feeling of family; and people . . . might shake each other's hands on the way down, and that's just really an important thing here.[85]

When I asked him why this piling into the aisles is so important to them, he responded,

> . . . It's a coming together of something they thought would never happen, that they were so shameful or so bad that they would not be welcome in church. They couldn't come and receive the sacrament. And so I think what happens, at that moment in time, is an overwhelming emotion. They feel that this place welcomes them. And then there might be the start of a belief that I'm okay. . . .[86]

Invitation and response itself becomes a means of grace, a creation of family on the way to the Communion Table.

Other deep connections are experienced at the Lord's Table. Frank Walker said, "I always feel that Jesus is present there." He continued, "Jesus gave his life for us and I don't think there has been a communion I've been to in the last 10 years or longer that I haven't shed a tear."[87] Feeling has become religious affection, that is, an emotional response formed by deep and abiding encounter with the Gospel.[88] For him, tears are an offering of thanksgiving. Those who experience such formative grace in the sacrament are inclined to invite others to join them.

Garrett Eisner of St. Luke's Church, a World War II veteran who participated in the D-Day invasion of Normandy, related an experience of the communion of saints. After worshipers at St. Luke's receive communion at the chancel rail, they may either return to their seats or proceed through the choir space to the high altar, where they may kneel in prayer and remain as long as they wish.[89] Normally, Mr. Eisner does not go on to the high altar, but he did so when a communion service fell on the June 6 anniversary. Why? As he described it,

> I have only done it once or twice, on specific occasions.... D-Day is very vivid in my mind, because I was a parachutist and dropped into Normandy on the 6th of June. We lost a lot of people from my platoon; they were killed. So, I always remember the 6th of June. I pray for the souls of the people that were in my platoon, and died so young...[90]

For him, the Eucharist enabled this connection. It was a means of grace.

In similar fashion, a woman in the Rockview congregation said that she first became aware of her husband's cancer while kneeling at the communion rail. She said,

> When I was up at the rail, I really just felt a feeling, an uneasy feeling, a ...feeling of hurt...My father was ill at the time and I knew he was probably going to go through bypass and I thought that's why I was the way I was. But then I thought about it and as I was kneeling there at the rail, I knew it was my husband. I knew a little bit that my husband wasn't feeling well but I just got this feeling that something was wrong.[91]

He was diagnosed shortly thereafter. According to the testimony of these witnesses, God is at work in the Eucharist, drawing them into the dynamics of Christ's dying and rising. They experience the dynamics of conversion. Their testimonies reflect neither a vapid memorialism nor naïve cordiality. Entering communion can be a painful journey, but these Methodists cannot imagine denying anyone the opportunity to make it.

Communion as an Expression of God's Hospitality

Perhaps more than any other consideration, Methodist conviction about the hospitality of God, incarnate in Jesus Christ, shapes the church's *praxis* of the Lord's Table, including its passionate commitment to the open communion. I asked the Reverend Anna Freeman, senior pastor at Good Samaritan, what would happen if Jesus himself were to appear some Sunday morning. What would he do? How would he invite them to the Table? She responded,

> We know that he would break down barriers and he would pull in those who were left out and marginalized . . . I think Jesus would say, "I am here and this is the meal I have prepared for you . . . You are all welcome, especially those of you who are wondering if you are welcome . . ."

She continued,

> I imagine Jesus going along the altar rail and wiping the tears from people's faces and . . . putting his hand on the heads of the children, giving a special blessing, and just letting everybody know without a shadow of a doubt how much He loves them. . . . And then Jesus would send us out.[92]

When Marshall Williams, pastor of St. Luke's Church, invites his congregation to the Table, he does so with that rhetorical flourish well established in Methodist practice. He says, "This is not my table; this is the Lord's Table. This is not the St. Luke's Church table; it is the Lord's Table." "I make it sound almost like a litany," he said. "I'm basically saying that it is Christ who invites us to come and feast." When I asked him why it is important to make such a claim about Jesus, he responded, "Because it's true."[93] Such invitations, typical in United Methodism, arise from deep convictions about the nature and teaching of Jesus Christ.

Paul Skillman, senior pastor of Fellowship United Methodist Church, characteristically uses the language of market research and modern technology. Thus, he speaks of a need for a "user-friendly" worship service that will allow persons to be "comfortable."[94] Again, simply using such language is not a problem. When used in the context of church life, these culturally conditioned terms are used to express a Christian ethic of hospitality rooted in the Gospel narratives. Citing the New Testament as a primary witness, one might well argue that using language from our various cultural environments is a mark of healthy theological discourse. The problem comes when cultural considerations keep us from expressing the competing emphases of the Gospel. Thus we also need to speak those parts of the Gospel that call us beyond comfort to the cruciform life.[95] To say that Jesus "would make (people) feel comfortable," as one of the interviewees did,[96] can be supported by the Gospel narrative, especially when we equate "comfort" with the work of receiving guests. Hospitality is the art of receiving one's guests, caring for them, and putting them at ease. Indeed, when the multitude gathered in the wilderness became hungry, Jesus turned the wilderness into a banquet hall and he assuaged their hunger (Mark 6:30-44). He made them comfortable.

When seen in their wider context, terms like "user-friendly" and "comfortable" can hold significant theological weight. In the case of Skillman and pastors like him, they are part of a constantly expanding reflection about access to the church. As our conversation continued, for instance, he mentioned the need to provide gluten-free communion wafers to those who need them[97] as well as his conviction that Fellowship Church should begin a ministry of home communion serving for its shut-in members. He also mentioned the problem of persons living with agoraphobia, a debilitating fear of crowds. Note his use of the word "comfortable" in that context.

> What do you do with folks who really get bothered by crowds and have a hard time worshiping or have a hard time coming down to the front of the church? How do you deal with the sacrament with them in a place and a way that makes them comfortable?[98]

Using the language of his culture, Pastor Skillman was raising a serious evangelical question.

Attempting to remove such barriers stands at the very heart of Wesleyan identity and its ethic of inclusion. John Standing expressed this ethic when he told me that all those present at the service are invited to commune and "the infirm are served communion at their pew."[99] During the invitation the congregation at Fellowship Church is informed that trained Stephen Ministers will bring communion to the pew of any person who cannot come forward to the communion rail. Earlier in our interview, Mr. Standing related an incident that occurred at a meeting of the Methodist Men held during the early 1950s. A Church of Christ pastor had come to explain the beliefs of his church. As Mr. Standing described it,

> Now he didn't say it in concrete words, but he said to the effect, "If you don't believe what we do, you don't have a chance of going to heaven, you're not going to be saved." Well, I contained myself until after the program was over . . . [then] I engaged him in conversation and said, "Now, paraphrasing it, you were saying, to us, that unless we believe as you do, we don't have a chance of going to heaven. We're not going to

have salvation . . . How can you call yourself Christian when you believe us Methodists don't have a chance of salvation?" I didn't get an answer.[100]

In each case—the concern about those who cannot come to the communion rail and the debate with the Church of Christ pastor—he was expressing his commitment to a bedrock Wesleyan principle: The Gospel is for all persons and the generosity of God extends to all. Frank Walker of St. Luke's Church may have expressed this ethic best of all. When I asked him to share the gist of the communion invitation that he hears every month, he said, "We're guests of the Lord, that's exactly what we are!"[101] As we have seen earlier, (see Introduction) this Wesleyan phrase, "guests of the Lord," epitomizes the Methodist theology of invitation and demonstrates again that the practice of an open invitation is deeply rooted in Methodist piety.

Several of the interview subjects saw the communion of children as a significant expression of God's hospitality. Carlton Sachs was not allowed to receive communion in the Methodist Church of his youth, but he insists that the current practice of admitting children to the Table is entirely proper.[102] Another member of St. Luke's Church, Carole Agosto, enthusiastically supports giving communion to children even though she, also, was not allowed to commune when she was a young child. She said, "I like the way we do it here, because we offer it to little kids. Because, when I was a little kid I wondered why is it that the others were eating and I was not supposed to eat . . ."[103] Now she has a different experience. For her, open table means the admission of the children, and they become her teachers. When she takes communion, sometimes she becomes too solemn, almost sad. When that happens, she said, she remembers the little children and she "becomes elated like, 'Oh, I'm part of this big thing.' That's how I feel when I'm looking at these kids."[104] Her understanding of the Bible supports this practice. When I asked her to name some biblical stories that support the open table, she mentioned the feeding of the multitudes and then returned, once again, to the image of Jesus receiving the children, even in the face of the disciples' criticism: ". . . Let the children come to me, he was telling the disciples."[105] Both this practice of communing children and the biblical images used to support it are important manifestations of United Methodist identity.[106]

The wisdom of such hospitality to children is demonstrated in the testimony of Melody Smith, a young adult whose generation of United Methodists never knew a time when they were prevented from coming to communion. She said,

...I don't remember not taking communion...I just don't remember a time that I wasn't taking communion, if there was communion to be taken.[107]

An increasing percentage of the church's membership will have a similar testimony. We cannot know all of the implications of communing young children, but one can speculate that this practice will both deepen the church's commitment to the open table and will make attempts at fencing the Table seem even more unusual.

Stories Told: Indications of a Deeply Rooted Piety

Strong commitment to the open table has deep roots in the piety of United Methodists, thus the passionate reactions that come at the mere suggestion of a restricted practice. In the course of the interviews, I heard various stories that reflected this piety. Like all good stories, they are open to multiple interpretations. At the very least, they reveal the hearts of persons deeply formed by generous hospitality and thus more likely to practice an open table. Within these stories, I heard images that express beliefs about God's nature and the shape of God's reign. I will share three of them: (1) A story about an eccentric pastor with an open door; (2) a story about a woman who should have been invited to dinner; and (3) a story about a father who invited all manner of people to dinner.

A Story about an Eccentric Pastor with an Open Door

Like many of his generation, Carlton Sachs was not admitted to communion until he was confirmed in 1936[108] while he was a freshman in high school attending a Methodist Church on the prairies of North Dakota.[109] The minister who confirmed him in that church was a woman that he called "Hattie." A female pastor was an oddity in those days, but this one was facing an even bigger challenge. As Carlton told me, "... she was divorced and her husband, who was also a Methodist preacher, had committed suicide shortly after their divorce, so she came in with two strikes on her."[110] The nickname, it seems, was well earned. As he told me,

Her name was Hattie. She was a big woman, probably close to 6 feet tall ...and she would wear hats that were out of this world. She even wore a hat when she preached.[111]

What we wouldn't do for a photograph, but imagination will have to suffice. One can imagine the objections to this divorced woman who dared not only to speak in worship, but also to lead it; yet they could not accuse her of violating another Pauline dictum: she didn't worship with her head unveiled (1 Corinthians 11:13). One wonders if that was the point of the hats. Take that, you Pauline legalists—a covering for you, and an ostrich plume to boot! But I digress.

Eccentric persons with a questionable past have been known to make a deep impression on adolescent boys, although sometimes merely as an object of ridicule. According to Carlton, Hattie came to that church because "they couldn't get anybody else out there." Perhaps she had nowhere else to go. In any event, she left a deep and positive impression that remains with Carlton nearly seven decades later:

> She only lasted a couple of years . . . but she was a real doll, a fine gal. The parsonage was right next to the slope that we used in the wintertime for sledding and . . . the doors were always open. If she was busy or studying, why you just came in and made your hot chocolate and she'd always have cookies set out for us. After we stayed for awhile, we'd clean the place up and leave.[112]

Notice that the first person who admitted him to Holy Communion was a woman who lived in a house with an open door. She was a flawed woman, so it seems, yet she was free. The outrageous hats were an outward and visible sign of that freedom. In and around admitting him to the sacramental table, she invited him and others to come in out of the cold North Dakota winter and refresh themselves at her kitchen table. These stories of welcome, and the impressions related to them, are bound together in Mr. Sachs' memory. As he and other Methodists envision the welcome that God extends, it is not unlike the memory of that female pastor who admitted him to the mysteries of the Eucharist and the mysteries of the parsonage table. Perhaps God is a free woman who wears a large, jaunty hat and invites children to refresh themselves in her kitchen where the door is always open. She knows things that we don't know, and that fascinates us. She gives this welcome even though she knows the pain of rejection, disapproval, and even death.[113]

A Story about a Woman Who Should Have Been Invited to Dinner

As I shared earlier, in the course of my interview with George Thomas of Holy Pentecost Church, I learned that he had grown up in the church, albeit one in a sharply segregated context in rural East Tennessee. Much to his delight, as an adult he discovered that he has African American cousins. He has developed a relationship with some of these cousins, and particularly with an undertaker who continues to work in his hometown. He told me,

> My great-great uncle who established the town . . . impregnated one of his slaves at least twice and it may have been more than that. Five years ago I found out about this. I never knew it. My family didn't tell me about it. And I found one of them and we are cousins. When I see him, I'll holler "hey Cuz" and he does the same.[114]

According to George, distance and ill health have kept them from developing the relationship he would like to have.

> Yeah, if he weren't ill and about 600 miles away, we would know each other a lot better . . . He is an undertaker . . . Now he's got MS and he's not doing too well. He is in a nursing home. I called him the other night and we had a good time.

This story, which emerged when I asked him to describe his childhood memories of communion services, was one of a cluster of very interesting stories that nonetheless seemed somewhat tangential while he was telling them. Upon reflection, however, they made much more sense, as I will demonstrate below.

As with the other persons that I interviewed, I asked George, "What do you think would happen if Jesus were to appear in your midst some Sunday morning and make the invitation to communion himself? What would he say?" George responded,

> [Jesus would say] "Come all . . . Come, Come" and nobody would have to clean their life up. Nobody would have to do anything.

> Somebody would say, "You'd have to quit cussing wouldn't you?"

> And I'd say, "Well it would be very desirable but you wouldn't have to . . ."

> [Jesus would say] "Anybody that thirsts, come to me." He didn't say, "Come if you are good Jews . . ."[115]

When I first heard that response, it struck me as theologically much too indiscriminate. Was he entirely setting aside the call to repentance?

It occurred to me, however, that something more prophetic was happening. While the call to repentance is important, as with most religious practices, we can find good biblical reasons to suspect it. Even the call to repentance has been used to bolster the position of the privileged, to define sin as the lifestyle of the weak over against that of the powerful. Even more insidiously, it has been used to legitimize various purity codes, including the ones that bolstered American segregation and other forms of apartheid. In a political system in which violating segregation was the primary sin, skipping the call to confession might be the most liberating liturgical act of all. It was as if Jesus were saying, "We'll eat together first and sometime later we'll learn how to define sin."

This Jesus who says "Come all . . . Come, Come," who would not make anybody clean up before they took their seat at the table, seems to reflect the kind of childhood associations Mr. Thomas would have liked to experience in his hometown and church, like the relationship he now has with his undertaker cousin. As I said earlier, George told some other interesting stories that made more sense when I was able to reflect upon the whole interview. Early in the interview, he related the story of "an old black lady" who always came to their farm to help at hog-killing time. According to his story, she worked for them, but she did not otherwise associate with the family. She ate in a corner of the kitchen, away from the family, and she slept in the attic. George found the arrangements a bit curious. He told me,

> I asked, "Why is she eating over in the corner of the kitchen?"
> And they said, "That's where she wants to be."
> And I thought, "Come on . . . and why does she sleep in the attic?"
> They said, "That is where she wants to be."
> I wanted to dispute it. Of course, when you are twelve years old you have to be careful.[116]

The Jesus of his present experience stands beside the twelve-year old and says, "No, that's not where I want her to be." He tells George and the church, "She should have been invited to dinner and if you ever see her again, then let her eat with you." This vision—an open table indeed—is actualized in the multi-racial congregation that he now attends. It is the polar opposite of that troubling childhood memory. It is a vision of sin overcome. When understood in these terms, exceptions to the baptismal norm can function as deep and prophetic witness.

A Story about a Father Who Invited
All Manner of People to Dinner

For Mary Theodore, pastor of the Rockview congregation, her call to ordained ministry is directly related to her ministry at the Table. A successful executive with a high tech company at the time she began seminary, she began her studies on a part-time basis, looking toward a teaching career, possibly in academia. Her vocational epiphany occurred at a seminary chapel service, after she had begun attending school full-time. As she describes it,

> During that communion service I had this very strong sense that the rail was exactly where I was supposed to be . . . that I belonged in the parish . . . at the Table. The metaphor I use in talking about my calling is hospitality. I feel very much called to be an agent of God's hospitality. [My husband] and I for years have done a lot of entertaining. We have chosen homes that let us do table fellowship. That has always felt like where I belonged.[117]

Today she serves as pastor of a rural congregation which revels in its hospitality; indeed, they gather for breakfast every first Sunday of the month, their usual day for celebrating the Lord's Supper. If communion is moved to another Sunday, the breakfast—as much a ritual occasion as the Eucharist itself—is moved along with it. Pastor Theodore reflects the personality of her congregation and they reflect her convictions as well.

Her calling was clarified in that seminary chapel service and it is confirmed in her pastoral ministry; but she experienced it years before she arrived in seminary. She learned it from a father who invited all manner of people to dinner. He did not practice Christianity in a formal sense, but he kept an open door and an open table. Mary recalled,

> We had a house that always had extra people in it. We had dinner tables that always had extra people. You never had any idea who was going to be there. People came and lived at our house. My father was also an alcoholic. And it was a hidden thing . . .[118]

Her father was far from perfect. She endured the pain and confusion that comes to children of alcoholics. In some ways she is still working through it. During that experience at the seminary chapel communion rail, her first thought was about her father. She said to him, "This isn't where you expected me to be, is it?"

Maybe yes, maybe no. Mary described her father and their life together in that unusual household, and the effect it has on the way she lives today.

> I realized that he was never able to couch what he believed or did in terms of traditional Christianity. He said, "I will love my fellow man and God will deal with that."

> But he really taught me what it meant to welcome people...to welcome people without worrying about gender...about race...about economics. We had all sorts of people all over the place. And it took me a long time to understand that gift. Because it didn't come in the tidy package I wanted....

> And maybe there is a piece of me that says, "I am going to be open and it may not be the tidy package." But it is how you have to welcome people, because they are going to come from lots of different places.

His was not the first troubled generation, yet there was grace in the midst of dysfunction. In the midst of that difficulty something redemptive emerged.

> ...In all of that, he found a place to be himself by being extraordinarily welcoming, not judgmental. He gave lots of people places to heal and do what they needed to do.[119]

He was an official with the local school district, she said, "so all the teachers lived with us until they found housing." Various other people came to live with them and share their table, including "...a displaced couple from Hungary and multiple young Amish women." Their household was something like Noah's ark. When I asked her why all of these people came, she said,

> The young Amish women had housekeeping jobs or office jobs and couldn't get back and forth from the farm. We were in town. I think we were considered a nice, safe family to live with. I have no idea how the Hungarian family got to our house or where they went after they left. [They] came and then they left. In the meantime, I learned to love cabbage rolls. Cabbage rolls are maybe the closest thing to communion food I can get...[120]

Mary began this discussion about her father by asking me if I could accommodate "a digression." Assuring her that I had the time, she told the story of her father's hospitality. It was a profound "digression."

Quite significantly, Mary brought the conversation back to communion, at least as it relates to Hungarian cabbage rolls. In a sense, however, we never left our topic. The story about her father's hospitality reflects the very heart of Methodist identity. It is an image of God's reign not unlike Jesus' parable of the Great Banquet (Luke 14:15-24), in which broken people are invited to the table, perhaps even because of their brokenness.[121] That, it seems, was the way of life in Mary Theodore's childhood home. When such an invitation is presented over time—whether in the church or the household—it becomes the very image of that which is "meet, right, and our bounden duty."[122]

Observations Based upon these
Interviews of Contemporary United Methodists

But First, a Final Story

Another story that emerged in my interviews with Pastor Theodore's congregation shows how deeply the commitment to the open table resides in the piety of many United Methodists. Robert Strong, a Methodist for more than seventy years, is a self-styled theological and political conservative. At several points in our interview, he expressed anger and disappointment over the church's failure to address sin. When he was growing up, "the minister would give sermons about sins ...now it seems like we have feel-good sermons." Today's church practices a "pick and choose approach to the Bible," ignoring the demanding teachings that do not fit its worldview.[123] When I pressed him for specifics, he noted the growing refusal to condemn homosexuality, and, especially, the election of the Rev. Eugene Robinson as the Episcopal Bishop of New Hampshire. Of course, although the United Methodist Church has officially said, "...we do not condone the practice of homosexuality and consider this practice incompatible with Christian teaching,"[124] many in the church refuse to condemn them and focus, rather, on the statement "Homosexual persons no less than heterosexual persons are individuals of sacred worth."[125]

Although Mr. Strong wants the church to take a harder stand against gays and lesbians and their lifestyle, he would not exclude them from the Lord's Table. Earlier in the interview I had asked my hypothetical question about a more restricted invitation and he said, "I honestly believe that anyone, regardless of who you are, if you have the desire and the feeling to go up and participate, you should be afforded that opportunity."[126]

I pressed the question. If a gay couple began attending this church, and they insisted that their relationship represented a perfectly acceptable Christian way of life, what should the church do about them? He hesitated for a moment, and then he said, "That is a very difficult question... I think everyone should be welcome into the church. But I don't think that would say we condone it ..." His was a fascinating and revealing response. In one sense, he yielded no ground—the church should not condone homosexual behavior nor should it conduct same-sex marriage rites. Indeed, he even made something of an implied comparison between homosexuals and criminals, comparing them to bank robbers and child abusers. Even still, he insisted that they should be welcomed at the Table, essentially because the sacrament could function as a converting ordinance. That, of course, begs the question as to what effect a converting ordinance can have on persons who categorically insist that they have no need of conversion, at least in relation to their homosexuality. Like many questions, that one cannot be definitively answered. We can note, however, the fascinating way in which the opponents of homosexuality and those who urge its full acceptance argue for the same practice of open communion, yet they do so for radically different reasons.[127]

I make the following observations based on these interviews of contemporary United Methodist Christians:

1. Most United Methodists believe that any restriction of access to the Lord's Table is a serious injustice, and they will fight to defend an open table. Indeed, it is one of the few liturgical practices about which United Methodists will fight. Their passionate response to the very suggestion of fencing the Table indicates a significant commitment to it. This practice reflects this church's sense of the faithful.

2. In like manner, the positive images that emerged within the interviews suggest that the convictions about open table are deeply rooted in the corporate piety of the people. Although the practice is not without its problems, it is an expression of positive theological convictions.

3. While United Methodists disagree on many political and theological issues and they form factions relating to those disagreements, they are united in their commitment to the open table. Even though they practice it for different theological reasons, most members will vehemently oppose anyone who tries to restrict access to the Table.

4. If the United Methodist Church were to separate into two churches, one a more conservative body and the second a more liberal, progressive body, it is likely that each side would continue to practice the open table. Given that premise, reflection on the practice of the open table may suggest ways to reconcile the factions.

5. The Wesleyan concept of the Eucharist as a converting ordinance is known and believed by many United Methodists, clergy and laity alike, even though persons may or may not use the formal term. This belief provides an important theological foundation for the continuing practice of the open table.

6. In like manner, John Wesley's conviction that all persons could hear and respond to the Gospel is a benchmark belief shared by most United Methodists. It is expressed in the various concerns about cultural relevancy and in discussions about the need to make persons comfortable. This belief, also, provides an important theological foundation for the continuing practice of the open table.

7. The practice of the open table will continue in the United Methodist Church. Had the General Conference ruled against it, which they did not do, many would have protested the decision and then they would have ignored it.

Chapter Six

Open Table and the Suffering of Jesus

A CAUTIONARY WORD ON BIBLICAL GROUNDS

In the previous three chapters, I presented theological justification for the open table as sacramental exception. I described biblical witness to the hospitality of Jesus. I discussed implications of the theological trajectory begun by John Wesley's emphasis on Holy Communion as a means of grace and converting ordinance. I reported on the experience of American Methodist witnesses who have insisted that the Table belongs to the Lord and not to them; thus they declare it open. One of the most important conclusions that we can draw from these investigations is the obvious fact that the open table is a practice within the United Methodist Church; for better or worse, it is well-rooted in the church's piety. Given that piety, any who wish to challenge the practice will face a battle. Such opposition notwithstanding, we should raise questions about this exception to the norm. What are the negative consequences, albeit unintended, of setting aside all fencing of the Table? What values are misplaced when the church practices the open table?

With these questions in mind, in chapters six through eight I turn to a discussion of the problems and unresolved challenges that are presented by a practice of the open table. As I did in presenting the case for the exception, I will discuss biblical themes, Wesleyan themes, and the experience of the church. In this sixth chapter, I discuss the relationship of Jesus' suffering and Passion to our participation in the Table. In doing so, I present a cautionary word about the open table.

BEYOND THE PASSION NARRATIVE?

As we noted in chapter three, United Methodist liturgical reformers and hymn writers influenced by Vatican II attempted to widen the language used at celebrations of the Eucharist. They moved beyond the old focus on the passion narrative to a wider array of biblical themes, particularly invitation, banquet, and hospitality. It was a major shift. Thomas Cranmer's prayer of consecration, inherited by John Wesley and the Methodists, had focused almost exclusively on Jesus' passion and death, using language of sin, sacrifice, and blood. Here are the opening paragraphs of that prayer as they appeared in *The Book of Hymns* (1966), the last hymnal before the current reform:

> Almighty God, our heavenly Father, who of thy tender mercy didst give thine only Son Jesus Christ to suffer death upon the cross for our redemption; who made there, by the one offering of himself, a full, perfect, and sufficient sacrifice for the sins of the whole world; and did institute, and in his holy Gospel command us to continue, a perpetual memory of his precious death until his coming again:
>
> Hear us, O merciful Father, we most humbly beseech thee, and grant that we, receiving these thy creatures of bread and wine, according to thy Son our Savior Jesus Christ's holy institution, in remembrance of his passion, death, and resurrection, may be partakers of the divine nature through him:[1]

The prayer concluded with the Words of Institution. These were followed by the solemn cadences of the Prayer of Humble Access ("We do not presume...") and the *Agnus Dei* ("O Lamb of God..."). Then came communion, followed by the prayer of oblation,[2] which offered yet more reflection on the Passion and death of Christ, his blood and the forgiveness of our sins:

> O Lord, our heavenly Father, we, thy humble servants desire thy fatherly goodness mercifully to accept this our sacrifice of praise and thanksgiving; most humbly beseeching thee to grant, that, by the merits and death of thy Son Jesus Christ, and through faith in his blood, we and thy whole Church may obtain forgiveness of our sins, and all other benefits of his passion.[3]

The Cranmerian pattern expressed several important emphases:

- Christ's death upon the cross was the full and perfect sacrifice for the sins of the world.

- Christ's death is commemorated in the Lord's Supper and its benefits are received through it.

- There should be no understanding of the Lord's Supper as a repeatable propitiation for sins. Participants offer a sacrifice of praise and thanksgiving and they offer their bodies in service. Christ's sacrifice is not repeated.

- The primary benefit of the sacrament is the forgiveness of sins, which is received through faith in Christ's sacrifice, that is, "through faith in his blood."

Given his theological commitments and the controversies he was facing, Cranmer's focus on the passion of Christ was inevitable. He had to define the meaning of Christ's sacrificial death, which also involved stating *what it was not.*

Given different concerns and commitments, authors of the current rite muted the venerable connection of the Eucharist with the sacrifice and death of Jesus, although they did not entirely replace it. Blood and sacrifice are mentioned, but they are not emphasized. The whole life and ministry of Jesus is commemorated, with the Passion as one emphasis among many. The "suffering, death, and resurrection" of Christ is a "baptism" that "gave birth to [the] church."[4] The night of Christ's betrayal became "the night in which he gave himself up for us."[5] Sacrifice is mentioned, but not in relation to sin, nor is the term sacrifice directly related to Jesus Christ. Rather, Jesus makes an offering that we join through our worship:

> And so,
> In remembrance of these your mighty acts in Jesus Christ,
> we offer ourselves in praise and thanksgiving
>   as a holy and living sacrifice,
>   in union with Christ's offering for us,
> as we proclaim the mystery of faith.[6]

The blood of Christ is mentioned—it is the vehicle of our redemption—but we are not called to "faith" in it.[7] We become the body of

Christ for the world, but there is no longer the stark language about offering our souls and bodies as Christ's body had been offered.

There has been a purposeful, precise, and thorough shift in language categories, as the following anecdote from James White demonstrates. In the course of his October 2000 presentation to the Order of Saint Luke, he observed that many communion servers still say, "The blood of Christ, shed for you," even though the Word and Table text calls for them to say, "The blood of Christ, given for you."[8] "I guess they didn't get the word," he said.[9] Why the distinction between "shed" and "given"? White said,

> Hoyt (Hickman) and I had a long conversation about (these words), and we decided that we wanted to emphasize Christ's self-giving and not the passion narrative, so we put the words "given for you."[10]

Given the comprehensive scope of the biblical imagery present in the new texts, few would doubt that some correction was justified. But how much? To pose the question another way, what was lost in the correction?

The question of loss may be raised in relation to the decision to deemphasize the "Prayer of Humble Access." This venerable text has been part of the Anglican tradition since 1548, when the first authorized communion service was published in English. Due to the strong penitential language, however, the prayer was not included in the primary Word and Table pattern, even though many people requested it.[11] It remains in "A Service of Word and Table IV," an alternate service placed in the hymnal as a concession to the Methodist and Evangelical United Brethren (E.U.B.) traditions. That it is cast in Elizabethan language means that it will, most likely, fade from use. The current form of this prayer is as follows:

> We do not presume to come to this thy table,
>> O merciful Lord,
>> trusting in our own righteousness,
>> but in thy manifold and great mercies.
> We are not worthy
>> so much as to gather up the crumbs under thy table.
> But thou art the same Lord,
>> whose property is always to have mercy.
> Grant us, therefore, gracious Lord,
>> so to partake of this Sacrament of thy Son Jesus Christ,
>> that we may walk in newness of life,

> may grow into his likeness,
> and may evermore dwell in him, and he in us. Amen.[12]

The prayer is biblical, based on the story of the Syrophoenician woman who asked Jesus to cast an unclean spirit out of her daughter. Since she was a Gentile, Jesus dismissed her and then insulted her in the bargain: "Let the children be fed first, for it is not fair to take the children's food and throw it to the dogs" (Mark 7:27). Undeterred, she responded, "Sir, even the dogs under the table eat the children's crumbs" (Mark 7:28). Moved by this bold response, Jesus healed the daughter (Matthew 7:29-30; compare Matthew 15: 21-28). The woman became, as it were, an exception to the Jewish parameters of his mission. The prayer suggests that no one is worthy of admission; yet God's mercy makes it possible. God grants something like a sacramental exception every time we approach. In that sense, the Prayer of Humble Access expresses a quintessentially Methodist theme—undeserved grace is offered even to the outsiders. Nevertheless, this classic prayer is falling out of usage.

In like manner, the *Agnus Dei* ("O Lamb of God") does not appear in "A Service of Word and Table I," even though it has a long history of usage in the Western Church and was included in the 1966 Methodist *Book of Hymns*. It also finds its place in "A Service of Word and Table IV." Versions of this hymn could be used in the various modern language Word and Table rites, but a United Methodist congregation would have to make a decided effort in order to do so. *The United Methodist Hymnal* (1989) offers no settings other than the John Merbecke setting (1550), printed in the 1966 book, even though ten settings are provided, for instance, in *Hymnal 1982* of the Episcopal Church.[13] In fact, Good Samaritan United Methodist Church in Houston has used the English Language Liturgical Consultation (ELLC) version of the *Agnus Dei* since the early 1970s. This text softens the classical *Agnus Dei* through use of contemporary language and by addressing "Jesus" directly, thereby shifting emphasis from the more sacrificial phrase "Lamb of God."

> Jesus, Lamb of God: have mercy on us.
> Jesus, bearer of our sins: have mercy on us.
> Jesus, redeemer of the world: give us your peace.[14]

Their use of Betty Pulkingham's lyrical musical setting softens the text even further.[15] It has become a high point of their service. Although

Pulkingham was working at a nearby Episcopal church when this hymn was introduced at Good Samaritan, this congregation would not continue singing it were it not a significant expression of their piety.

While they differ stylistically, both the contemporary and the classical text draw upon primary biblical images and phrases (Exodus 12:1-13; Psalm 51:1-2; John 1:29, 36; Mark 10:47-49). Given that biblical foundation, it seems odd that neither text is part of the mainstream United Methodist *ordo*. Indeed, its penitential tone is but one aspect of the *Agnus Dei*. It reminds the members of Good Samaritan Church that they come to the Table as a gift of God's mercy. All who commune do so by a surprising exception that they do not deserve. Thus its penitential language is not contrary to the experience of gracious feast, it may even deepen it. Loss of penitential language may even compromise that depth. In order to avoid that compromise, we must define "grace" and "gift" according to the context of the Gospel.

GRACE AS PARTICIPATION IN THE PASCHAL MYSTERY OF JESUS CHRIST

As I have established earlier, many will defend the open table by observing that Holy Communion is a means of grace or gift.[16] As with most theological language, these terms are useful "in Christ," that is, when they are used to illumine key dynamics within the biblical narrative of our salvation, and they are less helpful when abstracted from it.

A problem arises if we view grace as some type of objective substance, available through a variety of means, including Holy Communion. According to this understanding, communion is "good for us" in a vague sense, akin to eating one's spiritual vegetables. Communion becomes, as it were, a helpful spiritual "thing." Sacraments use matter, of course, but they are far more than holy water and consecrated bread and wine. As Catholic theologian Edward Schillebeeckx insisted, they are not "things," but they are "encounters" of human beings with the living Christ.[17] They involve matter and gracious action related to it, and they are inextricably rooted in the biblical narrative. Sacraments are like the steps to a dance that begins with the narrative of the covenant people and Jesus, continues in our liturgical assemblies, and then permeates all of our living. In this sense, one does not simply receive the grace of a sacrament as one would receive a valuable commodity; rather, one enters the sacramental action and *participates* in it. The Eucharist is not primarily a thing, but it is a way of life rooted in Jesus Christ.

The ritualization of sacrament and grace as "thing" and "substance" reaches its ridiculous extreme in "come and go" communion rites. I remember attending one of them. I was greeted not by my sisters and brothers, but by an empty chapel and an altar on which a plate full of bread pellets and a tray with small cups of grape juice had been placed. No one proclaimed the Gospel to me, no one called me to repentance and reconciliation, and no one prayed for the blessing of the Spirit. No one fed me and no one sent me to feed anybody else. I did the best I could, I suppose; I took my bread and juice and tried to think holy thoughts, but I would not say that communion happened.

Did an elder speak a prayer of consecration over the elements before leaving them there on the altar? Perhaps so, but that does not change the issue. One cannot celebrate communion by oneself, without the community and its biblical narrative.[18] By themselves, consecrated elements are no means of grace, else the Corinthians who arrived at the meal early and gorged themselves would have been the holiest Christians of all. Instead, Paul rebuked them (1 Corinthians 11:17-34).

What, then, is grace? "Grace" is a way for Christians to describe the dynamics of our life in Christ and thus our understanding of it cannot be separated from him, especially his Passion, Death, and Resurrection. We are crucified with Christ (Galatians 2:19) and we find the promise of new life in his resurrection. All truly Christian meaning is revealed and constructed according to this narrative. Even the simple phrase "Jesus loves me" is defined not according to the saccharine, greeting card intimacies of modern culture, but according to the cross and the hope of resurrection. Jesus loves us by standing with us in the place of struggle and leading us to new life. Jesus loves us by placing us in a fellowship open "to people of all ages, nations, and races,"[19] where we die to constricted views of the world and are raised to a new appreciation of the other. Grace is the call to participate in Christ's ministry with "the least of these" (Matthew 25:31-46). Grace is God's work of judging inadequate dreams, even shattering them, and then giving us new dreams. Means of grace lead us into these dynamics of conversion, into this dying and rising, which is precisely why churches need to invite seekers truthfully. Not all will wish to go where they lead.

At this point in our discussion, we must confront the ancient problem of docetism. The term docetism (or docetic) derives from the Greek verb *dokein*, "to seem." Docetism is related to Gnosticism, that ancient dualistic tendency that equates salvation with escape from the bondage of creation, and particularly from the human body. Persons given to a gnostic worldview were troubled by claims that God had redeemed the world through the Incarnation, Death, and Resurrection of Jesus Christ. Thus some developed a docetic explanation of the Gospel narrative, saying that Christ only appeared to assume human flesh. Others insisted that Christ did not suffer, but that someone else, perhaps Simon of Cyrene, suffered and died in his place. The writer of 1 John was addressing docetic claims when he wrote the following:

> Beloved, do not believe every spirit, but test the spirits to see whether they are from God; for many false prophets have gone out into the world. By this you know the Spirit of God: every spirit that confesses that Jesus Christ has come in the flesh is from God, and every spirit that does not confess Jesus is not from God. (1 John 4:1-3a)

The second-century martyr Ignatius warned against the same tendency. In his letter to Smyrnaeans, he wrote,

> For [Jesus Christ] suffered all these things for our sakes . . . and He suffered truly, as also He raised Himself truly; not as certain Unbelievers say, that He suffered in semblance . . . For I know and believe that He was in the flesh even after the resurrection.[20]

A docetic reading of the Gospel presented ethical problems as well as theological problems. Ignatius observed that those who refused to acknowledge the suffering of Christ often denied the suffering that occurred in other places as well.

> But mark ye those who hold strange doctrine touching the grace of Jesus Christ which came to us, how that they are contrary to the mind of God. They have no care for love, none for the widow, none for the orphan, none for the afflicted, none for the prisoner, none for the hungry or thirsty. They abstain from eucharist (thanksgiving) and prayer, because they allow not that the eucharist is the flesh of our Saviour Jesus Christ, which flesh suffered for our sins, and which the Father of His goodness raised up.[21]

In time, such docetic beliefs were excluded by the emerging doctrinal and creedal consensus of the church, and so the Nicene Creed proclaims that the Son of God "became truly human," that "he suffered death and was buried."[22]

While a docetic interpretation of the Gospel is no longer a serious doctrinal option, a type of *docetic spirituality* remains. Like Peter, we proclaim Jesus as Christ, but we are scandalized by his message of suffering and the cross, particularly the assertion that faithful disciples will "deny themselves and take up their cross and follow (Jesus)" (Mark 8:34). The call to embrace suffering and pain is avoided in numerous ways. We ignore the homeless and those with AIDS or we find ways to blame them. We discourage grief and sometimes we deny it altogether. Funerals become a denial of death. Death only *seems* painful. We look at tragedies and call them acts of God. We define ecclesiastical success according to the canons of Madison Avenue—bigger, better, more visible. Some insist on singing upbeat songs only, nice little jingles free of poetic and tonal complexity. We ignore Advent. We avoid silence. We glibly dismiss the call to Lenten fasting, either joking about it or ignoring it altogether. We celebrate Palm Sunday and then Easter, forgetting the Passion Narrative and the solemn weekdays of Holy Week. We do not learn how to lament. We think denunciation and cursing is unseemly, so we ignore evil and, polite people that we are, we hope it will go away.

Indeed, Eucharist is banquet and feast—the joyful marriage supper of the Lamb—yet it is not as if these are free-floating images that exist outside of the biblical narrative. Disciples ate with Jesus on the way to the cross, at the Last Supper, and on the way from it, at Emmaus (Luke 24:13-35). The host of that great marriage supper is the Lamb that was slain (Revelation 5:6). If emphasized to the exclusion of other themes, focus on banquet and feast can drift toward a new form of docetism, to a muting of the Paschal character of Christian life or an outright denial of it. Those who eat with Jesus enter the dynamics of his death, seeking a new life that follows the contours of the Gospel narrative. Thus the Eucharistic mystery is far deeper than the conviviality shared at a church coffee hour.

In that light, those who eat and drink with Jesus may well be warned as well as invited. The church has long understood this dynamic. Most rites of the Reformation era included exhortations warning persons against a presumptuous receiving of communion. This text from *The Book of Common Prayer* (1552) is typical:

If any of you be a blasphemer of God, an hynderer or slaunderer of his worde, an adulterer, or be in malice or envie, or in any other grevous cryme, bewayle your sinnes, and come not to thys holy Table; lest after the takyng of that holy Sacrament, the Devill entre into you, as he entred into Judas, and fyll you ful of al iniquities, and bryng you to destruccion, both of bodye and soule. Judge therefore your selves (brethren) that ye bee not judged of the Lorde. Repent you truely for your sinnes paste have a lively and stedfaste fayth in Christe our savioure. Amende youre lyves, and be in perfecte charitie with al men, so shall ye be meete partakers of those holy misteries.[23]

John Calvin had expressed a similar spirit.

We have heard, brethren, how our Lord celebrated his Supper with his disciples, thereby indicating that strangers, and those who are not of the company of the faithful, ought not to be admitted. Therefore, in accordance with this rule, in the name and by the authority of our Lord Jesus Christ, I excommunicate all idolaters, blasphemers, despisers of God, heretics, and all who form private sects to break the unity of the Church, all perjurers, all who rebel against parents or their superiors, all who are seditious, mutinous, quarrelsome or brutal, all adulterers, fornicators, thieves, ravishers, misers, drunkards, gluttons, and all who lead a scandalous and dissolute life. I declare that they must abstain from this holy table, for fear of defiling and contaminating the holy food which our Lord Jesus Christ gives only to his household and believers.[24]

According to these exhortations, something deeply important is occurring at the Table, and the prospective communicant must not take it lightly. Unfortunately, the primary focus of these particular warnings fell on issues of personal sin and penance, and thus most contemporary theologians find them inadequate.[25] As we noted earlier (see chapter 3), John Wesley rejected them as well.

The precedent of warning communicants is as old as the Gospel tradition itself and the concerns one finds in the Gospel narratives range much wider than the individualistic focus of the sixteenth century. Those who eat and drink with Jesus should hear the question that he posed to his disciples when they asked for special privileges: "Are you able to drink the cup that I drink, or be baptized with the baptism that I am baptized with?" (Mark 10:38). The Gospel speaks this question to the whole church. Like the other Gospel texts about eating and drinking with Jesus, it also should be heard in light of the early church's experience of the Eucharist.[26] That first-century community, facing the distress of persecution, was reminded that disciples are called to follow Jesus in the way of Passion and cross.[27] Their Eucharist was not, therefore, primarily a means to self-fulfillment and spiritual peace, but a means for drawing them ever deeper into the Paschal mystery. The Eucharistic cup is the cup that Jesus drank, and no other.

The plea of Jesus in the Garden of Gethsemane should also be heard in relationship to the Eucharist. Facing the prospect of his death, Jesus prayed "Abba, Father, for you all things are possible; remove this cup from me; yet, not what I want, but what you want" (Mark 14:36). Raymond Brown points out the irony of this prayer that occurs in the pericope immediately following the institution of the Lord's Supper:

> At the supper a complete self-giving was symbolized by the cup of wine/blood, and now Jesus asks the Father to take away the cup![28]

We may wish to offer the same prayer. Indeed, only God's grace makes us able to drink the Eucharistic cup, but the grace that we receive there does not excuse us from the dynamics of Christ's passion, death, and resurrection. In the Eucharist, we are entering something deeply serious. We become connected to Christ and his mission, connected to all others who commune with Christ. This insight bears directly on the open table question.

I think of James, an older adult with Down Syndrome and a member of a church I once served as pastor. James loved to worship, so much so that he attended both the 8:30 and the 10:50 A.M. services, even though we used the same order of worship in each. He sang the hymns lustily, each time in his own unique way. That means that he would hang onto the last note for two or three beats after the rest of us were finished. Why stop? Some of us more orderly brothers and sisters wondered whether someone should teach him when to quit; but the teaching didn't work very well, so he kept on singing in his own unique way. On our better days, we came to expect such singing, even to cherish it. Since we were in communion with James, there was really no choice, was there? The fact that we are placed in church with persons like James, which changes us, *is* the grace of communion. It is an experience of dying and rising with Jesus Christ.

As my colleague John Thornburg has said, perhaps we should think of invitation to communion as the ultimate altar call. Instead of saying "Y'all come," we might say something like the following:

> I invite you to come to this table. This is not coffee hour. This is not social club. This is not a "feel good about yourself" place. This is a place in which you get amazing life-changing gifts given to you, and then, in a split second, you get the word that you're being sent to the war zone to work in a field hospital. If you are willing to be dispatched, come on. If you're not, we're ready to surround you with people who've been there. They will tell you what it's like. Then you'll know whether you are ready.[29]

Thornburg offers an intriguing thought here, one that combines an understanding of communion as means of grace with the Wesleyan dynamics of missional service, the offering of our bodies in Christ's name. Such a double emphasis is a worthy one. The Wesley brothers spoke eloquently about the Eucharist as a means of grace and foretaste of the celestial banquet, so we are right to do the same. They also understood the Eucharist as missional identification with Christ's sacrificial death, as we shall see in the next section.

THE WESLEYS AND EUCHARISTIC HYMNS ON SACRIFICE

The language of sacrifice is rooted in the Old Testament narrative, occurring as early as the story of Cain and Abel (Genesis 4). Israel's deliverance from Egypt was sealed through the blood of sacrificial lambs and their remembrance of that deliverance involved the annual sacrifice of lambs (Exodus 12). Leviticus describes the various types of sacrifice: burnt offerings (Leviticus 1), grain offerings (Leviticus 2), offerings of well-being (Leviticus 3), sin offerings (Leviticus 4:1-5:13), and the guilt offering (Leviticus 5:14–6:7). Priests were instructed on the proper ritual action for each (e.g., Leviticus 6:8-7:38; 14:10-20; 16:1-34). Alongside the priestly cult grew a prophetic critique. "With what shall I come before the LORD?" asked Micah (6:6). Not with "thousands of rams" (Micah 6:7) but with righteous living:

> He has told you, O mortal, what is good;
>   and what does the LORD require of you
> but to do justice, and to love kindness,
>   and to walk humbly with your God? (Micah 6:8)

In like manner, the prophet Hosea spoke, "I desire steadfast love and not sacrifice, the knowledge of God rather than burnt offerings" (Hosea 6:6). The meaning of Temple rites and ritual was deepened and redefined. A similar dynamic was at work in the New Testament, where the death of Jesus was described in cultic language—Christ is the Lamb of God that takes away sin (John 1:29-36; 19:14-18, 30). Christ is the perfect sacrifice offered once for all (Hebrews 9:26). Even so, the language and spiritual dynamics of sacrifice did not end, but the church used them to speak about discipleship. The prophetic critique was fulfilled:

> I appeal to you therefore, brothers and sisters, by the mercies of God, to
> present your bodies as a living sacrifice, holy and acceptable to God,

which is your spiritual worship. Do not be conformed to this world, but be transformed by the renewing of your minds, so that you may discern what is the will of God—what is good and acceptable and perfect. (Romans 12:1)

For the bodies of those animals whose blood is brought into the sanctuary by the high priest as a sacrifice for sin are burned outside the camp. Therefore Jesus also suffered outside the city gate in order to sanctify the people by his own blood. Let us then go to him outside the camp and bear the abuse he endured... Through him, then, let us continually offer a sacrifice of praise to God, that is, the fruit of lips that confess his name. Do not neglect to do good and to share what you have, for such sacrifices are pleasing to God. (Hebrews 13:11-13, 15-16)

In what sense is the Eucharist a sacrifice? In what sense do Christians participate in that sacrifice? Because of its integral connection to the sacrificial death of Jesus, many came to view the Eucharist itself as a sacrificial offering for sins; indeed, much of the late medieval ecclesiastical culture was built on the idea that masses could be offered as payment for the sins of souls in purgatory.[30] Following the logic of Hebrews 9:26, Cranmer and the principal Anglican reformers insisted that the sacrificial death of Christ was offered once for all time, "a full, perfecte, and sufficiente sacrifice, oblacion, and satisfaccion, for the synnes of the whole worlde."[31] Continuing in the language of Romans 12:1-2 and Hebrews 13, however, they insisted that Christians who participated in the Eucharist made a "Sacrifice of prayse and thanksgeving," one that involves even "[their] soules, and bodies" as "a reasonable holy, and lively Sacrifice" to God.[32] In the Anglican understanding, there would be no propitiatory offerings for souls living or dead; rather, they would celebrate the Lord's Supper as a way of pleading for the present benefits of that one sacrifice. It was important that they remember that sacrifice in its details, for it showed them the depths of God's mercy and in some measure the shape of their own discipleship.

Each of these primary themes is expressed by the Wesley brothers (again, primarily Charles) in *Hymns on the Lord's Supper.* Section IV (116-127) presents hymns on "The Holy Eucharist as it Implies a Sacrifice" and Section V (128-157) presents hymns "Concerning the Sacrifice of our Person." Before looking at three of these hymns, fairness requires my conceding that the language of sacrifice is present in the "Word and Table I" text. We speak there of "[offering] ourselves in praise and thanksgiving as a holy and living sacrifice, in union with

Christ's offering for us . . ."[33] In like manner, there is some mention of blood. The church is "the body of Christ, redeemed by his blood."[34] While present in this text, however, these images are not emphasized there. The weight of this claim will become clear as we look at the Wesley hymns, where such themes hold center stage.

"Victim Divine" (*Hymns on the Lord's Supper*, 116)

"Victim Divine" is included in the recently published *The Faith We Sing*. Thus its imagery can be recovered for contemporary Methodist usage.[35] The fact that it was included in the collection at the urging of James F. White suggests some softening of the linguistic agenda noted earlier.[36] What follows are the first, second, and fourth stanzas of the text as we find them in the 1745 version.[37]

> Victim Divine, Thy grace we claim
>   While thus Thy precious death we show;
> Once offer'd up, a spotless Lamb,
>   In Thy great temple here below,
> Thou didst for all mankind atone,
> And standest now before the throne.
>
> Thou standest in the holiest place,
>   As now for guilty sinners slain;
> Thy blood of sprinkling speaks, and prays,
>   All-prevalent for helpless man;
> Thy blood is still our ransom found,
> And spreads salvation all around.
>
> He still respects Thy sacrifice,
>   Its savour sweet doth always please;
> The offering smokes through earth and skies,
>   Diffusing life, and joy, and peace;
> To these Thy lower courts it comes,
> And fills them with divine perfumes.[38]

The linking of "Divine" to "Victim" may surprise us. We are becoming more aware of the damage done to victims of child and spouse abuse, and thus we are reluctant to use images that may deify victimization. In this text, however, there is no strong man oppressing the weak. The sacrifice of Christ is offered in strength, thus breaking the power of oppression.

The victim language is deeply Eucharistic. Indeed, "victim" is the English translation of the Latin term "hostia," from which comes the word "host," the Catholic term for the consecrated communion bread. Thus the phrase "Victim Divine" refers to the sacrifice of Jesus on the cross, that "full, perfect, and sufficient sacrifice" once offered yet commemorated in the Lord's Supper. It suggests, also, a real presence of Christ offered to the church in the sacramental bread. The host, that is, the Victim, is presented as God-filled, as divine. That Charles Wesley used such an obviously catholic term to describe the sacrament reminds us once again that persons of Methodist heritage should not speak of the sacraments as empty signs.

Of greatest importance for our current discussion is the sacrificial imagery of this hymn text along with its realistic language about blood. Wesley insists that Christ the spotless Lamb of God has been offered as an atoning sacrifice—his life given in the place of ours. The gift is costly. He was slain for our guilt, just as the guilt offerings were offered on the altar of the Temple. Blood was drawn and sprinkled about, and that blood is the ransom paid for our salvation, even now. There is no freedom without this shedding and sprinkling of blood, and God still "respects the sacrifice," honoring it as if it had just been offered. Even with the language of Temple sacrifice and pleasing odors to God (e.g., Leviticus 1:17, 2:16), this hymn allows no docetic avoidance of the Passion Narrative and its implications. We are saved by blood.

Other hymns in Section IV are more graphically realistic. In hymn 122, Wesley calls God (and us) to view the wounds of Jesus. We gaze on something like a verbal crucifix:

> Still the wounds are open wide,
>   The blood doth freely flow
> As when first His sacred side
>   Received the deadly blow:
> Still, O God, the blood is warm,
>   Cover'd with the blood we are;
> Find a part it doth not arm,
>   And strike the sinner there![39]

There is healing for us in these open wounds so graphically and sensuously expressed. The verbal crucifix calls forth such faith. We see the blood flowing like a river of life and we feel its warmth as it covers us. Perhaps this excursion into the medieval piety of the wounds is more than we can bear, but the imagery of divine generosity and cost is too strong to avoid; in a sense, our revulsion reveals its value. Hymn 124 is equally strong. It presents the standard view of the Eucharist as commemoration of the "complete" sacrifice "once offer'd," yet made available to us.

> Yet may we celebrate below,
> And daily thus Thine offering show
>   Exposed before Thy Father's eyes;
> In this tremendous mystery
> Present Thee bleeding on a tree,
>   Our everlasting Sacrifice.[40]

Again, Wesley's imagery provides us with a poetic crucifix. We see him "bleeding on the tree," and this vision redeems us.

How do these realistic, even graphic, images function in the life of liturgy and prayer? Even though we proclaim a sacrifice once offered, the details of that offering remain an essential part of our anamnesis. The blood images remind us that Christ's sacrifice was costly; therefore we should give thanks. The suffering was real and not illusory; therefore we must realize that the suffering of our generation is real. It is not simply an inconvenience some face on their way to heaven. Suffering presented realistically calls for serious, committed response; and it reminds us that such response is costly. The Wesleys show us where full, active, and conscious participation in Christian liturgy can lead us.

"Would the Saviour of Mankind?" (Hymns on the Lord's Supper, 131)

In section V, entitled "Concerning the Sacrifice of our Persons," the Wesleys insisted on the connection between Christ's sacrifice and Christian discipleship. The hymn "Would the Saviour of Mankind" provides a clear example. Again, we are confronted with Christ's Passion in all its details, with references to the altar and a slaughtered lamb, suffering and blood. We are called to participate in that Passion, presenting our souls and bodies in sacrifice. Charles Wesley wrote,

> Would the Saviour of mankind
>   Without His people die?
> No, to Him we all are join'd
>   As more than standers by.
> Freely as the Victim came
>   To the altar of His cross,

> We attend the slaughter'd Lamb,
> And suffer for His cause.[41]

Wesley's question invites us to imagine a story line different from the one we find in scripture. According to Mark's account, Jesus did die alone; the disciples scattered and deserted him (Mark 14:26-30). While he suffered, they looked on from a distance, doing their best to avoid identifying with him (Mark 14:66-71, 15:40).[42] Christ endured in spite of their desertion, and that is good news for us; so is the continuing call to take up the cross and follow. Wesley reminds us that Christ's disciples are given an opportunity to reenter the story and live a more faithful ending. Through our participation in the Eucharist, we stand beneath the cross and join in his suffering.

According to this hymn, the Christ whom we see sacrificed on the cross is like the scapegoat of the Levitical rites (Leviticus 16:5-10, 20-22); he is the sacrificial Victim who bears the burden of our sins.

> Him even now by faith we see;
> Before our eyes He stands!
> On the suffering Deity
> We lay our trembling hands,
> Lay our sins upon His head,
> Wait on the dread Sacrifice,
> Feel the lovely Victim bleed,
> And die while Jesus dies![43]

It is not, however, as if Christ simply bears them away while we live "happily ever after." Our hands tremble in fear for good reason, for we, too, must die if we are to live. According to Wesley, there is no way to holiness except through the blood of this sacrifice. We are called to participate in it—to exult in this blood, identify with it, bathe in it, and share in the death that it signifies. Most certainly, Wesley allows us no avoidance of the cross, as if Christ's work had excused us from the call to join in his sacrifice.

> Sinner, see, He dies for all
> And feel His mortal wound,
> Prostrate on your faces fall,
> And kiss the hallow'd ground
> Hallow'd by the streaming blood
> Blood whose virtue all may know,
> Sharers with the dying God,
> And crucified below.[44]

Our sin is cleansed by Christ's blood and then we join him as faithful disciples, taking up the cross and following. Only in this way, insisted Wesley, the way of Passion, death, and resurrection, do we know the deep joys promised in the Gospel.

> Sprinkled with the blood we lie,
>   And bless its cleansing power
> Crying in the Spirit's cry,
>   Our Saviour we adore!
> Jesu, Lord, whose cross we bear
>   Let Thy death our sins destroy
> Make us who Thy sorrows share
>   Partakers of Thy joy.[45]

Participation in Holy Communion leads us into these Paschal dynamics. Such participation makes us Christ's people, joined to his cruciform narrative. If United Methodists insist on a radically open table, then they should (at least) proclaim this Paschal dynamic as part of their invitation. At the very least, those who eat and drink with Jesus are entering a realm where costly love is demanded, where they will be called to repent and love the unlovable. It is a converting ordinance in the deepest biblical sense, one that redefines the very meaning of happiness. We see these claims in this next hymn text.

"Happy the Souls that Follow'd Thee"
(*Hymns on the Lord's Supper*, 141)

Again, Wesley insists that participation in the Lord's Supper brings us to the foot of the cross. Here we find echoes of the Johannine Passion, with its more positive examples of discipleship. We become like the mother of our Lord, Mary the wife of Clopas, Mary Magdalene, and the beloved disciple who stood near the cross (John 19:25-27). They lamented, yes, but we can see God's promise embedded in that lamentation. In that place of death they saw a glimpse of God's promises fulfilled. Wesley's use of "happy" suggests another promise spoken by Jesus: "Blessed (happy!) are those who mourn, for they will be comforted" (Matthew 5:4). According to Charles Wesley, those who stood near the cross were the privileged first participants in his sacrifice, yet Christians find the same blessing as we draw near through the ordinance of the Supper. It brings us to the cross, into the dynamics of the crucifixion.

Happy the souls that follow'd Thee,
    Lamenting, to th' accursed wood;
Happy, who underneath the tree
    Unmovable in sorrow stood.

Not all the days before or since
    An hour so solemn could afford,
For suffering with our bleeding Prince,
    For dying with our slaughter'd Lord.

Yet in this ordinance Divine
    We still the sacred load may bear;
And now we in Thy offering join,
    Thy sacramental passion share.

We cast our sins into that fire
    Which did Thy sacrifice consume,
And every base and vain desire
    To daily crucifixion doom.

Thou art with all Thy members here,
    In this tremendous mystery
We jointly before God appear,
    To offer up ourselves with Thee.

True followers of our bleeding Lamb,
    Now on Thy daily cross we die
And, mingled in a common flame,
    Ascend triumphant to the sky.[46]

The images pile up in typical Wesleyan style: suffering, dying, slaughter'd Lord, a bleeding Prince, a bleeding lamb, sacrificial fires accepted by God, cross and death for Christ and those who follow him. Wesley's imagery allowed no docetic avoidance of the truth he believed, for him disciples are called to behold this bleeding lamb and follow in his way. So yes, Eucharist is a means of grace, one that helps its participants join in the triumphs of Christ; but through the imagery of this hymn, Wesley reminds us that the triumph is a *Christian* triumph, one rooted in the cross.

CONCLUSIONS

In this chapter, I have argued that we must use references to the Passion Narratives when we talk about the grace afforded by Holy

Communion. Such references should shape our invitations to the Table. I have demonstrated how such imagery was used by the Wesley brothers in sections four and five of *Hymns on the Lord's Supper*.

Analyzing these texts is an effort; section II ("As it is a Sign and a Means of Grace") and section III ("The Sacrament as a Pledge of Heaven") resonate with the deeper streams of my Eucharistic piety. The sections on Eucharist as sacrifice do not resonate so deeply; yet when I came to a renewed study of them several years ago, I realized that they had something important to say to the question of the open table. Nonetheless, I admit that reading them is painful, analyzing them an effort.

My formation has led me to dislike "blood hymns," to view them as inadequate theologically and liturgically. I think there will be wild palm trees growing in Alaska before I will use "Power in the Blood" at a celebration of the Eucharist, but I am prepared now to use "Victim Divine" and "Would the Saviour of Mankind?" (although we would have to update the language and find a proper tune).

Life teaches us. During part of the time I was writing this chapter, my third grade son was home for a few days with a touch of the flu. Of course, when one is writing, caring for a sick child is something of a distraction; but there can be an upside, like mid-morning breaks for juice and cookies and lunches together. These were shared banquets in the best sense. Much of the time, however, I wrote and revised, and he sat in the next room watching The History Channel. One day there was a stretch of documentaries on Adolf Hitler and the Holocaust, followed by films about the Ku Klux Klan and their atrocities. Perhaps I should have turned off the television and played a Disney movie, but I did not. These are stories he needs to know, I thought, because disciples need to know what evil looks like if they are going to resist it. Thus he came to lunch wondering what God would do to those people "who broke the sixth commandment." So we talked about evil and murder and how God and Jesus relate to them. There was no "happily ever after" conclusion, but we did talk about the Gospel, about Divine judgment and liberation. Upon reflection, it occurs to me that my son and I were talking about blood—the bloodshed of the oppressed, the bloodshed of their advocates and liberators, the blood Jesus shed for us.

Discipleship involves dealing with blood, metaphorically and literally. We donate blood for use in the healing process. We are called to bind up the bloody wounds of earthquake and hurricane victims, to stand with children and spouses who have been beaten bloody by their abusers, to bury the bloodied victims of war, and to uncover the blood that has been shed and hidden by totalitarian regimes. In these days of the continuing AIDS epidemic, we are called to stand with those whose blood itself has become a threat. Discipleship brings us face to face with blood. Christians given to a docetic spirituality—who grow faint at the sight of blood—can hardly witness effectively. Fortunately, the tradition can save us.

Wesley's hymns on sacrifice remind us that the grace rooted in cross and resurrection is the only grace that Christians know and the only one we are given to proclaim. We must see and proclaim the blood of Jesus, Wesley would argue, and the Eucharist does both. It is a means of grace insofar as it allows us to participate in this dynamic of shed blood. Knowing what we know about the costly nature of Christian discipleship, in what sense do we invite persons to the Table?

As we have described earlier, the traditions of the church include warnings about approaching the Table presumptuously, but that tradition offers us little help. It was much too concerned with personal sin and it discouraged those who needed communion the most. We should not imply that persons who commune unworthily will be punished by God; nor should we imply that anything particularly awful will happen if some non-baptized persons approach the Table. Quite the contrary, the narrative of Jesus gives us ample reason for feeding all of those who approach.

Our response to such seekers should be a modest one, much less confrontational and less negative than the old fencing strategies. We should, simply yet profoundly, tell the truth about life in Christ. In the ongoing process of inviting persons to the Table, we need to tell them that the Christ whom they meet there will lead them to new life by the way of the cross, through the blood of Jesus found at the altar and in the world. It is a cautionary word. Participation in the Eucharist takes Christians into the same deep waters that one enters in baptism, into the depths of covenant responsibility for and with one another.

Chapter Seven

Formation as a Means of Grace

CHALLENGING AN OPEN TABLE ON
WESLEYAN GROUNDS

A s we have established, John Wesley believed in preaching the Gospel to all people. Methodists have adopted that logic, applying it to many aspects of their life and witness; it supports their evangelistic appeal, their witness for social justice, and yes, the way they invite persons to the Lord's Table. Although Wesley believed in preaching to all people, his work did not end with the spiritual awakening of seekers. Rather, Wesley called them into disciplined communities of accountability, where they would watch over one another in love.[1] In Wesley's day this oversight was provided through the Methodist class system which he described in his treatise "The Nature, Design, and General Rules of the United Societies in London, Bristol, Kingswood, and Newcastle upon Tyne (1743)," hereafter known as "the General Rules."

> In the latter end of the year 1739 eight or ten persons came to me in London who appeared to be deeply convinced of sin, and earnestly groaning for redemption. They desired (as did two or three more the next day) that I would spend some time with them in prayer, and advise them how to flee from the wrath to come, which they saw continually hanging over their heads. That we might have more time for this great work I appointed a day when they might all come together, which from thenceforward they did every week, namely, on Thursday, in the evening. To these, and as many more as desired to join with them (for their number increased daily), I gave those advices from time to time

which I judged most needful for them; and we always concluded our meeting with prayer suited to their several necessities.

This was the rise of the United Society, first at London, and then in other places. Such a Society is no other than 'a company of men "having the form, and seeking the power of godliness", united in order to pray together, to receive the word of exhortation, and to watch over one another in love, that they may help each other to work out their salvation.'[2]

Here we see a formational structure that functioned as a means of grace. Persons had been awakened to their need for salvation but they did not know what to do next. So Wesley brought them together for the advice and prayer that would support their growth and their meeting together became an accountability structure that encouraged them to continue. This combination of invitation and discipline is essential to a full expression of Methodist ecclesiology. The General Rules present a vision of mature Christianity and they provide the means for moving toward that goal. Of course, conversion and maturity come by the grace of God, but members prepared to receive that grace according to the pathway prescribed within the Rules. The pathway is significant.

The first rule involved turning away from sin and evil. Members were called to demonstrate their desire for salvation "By doing no harm, by avoiding evil in every kind—especially that which is most generally practised."[3] Wesley named some of those practices. Among these were several rather obvious prohibitions. There was to be no "taking the name of God in vain . . . drunkenness . . . fighting, quarrelling, brawling, brother 'going to law' with brother . . . [and] laying up treasures upon earth."[4] We might address these today in similar terms. Others were specific to that time and place, such as the prohibition against "The 'putting on of gold or costly apparel', particularly *the wearing of calashes, high-heads, or enormous bonnets.*"[5]

Such naming of forbidden practices is prone to legalism, but avoiding specificity is no better. For instance, in recent years the church has been forced to identify and proscribe that set of actions and attitudes that we now call "sexual harassment." Such analysis is necessary even though the call for justice can devolve into legalism. The church cannot avoid the call to discernment simply because it is difficult.

The second Rule called people to do good. Members were to show their desire for salvation "by doing good . . . of every possible sort . . . "[6] as often as they had opportunity. They were charged with doing the corporal works of mercy described in Matthew chapter 25: "Doing good...by giving food to the hungry, by clothing the naked, by visiting or helping them that are sick, or in prison."[7] In Wesley's understanding, "doing good" also meant offering faithful Christian instruction.

The third Rule offered spiritual resources for keeping the other two. Society members were called "to evidence their desire for salvation...by attending upon the ordinances of God."[8] Again, Wesley delineated the specifics. They were to observe the following means of grace:

> The public worship of God;
> The ministry of the Word, either read or expounded
> The Supper of the Lord;
> Family and private prayer
> Searching the Scriptures; and
> Fasting, or abstinence.[9]

Wesley viewed these Rules as a unit, one not making sense apart from the others, and as norms for the Society. Those who did not follow them would be warned about their negligence and those who persisted in their disobedience could be expelled. He wrote,

> These are the General Rules of our societies...If there be any among us who observe them not, who habitually break any one of them, let it be made known unto them who watch over that soul, as they that must give account. We will admonish him of the error of his ways. We will bear with him for a season. But if he then repent not, he hath no more place among us.[10]

And he did, in fact, expel some who did not conform.[11]

We can see two important dynamics at work in the General Rules. First, the Society offered clear ethical, devotional, and liturgical norms, and they expected persons to follow them within a specific accountability structure. Meeting together was not optional. Second, if persons refused to keep the Rules, they would be asked to leave the Society. Each of these classic Wesleyan dynamics presents a significant challenge to the contemporary United Methodist practice of the open table. I will discuss each in turn, first, the call to Christian formation as it relates to the communion invitation, and second, the necessity of maintaining a discipline of expulsion—that is, excommunication—as a measure of last resort.

CHRISTIAN FORMATION AND ITS RELATIONSHIP TO THE COMMUNION INVITATION

Unlike many witnesses before and since, Wesley did not require a profession of faith before he would admit a person to Holy Communion. He required, rather, a desire for saving grace and a willingness to commit to the lifestyle expressed in the General Rules. Members would receive Holy Communion throughout this journey, believing that it would bring them to conversion and, once that was experienced, deepen their relationship with God. Holy Communion was a converting ordinance. That did not mean that it worked in some magical way, that one could expect conversion even if one willfully opposed God's will; thus the behavioral expectations found in the Rules.

If not magically, how then does participation in the Eucharist contribute to our conversion? That is a complex question that cannot be answered precisely, but we can make some relevant observations about conversion in general and the Eucharist in particular. In some conversion experiences, like that of St. Paul on the Damascus Road and John Wesley at Aldersgate, persons seemingly experience conversion in an instant. We must remember, however, that neither experience occurred in isolation from a wider context. Paul had been deeply formed in the Hebrew Scriptures and Jewish tradition, the narrative rooted in God's promise to Abraham and his family. In his encounter with the risen Christ, Paul's relationship to that narrative was radically rearranged and updated, but it was not replaced. In like manner, Wesley had been shaped by the classic formularies of the Church of England and he was deeply rooted in the Scriptures. In his heart-warming experience, he came to understand both in a radically different way, but he did not change narratives. In both of these well-known cases, conversion was not discontinuous with previous experience. It is often the same with our lives; intense life-changing moments of spiritual insight rarely occur outside of an extended context of thought and experience. Such moments rearrange and refocus what we already know. When we understand conversion experiences in this way, it is unrealistic to expect persons to be thus converted on their first encounter with the Eucharist. It is possible, yes; but not likely. We should differentiate between conversion itself and conversion experiences. Normally, conversion through the Eucharist happens over time, even though there may be an intense moment—a conversion experience—that crystallizes emerging insights and changes.

Neither does conversion occur outside of our bodies, a critical insight when attempting to understand Eucharist as a converting ordinance. Just as Christians should not understand the body as a mere shell that carries the soul, perceived to be the real and essential person, so we should not understand the Eucharist as some sort of dispensable package that delivers a measure of ethereal divine stuff called grace. The Eucharist is an embodied liturgical act—we do it in our bodies in the presence of other bodies. The particular grace revealed here is found within the practice itself. The Eucharist converts us, if you will, in and through what we do with our bodies. Through faithful practice of it, we are formed—embodied—in a new way. Our bodies—even though they remain individual bodies—become members of the Body of Christ; and together we learn to discern that Body (1 Corinthians 11:17-12:31). The Eucharist is not simply consecrated bread and wine that we eat like some sort of holy medicine, a thing that will automatically make us well, without the full cooperation of our bodies.[12] Few medicines, of course, work well without our cooperation, as if simply ingesting them were all that mattered. We take our medicine and we also rest, eat properly, and do our exercise. We take our medicine and, for lack of a better word, we repent, forsaking behaviors that contributed to the illness and learning new ones. Healing emerges within this combination of medicine and therapeutic action.

The Eucharist in its fullness—holy food taken in the midst of sacred action—is the means of grace that converts us. In the Eucharist, we learn how to handle created things and offer them to God. God meets us in the midst of that action and converts us in and through it, changing our relationship with all creation. The communion ritual calls us to exchange the peace with our sisters and brothers and thereby we practice a way of life that begins to show up in our relationships; practicing the Eucharist shapes and converts us, in our bodies. We learn how to approach God along with our sisters and brothers and we meet God within this meeting of bodies. We eat in a nonanxious way, knowing that we will receive our share of the meal as will everyone else in the church; thus we learn to receive God's gifts in a similar nonanxious way. Like this, the Eucharist converts us over time, shaping communicants to see the world in an increasingly new way. We do not wish to limit God by ruling out the miraculous; stunning new insight can arise quickly. Even then it is often a matter of pieces that were there all along fitting together in new ways. Under ordinary circumstances, conversion occurs in the slow, incremental way described here. The Eucharist is a converting ordinance primarily for those who commit themselves to its practices over time. We can even say that Christian discipleship has a Eucharistic shape; that is, faithful discipleship bears many of the same dynamics one practices in the Eucharist. We meet God in the midst of both.

Although Wesley believed that Christian discipleship is shaped in the midst of Eucharistic practice—in combination with the call to resist evil and do good—many Christian churches have believed that the primary work of formation should occur prior to baptism and admission to first communion. The Roman Catholic *Rite of Christian Initiation of Adults (RCIA)* provides the foremost contemporary example. Along with their Methodist sisters and brothers, contemporary Catholics assume a Eucharistic shape to conversion and Christian discipleship, but there are crucial differences. Foundational to the *RCIA* are the assumptions that life in Christ is counter-cultural and full conversion to it is a long process.[13] An adult who enters the church is taking up a radically different way of life and thus he or she must undergo what Aidan Kavanagh calls "conversion therapy,"[14] the unlearning of old habits and the learning of new ones. According to this perspective, admitting someone to baptism and Eucharist prior to such conversion therapy is like sending them on a missionary journey with no understanding of the new culture, its language and its grammar. To use another metaphor, premature admission to the sacraments is like entering a marriage unadvisedly, without an adequate knowledge of the prospective spouse and sober consideration of the marriage vows. Working within this understanding of conversion and its relationship to the sacraments, the *RCIA* calls for a long period of preparation—a long courtship if you will—before one enters the blessings and responsibilities of participating in the sacraments.

The *RCIA* is based on ancient models of the catechumenate and the rites of Christian Initiation. I described this process in my earlier book:

> The journey began with a clear demand for repentance. Gladiators, prostitutes, and wizards (that is, practitioners of pagan religions) were told to renounce those practices immediately or else go home . . .

> Upon entering the catechumenate, people began a long process of formation. Catechumens attended the reading and preaching of the Scriptures and were encouraged to practice what they had heard . . . Their period of formation lasted as long as three years. When the catechumen was deemed ready, he or she was brought to the bishop on the first day of Lent and enrolled for baptism, thus beginning the final intensive preparation for baptism. Candidates received further instruction in the

Scriptures. They learned the Apostles' Creed and the Lord's Prayer. They fasted. The bishop offered prayers of exorcism on their behalf...

In the early hours of Easter morning (at the Easter Vigil) the candidates were baptized . . . Then . . . the newly baptized participated for the first time in the prayers of the people, the kiss of peace, and the Eucharist... Nevertheless, baptism did not complete the process. The new baptisands were reminded that the church's liturgy would shape them for the rest of their lives. As a beginning step...the newly baptized attended a series of mystagogical lectures, that is, lectures on the sacraments...

This system shows us that preparation for baptism involves moral and spiritual formation and not just the accumulation of knowledge...[15]

The *RCIA* has reintroduced a similar pattern to the contemporary church. Inquirers are enrolled in the catechumenate, where their conversion is nurtured and deepened. They remain for an indefinite period of time, but normally for at least one year. When church and candidate deem them sufficiently formed, they are enrolled for baptism. During Lent, they proceed through that final "Period of Purification and Enlightenment" after which they receive the sacraments of initiation— baptism, confirmation, and first communion—at the Easter Vigil. Mystagogy follows during the Great Fifty Days of Easter.[16]

While Anglicans and Methodists have never practiced such an extensive pre-baptismal (and pre-Eucharistic) discipline, the logic is not entirely absent from their traditions. At various points in their history, confirmation has been required for admission to communion. A rubric requiring confirmation was in place as early as the 1549 *Book of Common Prayer* and we have seen relatively recent evidence of the practice in the interviews of Tom Lightner,[17] an Episcopalian in his youth, and Carlton Sachs,[18] who grew up in the Methodist Church (see chapter 5). In those cases, there was no communion before confirmation. While Wesley rejected confirmation and American Methodism did not officially restore the practice until 1964, it existed in parish practice before that time, functioning much as it did in the Anglican tradition.

Long before they had confirmation, Wesley and the early Methodists had their practice of communion tickets. Anglican rubrics also called their priests to warn estranged parishioners to seek reconciliation before coming to communion, an insight not lost on Methodists as demonstrated in their long use of the "Ye that do truly and earnestly repent" invitation. Each of these historic disciplines witnesses to an important relationship between Christian formation and the Eucharist.

Christian discipleship is given its clearest expression at the Eucharist and grace to sustain such faithfulness is received there; but one cannot expect to receive that grace while willfully resisting the love of God and neighbor. God's grace is not limited, but it does not work magically, either. It bears its greatest fruit in those who "truly and earnestly repent of [their] sins," who "are in love and charity with [their] neighbors, and intend to lead a new life, following the commandments of God."[19] Modern pre-Eucharistic disciplines express similar insights. To that end, Episcopalians and United Methodists have made initial attempts at recovering the catechumenate.[20]

Although done with good intent, these disciplines sometimes yield a problematic result. The catechumenate, properly understood, is not a class but rather formation in a Christian lifestyle. Unfortunately, the membership class model is so deeply entrenched in the church's mindset that it is difficult for some parishes to move beyond thinking of the *RCIA* as a class that one takes to become a Catholic. In that model, the Easter Vigil and its rites of Christian Initiation become a graduation exercise, with first communion the reward for passing the course. Anglicans and Methodists have faced a similar problem with their young confirmands; more than a few receive their confirmation certificate and become inactive shortly thereafter. After all, they took the course and they graduated.

The modern practice of the catechumenate poses other problems. Integral to its logic is the *disciplina arcani* (secret discipline) of the early church under which the sacraments were not celebrated in public settings and only the fully initiated knew about the mysteries. Catechumens and other seekers were dismissed before the intercessions and the Eucharist. The *disciplina arcani* no longer exists, yet as part of its current practice, the *RCIA* commends a similar dismissal of the catechumens.[21] It is an odd ritual for a church that no longer practices its sacramental rites in secret; one can imagine that more than a few have witnessed baptisms and the Eucharist in other settings, even in Catholic settings. Indeed, casual visitors in the congregation—those not yet admitted to the catechumenate—are not routinely dismissed along with the catechumens. The long waiting period before baptism and first communion can seem equally strange. For most Americans, conversion to Christianity is not a matter of grave risk, even though they should perhaps see it as more of a risk than they do (see chapter 6). Is there, in fact, a much more pragmatic reason for the long delay? Is the church, in fact, withholding the desired prize until the end of the class, so that baptismal candidates will stay and fulfill all of the course requirements?

One might argue that something like the early Methodist pattern—an earlier celebration of the sacraments followed by extensive reflection, support, and *praxis*—could provide an equally effective formation process.

To return to the marriage analogy used earlier, while the church does what it can to prepare couples for marriage, married persons know that most of their learning about the marital *disciplina arcani*, so to speak, occurs in the months and years following the ceremony. We engage married couples in formational work in the months before the ceremony in part because we can require it as a condition of their receiving a church wedding. It may not, in fact, be the optimum time for such formation. Acknowledging this reality, for a while I tried scheduling couples for a follow-up session six months after their wedding; but most of them cancelled or simply did not return. Not finding the time or the energy to press the issue, eventually I gave up on the practice. Would neophytes also fail to return?

Regardless of the problems inherent in them, Wesley's class system and the catechumenal pattern embody a serious ethic of Christian formation related to the Eucharist. They remind us that, whatever else it might mean, an open communion table cannot mean the forsaking of all discipline. A church cannot sustain its integrity with an entirely unconditional invitation to communion. An authentically Wesleyan church must do the intentional work of formation at some point in its common life and that work must be done in relation to the Eucharist.

As part of its discipline, the church must define the outer limits of its fellowship and toleration. Although decidedly unpleasant work, Wesley and Christians of every generation have understood this need. As I will demonstrate in the next section, the church must at least consider the possibility of excommunication. This insight may present the most severe challenge to the practice of the open table. Having made the case about excommunication, I will close this chapter in a more positive way, by suggesting several "cultures" that would shape and discipline our practice of the open table.

EXCOMMUNICATION AS A MEASURE OF LAST RESORT

Contemporary Methodists cannot avoid the fact that Wesley practiced the discipline of expulsion—a form of excommunication—in relation to the General Rules; thus it is part of our tradition. Society members who refused to practice the Rules could be expelled.[22] Early American Methodists practiced a similar discipline, most notably in relation to its rules about slaveholding and manumission.[23] Ineffective enforcement of these rules led to the 1844 division of the Northern and Southern branches of the Methodist Episcopal Church.

Excommunication is based on the New Testament witness. The best-known example is the three-step outline presented in Matthew:

> If another member of the church sins against you, go and point out the fault when the two of you are alone. If the member listens to you, you have regained that one. But if you are not listened to, take one or two others along with you, so that every word may be confirmed by the evidence of two or three witnesses. If the member refuses to listen to them, tell it to the church; and if the offender refuses to listen even to the church, let such a one be to you as a Gentile and a tax collector. (Matthew 18:15-17)

That Matthew's Jesus refers to "the church," one of only two such references found in the Gospels (see also Matthew 16:18), leads some to conclude that the saying did not originate with the historical Jesus. Adjudicating that question lies beyond the scope of this project; at the very least this saying represents the ecclesiology of the Matthean community, their attempt to embody Christ's teaching. What did they teach? An offender should be addressed first in a private conversation, thus protecting the reputations of the parties involved while encouraging repentance and reconciliation. If that approach does not yield a positive result, says the text, one should try another conversation, this time in the presence of a small party of witnesses. If that attempt fails, the process goes public, possibly resulting in expulsion. Each step in this Matthean *ordo* protects the integrity of the church and its members while also seeking the repentance of the offender, whose situation is far from hopeless. The possibility of reconciliation is stressed at every point. The implication of the teaching is clear, however—some behaviors cannot be tolerated. Exactly what actions should lead to disciplinary action is a matter for the church's continuing discernment, its work of "binding and loosing" (Matthew 18:18).[24]

First Corinthians, a text replete with rules and guidelines for eating together,[25] insists that some persons should be sent away from the community table. Upon hearing that a church member was involved in a sexual relationship with his stepmother, Paul rebuked all attempts to justify that behavior and insisted that they expel the man from their fellowship. Tolerating such behavior would compromise the integrity of the church and thus they should be excommunicated:

> Now I am writing to you not to associate with anyone who bears the name of brother or sister who is sexually immoral or greedy, or is an idolater, reviler, drunkard, or robber. *Do not even eat with such a one.* (1 Corinthians 5:11, italics added).

In the same epistle Paul insisted that Eucharistic fellowship required the church to make moral distinctions about what and whom they could receive at the table. They could not receive meat offered to idols because "You cannot partake of the table of the Lord and the table of demons" (1 Corinthians 10:21b). Those who participated in the latter could incite God's anger.

For Paul, excommunication was not irrevocable; some scholars believe that the remarks he made in the second chapter of 2 Corinthians referred to the excommunication noted in First Corinthians 5. He was distressed by the need to make that decision, and he did so "not to cause you pain, but to let you know the abundant love that I have for you" (2 Corinthians 2:4). According to Paul, they all suffered when the sinner was disciplined. Since the punishment had now worked its purpose—it had resulted in appropriate sorrow and repentance—their brother should be welcomed back into the fellowship of the church. "Anyone whom you forgive," said Paul, "I also forgive" (2 Corinthians 2:10). Indeed, the repentant sinner must be forgiven and restored. To preclude the possibility of reconciliation was to provide an opportunity for Satan and his divisive work (2 Corinthians 2:11).[26] Paul's witness insists that the exercise of church discipline must be mixed with compassion.

One finds a demanding rigorist Eucharistic discipline in various early church witnesses such as Hippolytus and *The Apostolic Tradition*, who presented an extensive pre-baptismal formation period. Tertullian accused the heretics of practicing an open communion table, of making no distinction between catechumens and the baptized, and he called them to greater discipline for the sake of the church's integrity.[27] In many cases, persons who committed serious sins were required to undergo an extensive penitential period.[28] Cyprian of Carthage demanded a rigorous penitential discipline for the lapsed but then he relaxed it when the church came under persecution. Penitents were reconciled before the completion of their discipline that they might receive the Eucharist as a source of strength for their ordeal.[29] Here one finds the needy multitude moving the heart of the church, just as it did Jesus. Compassion often moves the church to relax rules and become more permissive, erring, as it were, on the side of forgiveness.

Rigorists often protest, chiding the church for its laxity. Both witnesses are necessary. The pull of compassion often gains the upper hand, yet the discipline of excommunication persists, at least in theory.

The Reformers spoke openly of the practice, perhaps to excess. As noted earlier, *The Book of Common Prayer* charged priests to warn persistent sinners either to repent or avoid communion and it insisted that they call estranged persons to reconciliation.[30] John Calvin used the language of excommunication in the name of preserving the church's integrity.

> I excommunicate all idolaters, blasphemers and despisers of God, all heretics and those who create private sects in order to break the unity of the Church, all perjurers, all who rebel against father or mother or superior, all who promote sedition or mutiny; brutal and disorderly persons, adulterers, lewd and lustful men, thieves, ravishers, greedy and grasping people, drunkards, gluttons, and all those who lead a scandalous and dissolute life. I warn them to abstain from this Holy Table, lest they defile and contaminate the holy food which our Lord Jesus Christ gives to none except they belong to His household of faith.[31]

He quoted the 1 Corinthians 11 passage about self-examination and discerning the body. Although such a text is foreign to our modern experience, we should notice the strong call to integrity, an emphasis typical of the Reformation era.[32] As an aside, one wonders how anyone who heard that exhortation was able to gather up the courage to commune. Wesley deemphasized such exhortations; nevertheless, he was the exception to the rule.

Because it is foreign to our experience, one can hardly miss the call to Eucharistic integrity when it emerges in the modern era. German martyr Dietrich Bonhoeffer insisted that there is no authentic Christianity without discipline; otherwise, the church proclaims a "cheap grace"[33] that does not result in conversion. Bonhoeffer's treatise, of course, was forged in the context of Nazi Germany. It reflects his sharp disappointment at the German evangelical church, which was both unable and unwilling to defend its integrity. They believed, quite tragically, that the destiny of the church and the nation were one and so they failed to withstand the murder of millions. Could the tragedy have been averted had they exercised their discernment more faithfully and named the evil in their midst? Within this milieu, Bonhoeffer insisted that the church must practice excommunication when necessary, doing so for the sake of the sinner it hopes to redeem. Even as it excommunicates, it must seek his or her repentance and restoration, addressing the offender privately and humbly, as Matthew's Gospel teaches. Nevertheless, the church must not shrink from its duty.[34] If the sinner persists in rebellion, then the church must act.

> If he shows genuine repentance, and publicly acknowledges his sin, he then receives forgiveness in God's name. But if he is still unrepentant, the Church must retain his sin in that Name. In other words, the sinner must be excommunicated.[35]

According to Bonhoeffer, excommunication does not create the separation; rather, the church tells the truth about a separation that already exists.

Could excommunication be practiced in the contemporary American context, particularly within the United Methodist Church? Laurence Stookey has observed that excommunication would not be practical within a pluralistic, denominational church culture.[36] If one were expelled from a United Methodist congregation, one could go down the street and fairly easily join a congregation of another mainline denomination and perhaps even another United Methodist congregation. Excommunication would be difficult to enforce. Further discouraging its practice is the fact that it can easily become publicly controversial, as some Catholic bishops have discovered in their attempts to call elected officials to account. Excommunication should not, of course, be used as a partisan political tool, and if executed, should be done only as a measure of last resort, after due consultation and discernment. Even if churches would have difficulty enforcing it in the modern era, when used with the utmost restraint this discipline can make an important witness about the church and its values. The church that says "yes" to God, and "yes" to God's people and works of justice, must say "no" when those values are challenged. Inclusion without boundaries is meaningless, perhaps even dangerous. I am not advocating the exclusion of persons who merely struggle with sin; all of us face that problem. What shall we do, however, with the person whose public commitments openly defy the Eucharistic invitation that calls us to love God, repent of sin, and live at peace with our neighbor?[37] What shall we do with someone who not only refuses to resist evil, but also openly perpetuates it? What shall we do with the white supremacist, the person who openly refuses to accept the multi-racial and multi-cultural nature of the church? Again, I am not referring to the person who is struggling with her residual prejudices. The latter person needs communion along with a confessor, but the former should be confronted and, if he does not repent, then expelled. Allowing such persons to remain in the church can compromise its witness, wound the conscience of its members, and even compromise their safety. Such racists have willfully separated themselves from God and the church and the church must be able to proclaim that fact through excommunication.

Scott J. Jones, United Methodist theologian and bishop, offers a compelling discussion of these dynamics. As he relates, the church establishes official positions through the action of the General Conference and, to the extent that its rules allow, it may alter them. The church's decisions are recorded in *The Book of Discipline* and *The Book of Resolutions* and they are reflected in its official liturgical formularies. Any member of the church, clergy or laity, may try to change a doctrinal position, and, Jones argues, if they cannot accomplish the change, they should consider leaving the church.[38] The logic is persistent and difficult to refute, although historically there is an option that lies somewhere between obedience and open confrontation. Many church members have simply ignored those doctrines and liturgical formularies that they could not support.

Perhaps inevitably, Jones' argument about doctrine comes to focus on the conduct of the clergy, and especially on their preaching. According to *The Discipline* and the church's vows of ordination,[39] clergy are obliged to disseminate the official doctrine of the church and if they are unwilling to do so they should leave the church, or else face disciplinary charges. Jones wrote,

> There are certain beliefs like the Trinity and God's love for persons of all races that are so central to the United Methodist understanding of the gospel that fundamental disagreement with them requires the breaking of fellowship . . . In cases where doctrinal dissent is so fundamental and yet the dissenter will not voluntarily leave the Church, the Church must protect the integrity of its own witness by removing the person from its fellowship.[40]

This discussion of doctrinal standards and related discipline is at once courageous and problematic—courageous in its countercultural perspective and problematic when we consider the uneven way the church has administered its standards. Because of the church's recent battles over the issue of homosexuality, many will hear his argument in terms of that discussion even though, in all fairness, Jones does not mention that specific topic.

Indeed, the church opposes the practice of homosexuality, refusing to ordain or appoint self-avowed practicing homosexuals and forbidding the conduct of gay marriage ceremonies. Recent ecclesiastical trials and General Conference discussions about tightening accountability have focused on homosexuality. Conversely, one might argue that other doctrinal standards of the church are violated rather frequently yet no trials are brought and little outcry is raised.

Most do not want to create a culture in which ecclesiastical trials and disciplinary procedures are routinely threatened; nevertheless, calls to discipline such as that offered by Jones are important. As he suggests, the ultimate discipline of expulsion should be exercised only when the central values of the church have been violated in an egregious manner. Such considerations should, of course, be applied equally to the clergy and the laity. While a steady majority has consistently supported disciplinary rules on homosexuality, it remains debatable whether such a simple majority vote can be called a consensus. That question will remain before the church. It may be that our most obvious consensus is our commitment to open communion. Ironic as it may sound, we might find considerable support for expelling someone who publicly refuses to practice it. Whatever the shape of their central values, churches must hold out the possibility of disciplining those who violate them, even to the point of expulsion from fellowship. Such discipline is fully part of the Wesleyan heritage.

What would it look like today? The excommunication rite printed in the *Psalter Hymnal*, the official hymnal of the Reformed Church of America, provides a good example. The rite itself is biblically and theologically well-balanced and it speaks in a restrained voice. It presumes that members are bound to uphold their baptismal vows and profession of faith, in which they promise to repent and joyfully embrace Jesus Christ as Lord.[41] In like manner, members of that church promise to submit to the authority and governance of the church.[42] The excommunication rite publicly announces that these expectations have been violated and that the member persists in that sin, "despite [the church's] prayers and admonitions."[43] For reasons of compassion and legal prudence, their rules forbid the public announcement of the sin.[44]

The rite calls for the church to announce its intentions on three separate occasions, each time declaring the reconciliatory intent of the discipline. The second reading states,

> We inform you...with the advice of classis, that if our brother/sister does not repent, it may be necessary to exclude him/her from membership in the church of Jesus Christ.

Our Lord does not wish that sinners should perish but desires that they turn from their evil ways and live. Therefore, let us all continue to pray for our brother/sister and to plead personally with him/her to mend his/her ways and return to the Lord and his people in repentance and faith.[45]

Through this rite, then, the church expresses the serious nature of its expectations along with its pastoral intent.

In the third announcement, the church states the effective date of the excommunication and prayerfully expresses its grief at the need for the decision. The leader exhorts the faithful to maintain their own commitment to the church and its disciplines, including the duty to pray for the ultimate reconciliation of the excommunicated member.[46] The *Psalter Hymnal* presents its rite for readmission in the pages immediately following the excommunication rite, thus expressing the intended result of the excommunication process— renewed communion and fellowship. Penitents are restored through a reaffirmation of the membership vows that once again express the church's core values.[47]

Although it is unlikely that United Methodists will practice this ritual process developed by the Reformed Church of America, it bears the following important values worthy of our notice:

- Its teaching is biblical, expressing good balance among the justice and forgiveness proclaimed in the Gospel. (While the demand of the Gospel is expressed, so is its clear reconciliatory intent.)

- The church's ritual is directly related to its disciplinary and formational process. Membership expectations and related punitive disciplines are related to the vows for baptism and church membership. The expectations about the conduct of members are clearly and publicly stated.

- Implied within the process is the understanding that the Eucharist is not only a means of grace, but also a way of life.

- The disciplinary process is a public one that is properly regulated by church tradition and law. (While excommunication is not formally practiced by United Methodists, one fears that it is practiced informally. Through shaming and shunning, offending persons have been quietly but effectively driven from the church. With a ritual process like the one in *The Psalter Hymnal,* the church has an established means that allows it to process its indignation while keeping it in proper balance with mercy. It restrains vindictiveness and also places clear parameters on the punishment.)

- The rite of restoration signals a clear endpoint to the disciplinary process. In its own less satisfying way, the excommunication rite does the same. (As to excommunication, it announces that the painful time of discernment and decision-making is over. The church has taken action on the matter, doing what it can do. It must now step aside and move on to its more constructive work, allowing the Holy Spirit to work in the life of the excommunicated member. As to restoration, it announces the positive result of the disciplinary process and thus calls for the immediate suspension of any shunning.)

Given our predominant piety, it is unlikely that United Methodists will gain much practice in the discipline of excommunication, but it is important to maintain the possibility as a measure of last resort. The church does indeed have a system of trials that may be activated both for laity as well as for clergy.[48] If it is to have its fullest integrity, however, that process must at times be activated for issues other than sexuality and for persons other than the clergy. For instance, the church has stated its belief that "war is incompatible with the teaching and example of Christ"[49] just as it has continued to say "we do not condone the practice of homosexuality and consider this practice incompatible with Christian teaching."[50] The similarity in language is obvious—both are incompatible with the Gospel. Would the church be willing to bring charges against church members who lead us into ill-considered conflicts? Should we call persons to account for the former and not for the latter?

While a necessary discipline, discussing excommunication—not to mention actually practicing it—will always be difficult. Perhaps it should remain so. I will close this chapter with a somewhat easier discussion, in which I will suggest three "cultures," or habits of mind that should complement our continuing practice of the open table.

THREE CULTURES TO COMPLEMENT THE OPEN TABLE

First, a Culture of Serious Formation

As I noted earlier, in the early days of Methodism, the movement was defined by participation in the classes and their General Rules. While I am not advocating a restoration of the class system per se, its dynamics should be restored to the church. Churches could commit themselves to explore the meaning of the communion invitation, what it means to love God, earnestly repent of sin, and live in peace with each other.

The modern successor of the class meeting, the Covenant Discipleship Group, could be one option. Restoration of the catechumenate is another possibility; at the least, those who sponsor the baptism of infants could be expected to attend an extensive program designed to prepare them for their assuming the vows of sponsorship.[51] Such a requirement is not unlike the now well-established requirement of premarital counseling for those to be married in the church. The church could also create an environment in which all members were strongly encouraged to participate in one or several years of *Disciple Bible Study* process. In each of these cases, persons would be exploring the deeper implications of their membership in the Body of Christ, of their participation in the Eucharist. In congregations that developed such a culture, members would come to see serious formation not as extraordinary, but as a normal aspect of Christian life.

Second, a Culture of Mission Rooted in the Spirituality of the Eucharist

Participation in the Eucharist is intimately related to the rest of Christian discipleship. Thus we need a culture of mission rooted in the spiritual dynamics of the Eucharist. Leaders in such a church would continually tease out these implications. They would encourage the members to think about what it means to offer their best to God, to give thanks, to receive those gifts back from God, and to give them freely to others. Participation in the Eucharist would lead to deeper compassion for the hungry, not to mention the homeless.

Within their liturgies, they would pray for the hungry and the homeless and also for the sick and victims of abuse, that they might receive a full share of God's abundance. Such a church would do more, however, than pray within the liturgy. They would also pray with their feet, working to feed the hungry and provide a safe place for others in need.

Moreover, they would explore the political foundations of these problems and they would seek political solutions to them.

They would also explore the implications of the Eucharistic call to reconciliation and peacemaking. They would criticize militarism as bad stewardship, and also as a refusal to seek reconciliation. Within such a church, outreach like this would seem a normal result of participation in Holy Communion.

Third, a Culture of Discerning the Body of Christ

According to the teaching of St. Paul in 1 Corinthians 11, Christians are called to the work of discerning the Body of Christ. This is a twofold dynamic. First, discerning the body involves remembering the holiness of the Eucharist; to participate in the Lord's Supper is to participate in the Paschal Dynamic of Jesus Christ, with all that represents and demands. Second, it means following that most crucial Eucharistic rubric as found in verse 33 of that chapter: "So then, my brothers and sisters, when you come together to eat, wait for one another." The apostle told the Corinthian church to gather across economic lines, just as he told the Galatians to gather across racial and cultural lines (Galatians 2–3). For various reasons, and especially because of human sin, our gatherings often fall short of that ideal; but we must not become content with that condition. We should cultivate the discipline of asking ourselves, "Who is missing from this gathering?" Such a question comes naturally to Wesleyans, although they too must grow in their ability to ask it.

The first response to that question should lead the church into a ministry of taking communion to the unwillingly absent. In a sense, churches are responding to the same question when they design worship services for persons raised in a digital culture. If such persons are missing, the church is obliged to make room for them, and it must try not to drive other people away in the process. Churches should also look at the racial and ethnic demographics of their community and ask themselves, whom are we missing? When they discern an answer to that question, they will work at developing relationships with those missing persons, not only to make their attendance grow, but for the sake of justice.

Such a church will continue to welcome families that reflect mainstream ideals about traditional families, but they will also make room for single persons of all ages, for little people, for single parents and their children, for the elderly, for persons with physical disabilities and learning disabilities as well as those struggling with mental illnesses. If there are gay and lesbian persons living in their neighborhood, they will ask the question about them as well. They will make room for such people in their pews and in their leadership teams, and they will also welcome them as clergy.

Congregations that practice these cultures will be changed. When such Eucharistic habits are well-developed, it may not be necessary for the church to practice overt disciplines of excommunication, even though it must allow for them as a measure of last resort. Those who refuse to participate in the cultures named above will, in a sense, excommunicate themselves, even if they do not do so formally. The glare of such holiness will be too much to bear and they will simply remove themselves.

This discussion now moves us to the agenda of the next chapter, in which I will address the issue of open table and hospitality, particularly as it relates to the challenge posed by excluded and marginalized persons. This issue goes to the very heart of Wesleyan identity.

Chapter Eight

Open Table and Hospitality

THE CONTINUING CHALLENGE

The Eucharist reveals God's promise. As Christians participate in Holy Communion, they receive a foretaste of God's reign, a glimpse of the world that God desires. God's children are received in love; they are fed and they live together in peace. As we look around our congregations, we can point to friends whom we would not have were it not for the bonds of love established in the holy meal. Through the Eucharist, God draws us deeper into his promised reign, a reality Charles Wesley expressed in the following hymn:

> How glorious is the life above,
> Which in this ordinance we taste;
> That fulness of celestial love,
> That joy which shall for ever last!
>
> That heavenly life in Christ conceal'd
> These earthen vessels could not bear,
> The part which now we find reveal'd
> No tongue of angels can declare.
>
> The light of life eternal darts
> Into our souls a dazzling ray,
> A drop of heaven o'erflows our hearts,
> And deluges the house of clay.

Sure pledge of ecstasies unknown
Shall this Divine communion be;
The ray shall rise into a sun,
The drop shall swell into a sea.[1]

God's promise establishes a new world and bids us enter it, yet at times the church appears as if it is running away from God's reign. In this sense that we fall short of its vision, the Eucharist also reveals God's judgment.

Some Christians refuse to live in peace with their brothers and sisters, in spite of the communion invitation. In many cases our churches are less integrated than the neighborhoods they inhabit. Children with learning disabilities are misunderstood and their parents are blamed. Sometimes it becomes easier for them simply to stay at home on Sunday mornings. Single and divorced persons are ignored and misunderstood, gay and lesbian persons are feared and shunned. Both can find it difficult to remain. We are not the fellowship that Christ demands and we experience the gap between reality and aspiration. The Eucharist judges us.

Both the Eucharistic promise and judgment challenge our practice of the open table. The vision of God's reign reminds us that the open table must be about more than the simple cordiality appropriate to a church coffee hour. As we have seen earlier in this book (chapter 3), United Methodists have justified their practice of the open table by referring to the radical hospitality of Jesus. The argument is compelling. Indeed, Jesus made a banquet for the hungry multitude in the wilderness and he ate with sinners and tax collectors. He welcomed many persons, and that fact challenges us. Those who argue for the open table by citing the radical hospitality of Jesus have committed themselves to a daunting task; they must be far more than nice. They should feed the poor, and they should also learn their stories. Jesus called us to receive children, yet that very hospitality judges us, because sometimes we receive neither the children nor him.

In this chapter, I will discuss the continuing challenge of hospitality as it relates to the practice of the open table. The practice of Eucharistic hospitality will push us deeper and deeper into the reign of God, and it will make us confront our points of resistance. Such a discipline can be hard, unpleasant work, particularly as we are called to receive marginalized persons. I will use the lens of experience to challenge and stretch the practice of the open table just as in chapter 5 I used experience to support the practice. I will offer three short vignettes that discuss practices of hospitality, relating each of them to the practice of the open table. Important challenges arise from each. First, I will tell about a Catholic Worker house of hospitality, its director, and a Eucharist held there. Second, I will reflect upon some of the challenges presented to the church by children living with learning disabilities. Third, I will reflect on the pressing call to become more fully bilingual.

I will close this chapter by suggesting that the United Methodist position on the ordination of homosexuals stands in tension with its practice of the open table. There are, of course, two separate but inter-related sides to the Eucharistic table: the clergy's side, from which elders and deacons face the congregation across the Table, calling them to *koinonia* (communion) and *diakonia* (outreaching service), and the laity's side from which all ministries emerge, including those of the clergy. As I will argue, the church's practice pushes it to make both sides of the Table open. It is distressed when it ignores those implications.

EUCHARIST AT A CATHOLIC WORKER HOUSE

During the time that I served as associate pastor of First United Methodist in Chambersburg, I helped lead a work camp at the Llewellyn Scott Catholic Worker House of Hospitality in Washington, D.C., directed by the late Michael Kirwan (1945–1999). Finding Mike, the Catholic Worker, and the Scott House was one of the great serendipities of my life. First Church had done several work camps in rural settings and we were convinced that we should have an urban experience, but we had no idea where to find it. Then, on Easter Sunday 1987, I read a *Washington Post* editorial by Colman McCarthy in which he discussed Mike's ministry to homeless men and women in the District.[2] When I showed the piece to several of our leaders, we believed we had found our destination. I called Mike, made an appointment for a visit several weeks hence, and when the day came, several of us made the two-hour trip to Washington. He welcomed us into the Scott House that Saturday afternoon, then left us there in the small foyer while he went to solve a problem that was emerging somewhere else in the house. As we stood there, we saw two poorly kempt, unshaved men sleeping in the parlor. Another man sat, seemingly dazed, in what passed for a living room. The wall in the kitchen badly needed repairs, and there was an odd, musty smell about the place. I did not feel safe. Wary glances were shared among our group members, but no one said a word. When we shared our impressions later, we discovered that each of us was fighting the impulse to leave. Fortunately for us, we stayed.

Several moments passed in that hallway, then Mike finally returned and began sharing his story with us. We learned about his parents' involvement with the Catholic Worker movement, through which he became acquainted with its founder, Dorothy Day. He informed us that Catholic Worker Houses were not homeless shelters. We knew about homeless shelters and were involved in the work of our local shelter in Chambersburg, but the Scott House was different; it was a home. Some stayed until they died. Like any home, there were rules: use of alcohol and drugs was forbidden, and if one used either, then he or she had to find another place to sleep that night; weapons of any kind were forbidden and anyone found possessing one would be expelled; persons were expected to help around the house as they were able. This was no government-funded social service program, only a dignified yet realistic attempt to embody life in Jesus Christ. Soon we learned that Mike had no home other than the Scott House; even his clothing came from the same donated sources that the residents used. As we stood there our resistance began melting and our fascination with Mike and his ministry increased.[3]

Mike did not set out to become the director of a Catholic Worker house. In a sense the work found him. After returning from a hitch in the Navy, he became a graduate student in sociology at George Washington University. While walking to classes, he began to notice the homeless men living around the heating grates of government buildings and slowly his heart began going out to them. He began delivering soup and sandwiches to them, a practice that continued his entire life. One day, a man asked if he might come to his university apartment for a shower and shave. Reluctantly, Mike allowed it. He stepped out while the man was caring for himself and returned to find him washed and shaved, sitting there and listening to classical music. No longer was the man simply "homeless," a sociological category and object for charitable concern, but he was a person with a human face. Eventually several men took up residence with Mike. When university officials discovered the arrangement, he was evicted. Not long after, his ministry at the Scott House emerged.[4]

Michael Kirwan had provided my introduction to the Catholic Worker movement and its philosophy. I subsequently learned about the atheism and radical politics that Dorothy Day practiced as a young adult; yet when she found faith within the Catholic Church she did not lose her radical bent. I learned how the movement began during the Great Depression with a one-cent-per-copy newspaper, *The Catholic Worker*, through which she and her writers tried to raise the consciousness of the working classes, many of whom were unemployed.[5] Before long, she and others realized that conscientization was not enough, and the ministries of hospitality began.[6] I learned with delight about Dorothy's affinity with the Liturgical Movement, and the way she encouraged the corporate praying of compline in the Catholic Worker houses.[7] Mike told me a story about a time when Daniel Berrigan came to celebrate mass in a hospitality house where Dorothy was staying. When he came in street clothes, Dorothy insisted that he don proper vesture before beginning mass. Residents might draw their wardrobe from the used clothing barrel, but the ceremonial rubrics of the church would be properly observed.

Our work camp took place near the end of August 1987. Early one evening we celebrated the Eucharist in front of the Scott House, using a United Methodist order for Word and Table. Although Mike seemed a bit surprised when I told him that the Eucharist was an integral part of our work camp practice, he supported us fully, helped us purchase elements, and insisted that we hold our service on site. Our group was much too large to hold the service indoors, plus it was too hot, so we took two sawhorses and a piece of plywood and set up an altar in front of the house. First we shared dinner, then Word and Table. Neighbors and passersby watched and some joined us. Mike and most of the residents joined as well. The story of Sister Dorothy's admonitions notwithstanding, my only vestments were the work clothes that I had worn that day. For the service of the Word we shared Scripture verses along with related words of testimony and exhortation. Then we celebrated the service of the Table—in that very public place praying, confessing, passing the peace, proclaiming the Great Thanksgiving, breaking bread, lifting the cup, and sharing them in Jesus' name. Most of those present received communion, including Mike. It was open communion in the fullest sense—public and interdenominational, with no barriers to participation.

That event remains one of the most memorable Eucharists I have ever experienced, either as the presider or as a member of the congregation. It is memorable not only because of the unique setting, but because of all the theological and spiritual associations that I relate to it. There was no wall of separation between the Eucharistic gathering and the mission we shared in that place. Our group fixed some walls, built a porch, painted, and did other work, but Mike and the residents of the Scott House ministered to us even more deeply, by inviting us to imbibe the ethos of the Catholic Worker Movement. That experience crystallized my conviction that Eucharistic sharing calls us to a koinonia with the poor and the abused, wherever we may find them. It moves far beyond simple cordiality.

OPEN TABLE AND CHALLENGES PRESENTED BY CHILDREN WITH LEARNING DISABILITIES

Jesus calls the church to welcome little children. We know the story—Jesus was teaching and doing good when people began bringing children to him, ". . . that he might touch them" (Mark 10:13). We do not know exactly what the disciples said to those caregivers, except that they spoke sternly to them; Jesus heard about it and was indignant. So he taught them,

> "Let the little children come to me; do not stop them; for it is to such as these that the kingdom of God belongs. Truly I tell you, whoever does not receive the kingdom of God as a little child will never enter it." And he took them up in his arms, laid his hands on them, and blessed them. (Mark 10:14-16)

Church people have heard those words many times, have seen them depicted on countless Sunday School walls, and have accepted them in theory; nevertheless, practicing this commandment can be very difficult. Children move constantly and then they tire quickly, and they demonstrate that fact at inopportune times. They prefer cookies to vegetables. They get sick easily. They talk and ask questions when we want them to be silent. Their attention span is short. They must be accompanied at all times and driven everywhere they need to go. They fall short of expectations and then their parents must decide whether to push them harder or adjust their expectations. Knowing which is appropriate is not a simple matter. Indeed, receiving the children is an ascetical discipline, not one for the faint of heart. Such is the case especially when those children present learning disabilities.[8]

Along these lines it has been my challenge—and part of my ongoing conversion—to learn about Asperger Syndrome (AS), a neurological condition related to autism. Persons with AS display some of the following characteristics:

- A social deficit that makes it difficult for them to understand the social cues that most people read quite easily. A person with AS can learn to maneuver through everyday social situations, but must make a significantly greater effort to do so, not unlike that of a person learning to communicate in a second language.

- A tendency to focus on a particular area of interest and to talk incessantly about it, long after others have ceased being interested.

- Difficulty in making friends and sustaining relationships. Lacking a strong network of friends, AS children make easy targets for teasing and other forms of bullying.

- An apparent lack of flexibility.

- A tendency to have seemingly unpredictable temper tantrums, or "meltdowns." Many times, these are caused by fatigue related to the social deficit noted above. Again, AS children must work hard to keep pace with relatively normal social situations. As a way of avoiding meltdowns or quieting them when they begin, AS children learn to take "sensory breaks," a few minutes by themselves to do something relaxing. These breaks can seem counterintuitive to some, as if one were rewarding bad behavior.

- Unusual sensitivity to some external stimuli like bright lights and loud sounds. For them an activity pleasant to many, like a Fourth of July fireworks display, may become an ordeal, actually causing physical pain. Due to the fact that they react in ways that may seem unwarranted, the behavior of AS children can appear quite strange. At times, their parents are blamed or criticized for tolerating such odd behaviors.[9]

Children (and adults) with AS need people who understand that they experience the world in a way that is very different from the neurotypical majority. They need someone with a skill set and character not unlike that present in effective missionaries—a compassion rooted in the understanding that persons (and cultures) perceive the world in significantly diverse ways, yet God cherishes all. Such compassion works alongside a willingness to do the hard work of learning another's worldview and communicating effectively to it.[10] In many instances, persons with AS are brilliant people capable of unique insights—the kind of prophetic insight one can gain from viewing the world in an untypical manner, the kind of insight one gains from thinking about the same subject for long periods of time. Due to their quirkiness, AS people can also be incredibly lonely. Those who befriend them must work at it, but they need such dedicated and compassionate friends. The church can be the place where they find understanding, a people who will befriend and support them.

Becoming that type of community is a significant challenge, of course.

The Epilogue to *The OASIS Guide to Asperger Syndrome* offers "Fifty-four ways to make the world a better place for persons with Asperger Syndrome." I often share several of them with my students and I do the same with you now. These provide important guidelines for any church that takes Eucharistic hospitality seriously:

- Share your wisdom with one other parent.

- Commit random acts of kindness for other disabled children and their families.

- Thank people who are willing to see some of your child's "unusual behaviors" as positive variations on the norm.

- Teach tolerance for all disabilities and differences. Point out that everyone "has something." No one is spared.

- Don't force conformity on anyone, AS or NT (neuro-typical). Teach acceptance of all who think differently, have nonstandard reactions, or voice different points of view. New ideas are born that way.[11]

Having heard echoes of the Gospel, persons who are different sense that they will be welcomed in church. They sense that even more if they hear an open invitation to the Table. Welcoming such persons is a challenge, but blessed is the church that accepts it. When such persons are turned away, however, they may never gather sufficient courage to knock again.

OPEN TABLE AND THE BILINGUAL CHALLENGE

The church is called to proclaim the Gospel according to the linguistic and cultural forms of the people (1 Corinthians 14:1-19, Acts 15:1-35). God empowers us for this work (Acts 2:1-8). Fulfilling the task requires faith and perseverance, for those who do it must work hard and take risks. It also involves flexibility and a certain sense of adventure, for the cultural and linguistic landscape continues to shift.

The call to become bilingual applies almost anywhere, but especially in the Dallas-Fort Worth area where I live and work. This sense was brought home with particular clarity on the very day when our moving van arrived in June 2000. The driver for the moving company, who spoke only English, hired three dayworkers to help him unload the truck, of whom two spoke only Spanish. As the Spanish speakers brought items into the house it was left to me to point and say "*a la derecha*" or "*a la izquierda*" or "*por aqui, por favor.*" That is, "to the right," "to the left," or "in here, please." I was able to direct traffic on that moving day—the furniture and most of the boxes ended up in the right places, but I was hardly ready to proclaim the Gospel in Spanish. The challenge is upon us, however. Texas has always been a border state, but until recently the linguistic challenges related to that fact were experienced more in its southwestern regions—in places like San Antonio, Laredo, and El Paso—than they were in North Texas. That is no longer the case, however. The Dallas-Fort Worth metroplex is increasingly a bilingual culture and it seems that the rest of the United States is not far behind.

What shall we English speakers do, especially we United Methodists who proclaim an open table? Can we claim that we have adequately invited our Latin sisters and brothers to the Table if we do so only in English, or if we cannot converse with them further after they arrive there? Hardly. I am increasingly convinced that we should not wait until we are completely proficient before we use our Spanish. Otherwise, we may never begin. Not long ago, a student of mine invited me to speak at a bilingual Good Friday service on the seven words of Christ from the cross. My role was to offer a short historical introduction to the service. As a surprise to them and challenge to myself, I decided to render as much of my introduction in Spanish as I could. I prepared a written text that I delivered at the beginning of the service. I read it without any problem. Pleased with my effort, I sat down to enjoy the rest of the service, resolved to learn as much as I could. I did just that, but at the end of the service my student threw me a curveball: As we began singing the final hymn, he walked over and asked me to offer the benediction. I had not prepared to do that, which presented me with a problem—I insist that my students not read benedictions, but that they speak them directly to the congregation. So I thought about it as we quickly sped through the final stanzas of that hymn. Taking a deep breath, I stood up and spoke it: "La gracia del nuestro Señor Jesucristo, el amor de Dios, y la comúnion del Espíritu Santo sea con ustedes."[12] As far as I know, I communicated adequately, both in the introduction and in the benediction; at least I didn't say anything ridiculous that left them scandalized or, worse, laughing at me.

Perhaps we should just dive in and use what language skills we have;

such *praxis* usually leads one to proficiency much faster anyway. Commitment to the open table will stretch the church linguistically; without taking such risks, however, our talk about hospitality and open table will seem little more than lip service. Hospitable persons speak to their guests.

The three vignettes offered to this point provide challenges that call the church to explore the deeper implications of its open invitation. Good liturgists will challenge the church about such issues, to the end that its ethics and mission remain consistent with its liturgy and sacraments. In the final section of this chapter, I will discuss an arena, homosexuality, in which ethical statements and invitation appear to be significantly at odds with each other, much to the continuing distress of the church.

UNITED METHODIST POSITIONS ON HOMOSEXUALITY AND THE CHALLENGE OF THE OPEN TABLE: A CRITICAL INCONSISTENCY

The conservative wing of the United Methodist Church has chosen homosexuality as the primary battleground for its fight about biblical morality. Although these Methodists practice an open table even in relation to homosexuals, it is difficult to see how they reconcile their liturgical practice and their moral position. It seems inconsistent to welcome all persons to the Table, and then say "this far and no further," which is precisely what the church does when it baptizes homosexual persons, admits them to the Lord's Table, and then refuses to receive their gifts for ministry when they emerge. In the case of persons baptized as infants or young children, the church cannot know whether a particular child is homosexual or not. Nevertheless, when those persons grow up and gifts emerge, the church must not simply reject them. Even if one assumes that the practice of homosexuality is sinful, the church has an obligation to cherish and receive the gifts that emerge in its members. To do otherwise seems hypocritical, since the church overlooks many flaws in receiving its other ministers.

In spite of such arguments, these conservatives strictly oppose the ordination of homosexuals. They reject the premise that one's sexual orientation is a gift from God that cannot and should not be altered. Based on their reading of several biblical passages (for instance, Leviticus 18:22 and Romans 1:26-27), they label homosexuality as a sin that must be renounced. The evangelical conviction that sexual orientation can change is supported by conversion stories such as those told by Jeff Painter and Russ McCraw in *Good News*. According to their stories, both men had professed Christ, yet they remained homosexual. Both then sought a change in orientation and received help in the form of prayer, counseling, and accountability structures. Both testified to a change in orientation. Both began ministering to persons seeking to make the same transition.[13] Missing from these stories is the simple optimism about the effects of "accepting Christ" that one sees in many other evangelical conversion stories. Neither man claimed that accepting Christ led inevitably to a change in orientation. Rather, each described the type of difficult conversion therapy practiced by the various twelve-step groups. They did not say that it was easy for a person to change his or her homosexual orientation, yet they insisted that it is possible and necessary.[14]

In many ways, the official church position on homosexuality agrees with the conservative and evangelical views summarized above. The *Discipline* offers the following statement within its Social Principles:

> Although we do not condone the practice of homosexuality and consider this practice incompatible with Christian teaching, we affirm that God's grace is available to all. We implore families and churches not to reject or condemn their lesbian and gay members and friends. We commit ourselves to be in ministry for and with all persons.[15]

The Discipline forbids the ordination or pastoral appointment of "self-avowed practicing homosexuals" as well as the giving of church monies to any group that "[uses] such funds to promote the acceptance of homosexuality."[16] The language about "not condoning" the practice of homosexuality and considering it "incompatible with Christian teaching" suggests a call to repentance and renunciation, although the text stops short of saying it directly. The discussion of grace and the admonition about maintaining relationships with homosexual persons softens the impact somewhat. Nevertheless, one can read the disciplinary statement as a call to conversion—what else is one to do with a practice that is "incompatible with Christian teaching"?—and it seems that the Methodist evangelicals do so.

Although they insist that homosexuals need conversion, never do they suggest that they be excommunicated or refused membership. Ecclesiastical discipline related to moral failure is reserved for ordained ministers and ministerial candidates. For instance, the footnote to *Discipline* paragraph 306.4f discusses abstinence from tobacco and alcohol as a moral imperative for ordained ministers.[17] While the

Discipline insists that persons who desire to join the church take a vow "to renounce the spiritual forces of wickedness, reject the evil powers of the world, and repent of their sin,"[18] no *specific* moral issues are named as they are in the case of ordination.

Controversy over the 1987 death of Bishop Finis Crutchfield sharpened and personalized issues related to homosexuality and ordained ministry. Crutchfield died of complications related to AIDS, yet his illness was not reported until *after* his death. Controversy erupted after the publication of a *United Methodist Reporter* story in which Crutchfield's son, The Reverend Charles Crutchfield, reported "an extremely candid conversation" held with his father shortly before his death. According to his son, the Bishop denied having engaged in "homosexual or extramarital sexual conduct."[19] As *Good News* reported, that denial brought rebuttals and allegations from Houston area gay activists and from conservative United Methodists. Both groups claimed knowledge of homosexual activity by Crutchfield.[20]

It is not necessary to rehash the specific details of Crutchfield's personal tragedy, yet one particularly ironic statement invites reflection. *Good News* President James V. Heidinger II, mentioned that "(Crutchfield) was considered a friend by many of us in the Good News ministry."[21] His editorial applauded Crutchfield's emphasis on spiritual formation and church growth as well as his opposition to "political radicalism" in the church. In spite of that affirmation, one finds a post-mortem attempt to create some distance between *Good News* and the bishop. James Robb wrote,

> Though he was friendly and very supportive of a number of evangelical causes within the church, Bishop Crutchfield never fully identified himself as an evangelical or stated his full agreement with evangelical theology.[22]

How, they wondered, could one be a friend of evangelicalism and gay at the same time?

Many United Methodists experience a similar dissonance over the issue of homosexuality. They insist on saying that everyone is welcome at the Lord's Table, and are offended when anything less than that is said. United Methodists reveal some of their deepest convictions in that invitation. Persons on both sides of the homosexuality issue fight for the retention of such invitations, even though they may do so for divergent reasons. Evangelicals welcome gay and lesbian persons to the Table, believing that the encounter with Christ will bring conversion, delivering them from their homosexuality. Others in the church believe that persons can no more change their sexual orientation than a left-handed person can become right-handed; for these people, open table is a sign of God's affirming welcome. "God saw everything that he had made, and indeed, it was very good" (Genesis 1:31). What shall we make of it, however, when a self-centered and anxious homosexual person begins coming to church, enters a sustained practice of the Eucharist, and in the course of time shows the fruit of conversion in the emergence of faith, hope, and love, yet remains fully homosexual? Do we assume that the dynamics of conversion somehow bypassed his homosexuality, or do we assume with him that the homosexuality does not need converting? What shall we do if, in the course of time, such a person enters an exemplary committed relationship with a same-sex partner and then eventually presents gifts that indicate a call to a ministry of Word, Sacrament, and Order? At the present time, the rules of the church insist that he must be turned away from ordination. At best, it seems inconsistent.

Such a conundrum presents a sharp challenge to the practice of the open table. First of all, the practice of welcoming, nurturing, and then turning away persons seems dishonest. Perhaps the invitation to the Table should say, "Come this far and no further"? Yet the church should not say that when the theology inherent in United Methodist ordination rites insists that baptism and participation in the Eucharist is the highest expression of liturgical practice.[23] If one is morally unfit to preside at the communion table, then he or she is also unfit to receive communion at all. The converse would also be true: If one is morally fit to receive communion, then, assuming a call to the ordained role, he or she is also morally fit to preside as well.

Under this theology of Word and Sacrament, spiritual gifts that emerge in the course of Christian *praxis* must be taken seriously and should not be denied by the church. For support, we return to the classic case of St. Peter and his encounter with the Gentile God-fearer Cornelius (Acts 10:1-48; see also chapter 5). Peter was convinced that, by definition, an uncircumcised Gentile could not belong to the household of faith, yet God gave Cornelius the gift of the Spirit and Peter was forced to recognize it. Peter's response is enough to rock the most self-assured ecclesiology. He said, "Can anyone withhold the water for baptizing these people who have received the Holy Spirit just as we have?" (Acts 10:47). Cornelius and his fellow Gentiles were baptized, of course, and the church was radically changed. A similar logic has been employed in the case of the ordination of women. While many

Christians continue debating whether women should be ordained, for United Methodists and others, giftedness for ministry has become the primary consideration, regardless of gender. On the same principle, when our gay and lesbian members present gifts for ordained ministry, can the church legitimately withhold the sign of ordination? Indeed, Scripture calls the church to a more open table than it currently practices, one in which both the clergy and lay sides are open. Over the years, many gifted servants have been driven away.

Scripture also challenges the selective fencing that the church does. The church does not, in fact, apply the same strict standards to the treatment of divorced persons that it applies to gay and lesbian persons; yet Jesus, of whom the Gospels report no opinion about homosexuality, offered strongly worded teaching on divorce. The Pharisees reminded Jesus that Moses allowed a man to write a certificate of divorce and issue it to his wife, yet Jesus rejected that practice as inconsistent with God's intention for creation. He said,

> From the beginning of creation, "God made them male and female." "For this reason a man shall leave his father and mother and be joined to his wife, and the two shall become one flesh." So they are no longer two, but one flesh. Therefore what God has joined together, let no one separate. (Mark 10: 6-9).

According to this teaching, those who divorce and remarry, both husbands and wives, are adulterers (Mark 10:10-12, cf. Luke 16:18). This is a strongly worded prohibition, one that is only slightly softened in Matthew's version of it, which allows for divorce and remarriage when one of the partners has been unchaste (Matthew 5:31-32). In similar fashion, the author of 1 Timothy insisted that a bishop—which can be interpreted to mean a local church leader—be "married only once" (1 Timothy 3:2), that is, not divorced.

The biblical case for the exclusion of the divorced is quite strong, yet the modern church has not, by and large, incorporated these teachings into its canon law. On the contrary, it has made wide-sweeping exceptions to them both for practical reasons and as an expression of compassion. Even the Catholic Church practices a rather liberal understanding of annulment. Part of the concern is practical. If The United Methodist Church were to dismiss all of its divorced and remarried clergy and laity, it would be seriously understaffed and membership would be radically reduced. In the case of divorce, most pastors and theologians will insist that the church has let compassion have the last word, much as it has often done in relaxing penitential disciplines for the lapsed (see chapter 7). One could, of course, argue that the church has allowed cultural accommodation to have the last word, that we have reduced one's first divorce almost to the level of a rite of passage, and that we have been reluctant to discuss the large social cost of divorce, especially in the case of children. The church is vulnerable to such charges. I am not, however, advocating a punitive approach to divorced clergy and other members; our first response should be compassion. I raise this issue of divorce simply to point out the hypocrisy—if not outright schizophrenia—of the church's rules about gay and lesbians.

The church's current practice raises other as-yet-unanswered questions. What if, as some have claimed, persons are actually born with their sexual orientation? Many heterosexuals remember that they were attracted to the opposite sex at an early age, even if the attraction mystified them. Kindergarten crushes on the proverbial little red-haired girl suggest that such attraction is not simply a matter of choice. Could the dynamic be similar with same-sex attraction?[24] The mere possibility that persons may be born with their sexual orientation in place, the same as some are born left-handed and some right-handed, suggests a need for a greater ecclesial compassion and tolerance than often exists. At the least, taking a moratorium on discussing questions about homosexuality may be a good idea.[25] Let us keep silence for a while that we may think and reflect. John Wesley's call to do no harm may apply to this issue. Later generations may see ours as tragically intolerant of homosexuals, just as we now understand that previous generations were intolerant of their dyslexic children, labeling many of them either "slow" or "bad."

The issues discussed in this chapter have suggested the challenges and real difficulties inherent in exercising hospitality. They point out places where we seem to fall short of our optimistic rhetoric about the open table. The challenges expressed here remind us that our calling to radical hospitality goes much deeper than simply exercising common cordiality. Like all other genuinely Christian practices, invitation to the Table draws us into the dynamics of Christ's dying and rising. The practice, if it is authentically Christian, will cause us to die to our old restricted notions of family and then rise to a vision radically transformed. We will see the reign of God in our midst.

Chapter Nine

A Generous Reading
of the Final Rubric

The heart of Methodist identity is expressed in its invitations. United Methodists will insist that all people should be invited to hear and believe the Gospel and to participate in "the Gospel Feast," the Eucharist. This conviction is rooted in their reading of the Scriptures, their appropriation of key Wesleyan insights, and perhaps above all, their experience. As my interviews demonstrate, even thinking about a more restrictive type of invitation is a jarring experience for them. If they had to endure such an invitation, some would fight it and others would simply walk away sadly, wondering where their church had gone. Thus United Methodists practice an open table.

This practice must, however, exist in relationship with other Christian beliefs and practices, in what liturgical theologian Gordon W. Lathrop calls "juxtaposition."[1] For example, we have law and gospel, Word and Table, thanksgiving and lament, fasting and feasting, baptism and catechesis, and especially invitation and discipleship. Christians have long known that right practice emerges from the midst of such creative tension; when we break these pairs we spin out of balance and the integrity of the church is placed at risk. In seeking to maintain such a proper balance between open invitation and discipleship, I have noted some serious problems related to the church's practice of the open table (chapters 6 and 8). I have insisted that the call to communion must include teaching about the high cost of such participation. If any want to become followers of Jesus, they must take up the cross and follow him (Mark 8:34). In a Wesleyan understanding, the universal call to grace and faith must include an equally universal call to Christian discipleship.

A generous reading of the final rubric in the Service of the Baptismal Covenant allows the church to manage the tension between an open invitation to communion and baptismal discipline. That rubric states,

> It is most fitting that the service continue with Holy Communion, in which the union of the new members with the body of Christ is most fully expressed. The new members may receive first.[2]

This rubric reflects the ancient normative *ordo* of the church—admission to the Eucharist follows baptism—and there is good reason for the church to retain it as the norm. Indeed the church does so as a matter of course, both in its usual practice and in its official documents. In United Methodist services, the vast majority of those who present themselves at the Lord's Table are baptized. Both *By Water and the Spirit, A United Methodist Understanding of Baptism* and *This Holy Mystery, A United Methodist Understanding of Holy Communion* affirm the classical *ordo*, although each allows for the exceptional practice of the open table. *This Holy Mystery* says

> Nonbaptized people who respond in faith to the invitation in our liturgy will be welcomed to the Table. They should receive teaching about Holy Baptism as the sacrament of entrance into the community of faith— needed only once by each individual—and Holy Communion as the sacrament of sustenance for the journey of faith and growth in holiness— needed and received frequently.[3]

The relevant quotation from *By Water and the Spirit* follows that passage:

> Unbaptized persons who receive communion should be counseled and nurtured toward baptism as soon as possible.[4]

Again, each statement affirms the classic *ordo* while allowing for the occasional exception. At the deepest level of our being, turning people away from the meal seems to contradict the ways of Jesus, so if Methodists err, they choose to do so on the side of generosity.

THE CLASSIC *ORDO* MAY BE REVERSED, BUT NOT SET ASIDE

Generosity, however, is not permissiveness. A generous reading of the final rubric should not be construed as a disparaging of baptism or a rejection of it altogether. As noted earlier (see chapter 2), the danger in allowing for exceptional practices is that they can become new norms or pseudo-norms. This is why some are tempted by more of a hard-line approach about admission to the Table, saying, "Only the baptized may be admitted." Many would simply ignore such a rule. Moreover, if the church were serious about restricting access it would have to enforce it in some way. It could post deacons to guard the chancel or it could insist that prospective communicants register with the pastor before the service, as Church of England communicants were at one time required to do.[5] Many will want to opt for a more pastoral approach, although "pastoral" must mean more than "anything goes" or "never offend anyone." Although the church insists that it will not turn away anyone who responds to the communion invitation, ministers of the church should never take that to mean that baptism is optional. Baptism enables Eucharistic participation and discipleship in communion with Christ and the church; in the case of the non-baptized communicant we can argue that his or her participation partakes of the baptism that is to come, just as Cornelius and his household participated in the Spirit before they were baptized (Acts 10:44-48). In his case, baptism remained necessary, even though he had already received its sign; that remains so today. To teach some pathway other than baptism would be like saying that the children of Israel could escape Pharaoh and his charioteers by building canoes and paddling across the Red Sea on their own.

We proclaim, rather, that only God can deliver us from evil and sin, thus the necessity of God's gracious action, baptism. At the Easter Vigil, the church's classical rite for Christian Initiation, the church reads the Exodus 14–15 narrative about Israel's deliverance and then it prays "as once you delivered . . . Israel through the waters of the sea, so now deliver your Church and all the peoples of the earth from bondage and oppression . . ."[6] The phrase "so now . . ." refers to baptism, which follows later in the service. That point is made clear in the baptismal thanksgiving over the water that says "when you saw your people as slaves in Egypt, you led them to freedom through the sea."[7] Each of these texts points to the same idea: Through the gift of baptism, God delivers us from bondage to sin and brings us to freedom, into communion with Christ and the church where we participate in God's continuing work. Without God, we are backed up against the Red Sea with no way out. A classic understanding of sacramental grace says that only God can part the sea and take us safely through the waters. There are no canoes, no paddles. The church allows an occasional exception to the classical *ordo* and that must suffice. To say that baptism is somehow other than vitally important undermines the sacramental system and the theology of grace that it presupposes, and teaches that we can somehow find our own way through the waters.

MAGNIFYING THE CONNECTION

In addition to an occasional reordering of the classical *ordo*, a generous reading of the final rubric involves realizing that many members and constituents, including some pastors, are not sufficiently informed about the organic connection between baptism and Eucharist. We have not always thought about the intimate relationship between the two sacraments, nor have we done a particularly good job of ritualizing the connection. Some of the interview data points to this deficiency. Anna Freeman, pastor of Good Samaritan United Methodist Church in Houston, grew up in the Society of Friends, in which there is no formal practice of the sacraments. She did not become a Methodist until she was an adult. Today she understands the connection between baptism and the Eucharist, but she only became aware of it through the teaching of her seminary worship professor. At that point, she had been communing in the church for several years, oblivious to any problem with that practice. The worship of the church had failed to communicate any connection. She said,

> As soon as I came home from the hospital after I was born, my mom and dad took me to the church my dad pastored the next Sunday and I was dedicated to God . . . but I was not baptized until I was an intern pastor at [a United Methodist congregation] . . . I didn't know I was supposed to be baptized to be a Methodist. I do know now.[8]

If a person nearing the end of coursework in a denominational seminary did not realize the connection, then what can we expect of an average church member, especially when that member has joined the United Methodist Church from another tradition? When we have not properly ritualized the connection between the two sacraments, demands based upon that connection sound strange, if not hostile.

To say that the connection between the two sacraments is not always readily apparent to some members is not to say that baptism is unimportant to them. Many believe that it is very important. You may recall that Frank Walker of St. Luke's Church was deeply offended at the thought of a restricted communion invitation. He would consider any pastor who made such an invitation a "false prophet" (see chapter 5).

When he said that, however, he was not so much speaking against baptism as much as he was speaking for the open invitation. He told me that he and his wife have been raising their two granddaughters and he spoke about the hospitality that the congregation has shown them. Referring to their baptism at St. Luke's Church, he said, ". . . the whole congregation has helped. You know, they help when a child is born here. Everybody cares about that child. They just raise them right on. It's really neat."[9] There was no disparaging of the baptismal covenant; it was quite the opposite, in fact. His description of the church family and the care given to his two granddaughters demonstrates a solid sense of what the baptismal covenant effects. What we do not have in Mr. Walker and others like him is a clear articulation of the connection between baptism and Table.

That being the case, what is the best way to help United Methodists grow in their understanding of this connection? As we have noted, some United Methodist leaders want to approach the problem of the missing (or unperceived) linkage between baptism and Eucharist as a canon law problem, as if changes in *The Discipline* or the adoption of the correct resolution will solve the problem. I contend, rather, that a liturgical problem requires a liturgical solution. Along these lines, I will close this book by suggesting several ritual strategies that will enhance our understanding of the connection between baptism and communion:

- Let us not talk about the relationship of baptism to Eucharist in negative terms. "If you don't have A, you can't do B." (This strikes me as the canon law approach, one guaranteed to draw opposition and deepen suspicions).

- In like manner, let us find images other than the fence—perhaps the doorway—that focus on the Eucharistic privilege and responsibility granted in baptism.

- Let us celebrate the Eucharist immediately following every celebration of the baptismal covenant, according to the "it is most fitting" rubric described earlier and its call to commune the newly baptized first.[10] This practice will take the connection between baptism and Eucharist out of the realm of the theoretical and make it fully visible. To make the fullest connection possible, newly baptized infants and children should be communed also, even if the only way to do so is by touching a drop of communion wine to their lips.

- Let us preach about the connection between baptism, Eucharist, and discipleship. Such preaching should be invitational, not legalistic and didactic. The three great baptismal feasts of the Church Year—Easter, Pentecost, and Baptism of the Lord—provide the best opportunities, but creative homilists will see other possibilities as well. *Creative Preaching on the Sacraments*, by Craig A. Satterlee and Lester Ruth (Discipleship Resources, 2001) provides a good introduction to such preaching.

- Let us build strong liturgical centers for baptism, complete with immersion fonts and ample gathering space around them. Let us place such fonts at the primary entrance to our worship spaces or in the midst of them. Such architecture will help proclaim the centrality of baptism in all that the church does.

- Let us practice the catechumenate, with its full scope of transitional liturgies and formational processes involving the entire congregation. The catechumenate, drawn from ancient models for modern use,[11] clearly shows the connection between baptism and Eucharist as well as the relationship of each sacrament to discipleship and mission.

- Let us encourage use of the Easter Vigil and structure more and more of our initiatory and formational processes around it. Celebrating confirmations at the Vigil may be the most easily attained first step.

- Let us use other ritual action to magnify the connection between baptism and the Eucharist, such as placing a bowl of baptismal water in the aisle leading to the chancel, to be used for the remembrance of baptism as one moves toward the Table.

- Let us use hymns that magnify the connection between the two sacraments and let new ones be written. Good options currently available to United Methodists include "Wash, O God, Our Sons and Daughters" by Ruth Duck (*UMH* 605), "At the Font We Start Our Journey" by Jeffrey Rawthorn (*The Faith We Sing* 2114), and "We Were Baptized in Christ Jesus" by John Ylvisaker (*TFWS* 2251). The writing of hymns encourages the church to find fresh, positive ways to express the connection between the sacraments, forcing us well beyond the canon law approach.

- Let us use prayers that magnify the connection between baptism and Eucharist, and let new ones be written. In our public intercessory work, in addition to prayers for bishops and clergy, let us from time to time remember those who fulfill their baptismal vocation in particularly Eucharistic ways: home communion servers; nurses and hospital workers who help feed the sick and the infirm; nursing mothers and those who coach them; cooks in schools, hospitals, and prisons; those who work in food pantries and soup kitchens; and those who accept the cup of suffering (Mark 10:38, 14:36), to name but several.

- One could explore the connection between the two sacraments through the use of classical iconographic forms and contemporary artwork, including photographs and short films. The wedding feast at Cana in Galilee (John 2:1-10), with its interplay of water and wine, makes a promising subject.

- If we decide that sacramental integrity requires us to refuse Eucharist to the non-baptized, then let us turn people away in style, not with a terse announcement at the beginning of the Service of the Table, but with strong ritual action that celebrates their dignity. If we cannot offer them the Eucharist, then let hospitality abound in every other way.[12]

Practices such as these will help congregations see the connection between the two sacraments, and even more than that, will make the baptismal journey seem not like a barrier, but rather like a deeply gracious pathway. The whole journey will say, "Let every soul be Jesus' guest."

Notes

INTRODUCTION

1. Charles Wesley, "Come Sinners to the Gospel Feast," in *The Works of John Wesley*, Volume 7, *A Collection of Hymns for the Use of the People Called Methodists*, eds. Franz Hildebrandt and Oliver A. Beckerlegge with the assistance of James Dale (Nashville: Abingdon Press, 1993), 81-82. See a slightly updated contemporary rendering of this hymn in *The United Methodist Hymnal* (Nashville: The United Methodist Publishing House, 1989), 616. See also UMH, 339.
2. In *The United Methodist Hymnal*, the church has widened the language to say, "for God hath bid all humankind." See 616, stanza 1.
3. The Reverend Joanna Cornelius (pseudonym), Holy Pentecost United Methodist Church, Dallas, Texas area, December 2, 2001.
4. *This Holy Mystery: A United Methodist Understanding of Holy Communion* (Nashville: The General Board of Discipleship of The United Methodist Church, 2003, 2004), 14.
5. Mark W. Stamm, *Sacraments and Discipleship, Understanding Baptism and the Lord's Supper in a United Methodist Context* (Nashville: Discipleship Resources, 2001), 78-80. See also my discussion of style in the article "Developing Congregational Style," in *Worship Matters, A United Methodist Guide to Ways to Worship*, Volume I, ed. E. Byron Anderson (Nashville: Discipleship Resources, 1999), 86-92.
6. *The Works of John Wesley*, Volume 7, 79-82.
7. *Companion to The United Methodist Hymnal*, eds. Fred D. Gealy, Austin C. Lovelace, Carlton R. Young, [and] Emory Stevens Bucke, editors (Nashville: Abingdon Press, 1970), 151.
8. *The Methodist Hymnal* (New York: The Methodist Book Concern, 1905), 256; *The Methodist Hymnal* (Nashville: The Methodist Book Concern, 1935), 186; *The Book of Hymns* (Nashville: The United Methodist Publishing House, 1966), 102; *The United Methodist Hymnal*, 339, 616.
9. William Henry Meredith, *Jesse Lee: A Methodist Apostle*. (New York: Eaton and Mains; Cincinnati: Jennings and Graham, 1909), 77-78.
10. *The Constitution on the Sacred Liturgy of the Second Vatican Council and the*

Motu Propio of Pope Paul VI, with a commentary by Gerald S. Sloyan (Study Club Edition), (Glen Rock, N.J.: Paulist Press, 1964), chapter II, paragraph 51.

11. *The Works of John Wesley*, Volume 7, 81, 82.
12. Ibid., 7, 82.
13. Ibid., 81. See also *The United Methodist Hymnal*, 616.

1. WHAT IS REQUIRED FOR ADMISSION?

1. The possibility of "outsiders or unbelievers" being present in worship is raised in 1 Corinthians 14:22-25, within the discussion about speaking in tongues and prophecy.
2. See Gary Macy, *Treasures from the Storeroom, Medieval Religion and the Eucharist* (Collegeville, Minn.: The Liturgical Press, 1999), xiv, 30, 123. See also Paul F. Bradshaw, *The Search for the Origins of Christian Worship, Sources and Methods for the Study of Early Liturgy* (New York: Oxford University Press, 1992), 54, 204.
3. *Early Christian Fathers*, newly translated and edited by Cyril C. Richardson in collaboration with Eugene R. Fairweather, Edward Rochie Hardy, and Massey Hamilton Shepherd, Jr. (New York: Collier Books, Macmillan, 1970), 175.
4. *The First Apology of Justin Martyr* in *The Ante-Nicene Fathers, Translations of the Writings of the Fathers down to A.D. 325.* Eds. Alexander Roberts and James Donaldson. American reprint of the Edinburgh Edition, revised and chronologically arranged, with brief prefaces and occasional notes, by A. Cleveland Coxe, Volume I (Grand Rapids, Mich.: William B. Eerdmans Publishing Company, n.d.), chapters 66-67, 185-86.
5. Eamon Duffy, *The Stripping of the Altars, Traditional Religion in England, 1400–1580* (New Haven: Yale University Press, 1992), 93-95. Macy, 156-58.
6. *The Book of Common Prayer, 1559, The Elizabethan Prayer Book.* Edited by John Booty (Washington: The Folger Shakespeare Library, 1976), 282-83.
7. Ibid., 247.
8. *This Holy Mystery: A United Methodist Understanding of Holy Communion*, 15-17.
9. Justin pleaded for the lives of his fellow Christians: "And if these things seem to you to be reasonable and true, honour them; but if they seem nonsensical, despise them as nonsense, and do not decree death against those who have done no wrong, as you would against enemies. For we forewarn you, that you shall not escape the coming judgment of God . . ." *First Apology of Justin Martyr*, 186, chapter 68.
10. Ibid., 164, chapter 6; 168, chapter 17; 186, chapter 68.
11. Ibid., 172, chapter 29; 181-82, chapters 54-55; 184-85, chapter 64.
12. Ibid., 183, chapter 61.

13. Ibid., 185, chapter 65.
14. Ibid., 185, chapter 66.
15. Ibid., 185-86, chapter 67.
16. Ibid., 185, chapter 65.
17. Ibid., 172, chapter 29; 181-82, chapters 54-55; 184-85, chapter 64.
18. Ibid., 183, chapter 61.
19. Ibid.
20. Ibid., 185, chapter 66
21. Ibid.
22. Ibid., 185-86, chapters 65-67.
23. See my earlier discussion of this congregation in *Sacraments and Discipleship, Understanding Baptism and the Lord's Supper in a United Methodist Context* (Nashville: Discipleship Resources, 2001), 12-13. I was privileged to serve as Associate Pastor of First Church from 1985-90.
24. John Dromazos, Newsletter, First United Methodist Church, Chambersburg, PA. November 2002, 1. Used by permission.
25. Discussion of a Wesleyan "quadrilateral" came into the United Methodist Church with *The Book of Discipline* (1972) and the essay on "Our Theological Task" written primarily by Albert C. Outler of Perkins School of Theology. The essay proposed Scripture, Tradition, Reason, and Experience as "sources and norms," (pp. 75-79) and the combination became known as the "Wesleyan quadrilateral." The idea was a development of a venerable idea. For instance, in Book V, chapter 8 of *The Lawes of Ecclesiastical Polity* (1597), Anglican theologian Richard Hooker had proposed Scripture, Tradition, and Reason as the primary sources in an Anglican theological method. Outler had added Wesley's focus on experience as a fourth source.

Many theologians were troubled by the essay, both by its terminology and its implications, primarily because it seemed to hold the four sides as equally significant sources and thus did not place scripture as the primary source. The church officially moved beyond the idea of a quadrilateral with its 1988 statement that insisted, "Scripture is primary, revealing the Word of God 'so far as it is necessary for our salvation.' Therefore, our theological task, in both its critical and constructive aspects, focuses on disciplined study of the Bible." See *The Book of Discipline* (1988), 80, paragraph 69.

Tradition, reason, and experience remain as part of the method, but Scripture is the primary source and the others relate to it. This statement has appeared in all subsequent editions of *The Discipline*. See *The Book of Discipline* (2000), 76-77, paragraph 104. I agree with the current statement that Scripture must always be understood as the primary source for the church's theological reflection and discernment. That being said, however, I am insisting that experience is a deeply significant factor in the formation of the United Methodist theological mind.

26. *The Works of John Wesley, Volume 18, Journals and Diaries I (1735–1738)* (Nashville: Abingdon Press, 1988), 249-50.

27. For a thorough discussion of these dynamics, see *Aldersgate Reconsidered*. Maddox, Randy L., editor. Nashville: Kingswood Books, 1990.

28. *First Apology of Justin Martyr*, 185, chapter 66.

29. See Wesley's sermon "The Means of Grace." *The Works of John Wesley, Volume I, Sermons 1, 1-33*, edited by Albert C. Outler (Nashville: Abingdon Press, 1984), 376-97.

30. Exceptions may be noted, of course. Some American Christians do perceive the government as hostile: On one end of the theological-political spectrum, opponents of abortion and supporters of prayer in public schools, and on the other end, persons who have engaged in the sanctuary movement and those who oppose the military through various forms of civil disobedience.

31. *First Apology of Justin Martyr*, 185, chapter 66.

32. Dromazos, 1.

33. See my discussion in *Sacraments and Discipleship, Understanding Baptism and the Lord's Supper in a United Methodist Context* (Nashville: Discipleship Resources, 2001), 12-13.

34. See, for instance, "The Didascalia of the Apostles" and "The Apostolic Constitutions" in *Springtime of the Liturgy* by Lucien Deiss, translated by Matthew J. O'Connell (Collegeville, Minnesota: The Liturgical Press, 1979), 175, 224.

35. Charles Wesley, "O the Depth of Love Divine" (stanza 4), *The United Methodist Hymnal* (Nashville: The United Methodist Publishing House, 1989), 627.

36. That presentation, in a more mature form, was published in *Quarterly Review* under the title "Open Communion as a United Methodist Exception." See *QR* 22:3 (Fall 2002), 261-72.

37. *The Book of Common Prayer* (New York: The Church Hymnal Corporation, 1979), 330.

38. Caroline Westerhoff, *Good Fences, the Boundaries of Hospitality* (Cowley Publications, 1999), 86-89.

39. *Rite of Christian Initiation of Adults, Study Edition* (Chicago: Liturgy Training Publications, 1988), 40, paragraph 83; 59-60, paragraph 116.

2. SACRAMENTAL AND LITURGICAL EXCEPTIONS

1. See my earlier discussions in "Who May Receive Communion in The United Methodist Church?" *Quarterly Review* 21:3 (Fall 2001), 308-9 and "Open Communion as a United Methodist Exception" *Quarterly Review* 22:3 (Fall 2002), 266-67).

2. John Wesley, "The Duty of Constant Communion," *The Works of John Wesley, Volume 3, Sermons III, 71-114.* Edited by Albert C. Outler (Nashville: Abingdon Press, 1986), 427-39.

3. *Journal of George Fox*, edited by John L. Nickalls (London: Religious Society of Friends, 1986), 134.

4. This chapter comes from that section of canonical Isaiah commonly called "Second Isaiah" (chapters 40–66). The first section of the canonical book (chapters 1–39) was written during the eighth century B.C.E. It anticipates God's judgment. This second section, written after the deportation to Babylon (586 B.C.E.), reflects on God's judgment and mercy. For a good review see *The New Interpreter's Bible*, Volume VI (Nashville: Abingdon Press, 2001), 310-19.

5. Since we possess no text for their fasting ritual, we must infer its shape. For other biblical examples of ritualized practices related to fasting, see Leviticus 16 (Day of Atonement) and Zechariah 7–8. Knowing the exact shape of their ritual is not, however, essential to the argument I am making here.

6. See *The Book of Common Prayer* (New York: The Church Hymnal Corporation, 1979), 335.

7. *The United Methodist Hymnal*, 10, See also Matthew 26:26-29, Mark 14:22-25, Luke 22:14-23, 1 Corinthians 11:23-26.

8. I am aware that some traditions of the Eucharistic prayer do not include the words of institution, most notably the ancient liturgy of Addai and Mari. Therefore, one can argue against their being absolutely necessary. While an adequate Eucharistic prayer could avoid using them, one can hardly have an adequate Eucharistic prayer without substantial reference to the life of Jesus Christ and his ministry. For a text of the Addai and Mari Eucharistic prayer, see R.C.D. Jasper and G. J. Cuming, *Prayers of the Eucharist, Early and Reformed* (Collegeville, Minn.: The Liturgical Press, 1990), 39-44.

9. Ignatius, Bishop of Antioch, "Letter to the Smyrnaeans," circa 107 C.E., *Early Christian Fathers*, Cyril Richardson, editor (New York: Collier Books, 1970), 115.

10. John Wesley, "On Laying the Foundation of the New Chapel," *The Works of John Wesley, Volume 3, Sermons III, 71-114*, edited by Albert C. Outler (Nashville: Abingdon Press, 1986), 579-80.

11. John Wesley, "The Means of Grace," *The Works of John Wesley, Volume 1, Sermons 1, 1-33*, Edited by Albert C. Outler (Nashville: Abingdon Press, 1984), 376-97.

12. Ibid., 381.

13. Ibid., 383-84.

14. Ibid., 378.

15. Ibid., 381.

16. John Wesley, "On Laying the Foundation of the New Chapel," 588-89.

17. Ibid., 585.
18. Ibid., 584.
19. Frank Baker, *John Wesley and the Church of England* (Nashville: Abingdon Press, 1970) chapters 13-15 and Henry Rack, *Reasonable Enthusiast, John Wesley and the Rise of Methodism* second edition (Nashville: Abingdon Press, 1992), chapter 14.
20. Scott J. Jones, *United Methodist Doctrine, The Extreme Center* (Nashville: Abingdon Press, 2002), 246.
21. John Wesley, *Explanatory Notes Upon the New Testament* (London: Epworth Press, 1950), 632. Wesley's notes were originally published in 1754.
22. John Wesley to Mary Bosanquet, June 13, 1771, *The Letters of the Rev. John Wesley, A.M., Standard Edition*, Volume V, *February 28, 1766, to December 9, 1772.* Edited by John Telford (London: The Epworth Press, 1931), 257.
23. John Wesley to 'Our Brethren in America,' September 10, 1784, *The Letters of the Rev. John Wesley, A.M., Standard Edition*, Volume VII, *March 23, 1780 to July 24, 1787.* Edited by John Telford (London: The Epworth Press, 1931), 238.
24. Ibid.
25. Ibid.
26. That reluctance, by the way, was expressed by John Wesley himself, who was appalled at the American decision to give Asbury the title "Bishop." Here, he thought, was an unwarranted attempt at maintaining continuity. In his letter to Asbury dated September 20, 1788, Wesley wrote, "How can you, how dare you suffer yourself to be called Bishop! I shudder, I start at the very thought! Men may call me a knave or a fool, a rascal, a scoundrel, and I am content; but they shall never by my consent call me Bishop." *The Letters of John Wesley*, September 20, 1788, Vol. VIII (London, Epworth Press, 1931), 91.
27. For an insightful discussion of this topic see the article by Wanda Zemler-Cizewski, "The Eucharist and Celiac Disease: A Question of Access to Holy Communion," *Worship* 74:3 (May 2000), 237-47.
28. See my response to this topic in *Sacraments and Discipleship*, 104-5.
29. *The Book of Discipline of the United Methodist Church, 2000*, paragraph 103, p. 72.
30. Karen B. Westerfield Tucker, *American Methodist Worship* (Oxford: Oxford University Press, 2001, 151. For the full discussion, see 150-154. Robert C. Fuller, *Religion and Wine, A Cultural History of Wine Drinking in the United States* (Knoxville: The University of Tennessee Press, 1996), 88-89.
31. *The Methodist Hymnal* (1935), 523. *The Methodist Hymnal* (1905), 95.
32. "Regarding the Service of Holy Communion." *The Book of Resolutions of The United Methodist Church, 2000* (Nashville: The United Methodist Publishing House, 2000), 838.
33. Karen B. Westerfield Tucker, *American Methodist Worship*, 264-67. See also *The Book of Discipline, 2000*, paragraphs 317, 330-31, and 334.
34. Edward Schillebeeckx, *Ministry, Leadership in the Community of Jesus Christ,*

translated by John Bowden (New York: Crossroad, 1981), 72-3; 75-99.

35. *Baptism, Eucharist, and Ministry*, Faith and Order Paper Number 111 (Geneva: World Council of Churches, 1982).

36. *Churches Respond to B.E.M., Official Responses to the "Baptism, Eucharist, and Ministry" Text*, Volume II, edited by Max Thurian, Faith and Order Paper 132 (Geneva: World Council of Churches, 1986), 195.

37. *Daily Christian Advocate* 5:11 (May 7, 1956). See the speech by delegate Henry Lambdin printed on page 524, and the speech by delegate William Alderson, printed on page 531.

38. Lawrence Guderian, "Minneapolis Impressions," *The Versicle* 6:2 (Whitsuntide 1956), 2.

39. For a Catholic perspective see John R. Sheets, "Forum: The Ordination of Women," *Worship* 65:5 (September 1991), 451-61. See Carter Heyward's report of Episcopal Church opposition to her ordination in her book *A Priest Forever, One Woman's Controversial Ordination in the Episcopal Church* (Cleveland: The Pilgrim Press, 1976, 1999), 48-49.

40. For a full description of these events, see the book of Carter Heyward, one of the eleven ordinands. *A Priest Forever.*

41. Ibid., 38.

42. At its 1976 General Convention, the Episcopal Church did change its canons to allow the ordination of women. Some have argued that this change means that the 1974 ordinations were unwarranted, that the church would have changed without them. Others will insist that the 1976 change would not have occurred without the prophetic action of 1974. One can, of course, analyze only those events that actually occurred. See the discussion by Suzanne R. Hiatt, one of the eleven ordinands, in Heyward, *A Priest Forever,* 141-47.

43. *The Journal of George Fox*, edited by Rufus M. Jones with an essay by Henry J. Cadbury with New Glossary-Index (Richmond, Ind.: Friends United Press, 1976), 101.

44. Ibid., 82.

45. Ibid., 95, 205.

46. Ibid., 104.

47. Patrick J. Nugent, "Real Presence and First-Day Pitch-Ins: Why Quakers Are, and Must Be, a Eucharistic People," *Quaker Theology* Issue 7, Volume 4:2 (Autumn 2002), http://www.quaker.org/quest/issue7-2-nugent01.htm Accessed November 15, 2004.

48. Horton Davies, *Worship and Theology in England, Book II, From Andrewes to Baxter and Fox, 1603-1690.* (Grand Rapids: Eerdmans, 1996, originally 1975 by Princeton University Press), 515.

49. Ibid., 520-21.

50. Nugent, "Real Presence and First-Day Pitch-Ins."

51. Ibid.

52. "By Water and the Spirit: A United Methodist Understanding of Baptism,"

The Book of Resolutions of the United Methodist Church, 2000. (Nashville: The United Methodist Publishing House, 2000), 814.

53. Ibid.

54. Richard Fabian, "First the Table, Then the Font," *Sacramental Life* 15:5 (Summer 2003), 565.

3. THE MEALS OF JESUS:
JUSTIFYING AN OPEN TABLE ON BIBLICAL GROUNDS

1. Dennis E. Smith, *From Symposium to Eucharist, the Banquet in the Early Christian World* (Minneapolis: Augsburg Fortress Press, 2003), 9. Smith draws his insight from Mary Douglas, "Deciphering a Meal," *Implicit Meanings, Essays in Anthropology* (London: Routledge and Kegan Paul 1975), 249-75.

2. As we noted earlier (see Introduction), this parable inspired Charles Wesley's hymn, "Come, Sinners, to the Gospel Feast," about Christ's universal invitation.

3. *The New Interpreter's Bible*, Volume IX (Nashville: Abingdon Press, 1995), 301.

4. *The United Methodist Hymnal*, 340, stanza 1, with refrain. "Come, Ye Sinners, Poor and Needy" was written by Joseph Hart in 1759.

5. See discussion of this text in John Koenig, *New Testament Hospitality: Partnership with Strangers as Promise and Mission* (Philadelphia: Fortress Press, 1985), 54-55.

6. For an exegetical discussion of the boundary issues at work in First Corinthians, see the study by Dale B. Martin, *The Corinthian Body* (New Haven: The Yale University Press, 1995).

7. *The United Methodist Hymnal*, 9.

8. Ibid., 9-10.

9. Ibid., 10.

10. The preface (i.e., the opening section) of the Great Thanksgiving presents a similar attempt to remember the Hebrew Bible narrative. While such summaries will always be somewhat incomplete, their use implies an affirmation of the whole narrative. Thus the preface functions like a creed, fulfilling a function somewhat like Article VI "Of the Old Testament." "The Old Testament is not contrary to the New; for both in the Old and New Testament everlasting life is offered to mankind by Christ. . . ." *The Book of Discipline of the United Methodist Church, 2000*, paragraph 103, p. 61.

11. See, for instance, the Great Thanksgiving in *Book of Common Worship* (Louisville: Westminster/John Knox Press, 1993), 69-73. For other Presbyterian examples see pages 126-56. See Eucharistic Prayers C and D in *Book of Common Prayer, 1979*, 369-76.

12. Jasper, R.C.D., and G.J. Cuming, *Prayers of the Eucharist, Early and Reformed*, third edition, revised and enlarged (Collegeville, Minn.: The Liturgical Press, 1990), 35.

13. Ibid., 59.

14. Hoyt L. Hickman, "Word and Table: The Process of Liturgical Revision in the United Methodist Church, 1964–1992." *The Sunday Service of the Methodists, Twentieth-Century Worship in Worldwide Methodism*. Studies in Honor of James F. White. Ed. Karen Westerfield Tucker (Nashville: Kingswood Books, 1996), 123-24.

15. *The Book of Hymns of The United Methodist Church* (Nashville: The Board of Publication of the Methodist Church, 1966), 830. Proper prefaces are given for Christmas, Epiphany, Easter, and Pentecost. See #831.

16. Each of these follows the West Syrian pattern used in the Word and Table I prayer:

> SURSUM CORDA
> PREFACE drawn primarily from the Old Testament narrative
> SANCTUS AND BENEDICTUS
> POST-SANCTUS focused on the life of Jesus, including the Words of
>   Institution
> MEMORIAL ACCLAMATION
> EPICLESIS
> AMEN

17. *The United Methodist Book of Worship*, 56.

18. Ibid., 58-59.

19. Ibid., 54.

20. Ibid., 58.

21. Ibid., 60-61.

22. Ibid., 72.

23. Ibid., 58, 68, 70.

24. For an intriguing variation on this topic, see the Eucharistic prayers of lamentation and resistance composed by Marjorie Procter-Smith. *Praying With Our Eyes Open* (Nashville: Abingdon, 1995), 136-42.

25. For the full text and a comparison of the revisions, see Hickman, "Word and Table: The Process of Liturgical Revision in the UMC," 133-35.

26. James F. White, "Word and Table I: An Historical and Theological Commentary." Unpublished video recording of White's keynote address delivered on October 16, 2000, at the convocation of the Order of Saint Luke meeting at the St. Joseph Retreat Center, Greensburg, Pennsylvania. The exact quotation beginning at 1:23.35 and continuing through 1:24.02 is as follows: "Bill Farmer, who taught New Testament at Perkins, had preached a sermon in Perkins Chapel stressing that the one thing that we are absolutely certain about Jesus is that he ate with sinners; because this was such a scandal to the righteous Jew of his time that it gets mentioned prominently in all the Gospels. So I said, 'Why not? 'and put that line in, 'ate with sinners.'"

27. White, "Word and Table Commentary," 0:24.
28. Ibid., 0:59, 1:11.
29. Ibid., l:19.
30. Ibid., 0:37-38, 1:13. The original dialogical form is printed in *We Gather Together*, Supplemental Worship Resources 10 (Nashville: The United Methodist Publishing House, 1972, 1976, 1979, 1980), 11. It is listed as an "Alternative Act of Worship" in *The Book of Services* (Nashville: The United Methodist Publishing House, 1985), 45. According to White, Hoyt Hickman's congregation normally stood around the altar when they said the final prayer. Since they did not take their hymnals or bulletins with them, a dialogical form was not practical. For this reason, a version of the closing prayer was written that could be spoken by one person.
31. White, "Word and Table I Commentary," 1:37.
32. Ibid., 0:23.
33. In particular, the Presbyterian Church (U.S.A.) has adapted this insight into their praying of the Great Thanksgiving. Other mainline American churches seem a bit more reticent.
    See this sentence in "Great Thanksgiving: A": "He healed the sick, fed the hungry, opened blind eyes, broke bread with outcasts and sinners, and proclaimed the good news of your kingdom to the poor and needy." *Book of Common Worship* (Louisville: Westminster/John Knox Press, 1993), 70. One finds echoes of the phrase in "Great Thanksgiving: C": "He told your story, healed the sick, and was a friend of sinners . . . He is still the friend of sinners." (p. 131).
34. Norman Perrin, *Rediscovering the Teaching of Jesus* (New York: Harper and Row Publishers, 1967).
35. John Dominic Crossan, *The Historical Jesus, The Life of a Mediterranean Jewish Peasant* (San Francisco: HarperCollins Publishers, 1991).
36. Marcus Borg, *Meeting Jesus Again for the First Time, The Historical Jesus and the Heart of Contemporary Faith* (San Francisco: HarperCollins Publishers, 1994).
37. Crossan, 261-64.
38. Perrin, 102. Note his reference to N.A. Dahl, "The Problem of the Historical Jesus," *Kerygma and History*, ed. Carl E. Braaten and Roy A. Harrisville (New York: Abingdon Press, 1962), 138-71, esp. 158f.
39. Ibid., 103.
40. Ibid., 106. Crossan, 260.
41. Crossan 261-62.
42. Perrin, 107-8.
43. Ibid., 104-5.
44. Borg, 56.
45. Smith, 220.
46. Ibid., 2.
47. Ibid., 24, 27, 33, 37, 73, 79.

48. Ibid., 9.
49. Ibid., 102, 125.
50. Ibid., 64.
51. Ibid., 198.
52. Ibid., 201.
53. Ibid., 206.
54. Ibid., 219-20.
55. Ibid., 270.
56. *The United Methodist Hymnal*, 9.
57. The transmission and traditioning process is not, of course, free from error; nor has it always led to happy results for all. As Elisabeth Schüssler Fiorenza has asserted, the early church suppressed stories about women disciples of Jesus, most ironically in failing to remember the name of the woman who anointed the feet of Jesus (Mark 14:9). See *In Memory of Her* (New York: Crossroad, 1983).

    Marjorie Procter-Smith describes a service about the calling of disciples in which the biblical stories of male disciples are read followed by periods of silence kept to embody the missing call stories of women. See her "Beyond the New Common Lectionary: A Constructive Critique" *Quarterly Review* Volume 13 (Summer 1993), 56-57.

    In the case of the open commensality of Jesus, some argue that the historical witness to Jesus' eating with sinners has been to some extent suppressed. What remains, they argue, is a remnant of a much more radical portrayal. See reference to Norman Perrin in William R. Crockett, *Eucharist: Symbol of Transformation* (New York: Pueblo Publishing Company, 1989), 2.
58. George A. Lindbeck, *The Nature of Doctrine, Religion and Theology in a Postliberal Age* (Louisville, Kentucky: Westminster John Knox Press, 1984), 35-36.
59. Ibid., 81-82.
60. *The United Methodist Hymnal*, 614, 615, 617, 619, 625, 629, 630, 632, 633, 634, 636, 637, 640.
61. Ibid., 632, especially stanza 3.
62. Ibid., 638.
63. Ibid., 625
64. Ibid., 614, 620.
65. Ibid., 617, stanza l. I COME WITH JOY. By Brian Wren © 1971 Hope Publishing Co., Carol Stream, IL 60188. All rights reserved. Used by permission.
66. Compare the hymn phrase "Let all mortal flesh keep silence, and with fear and trembling stand . . .", translated from the fourth-century Liturgy of Saint James. See *The United Methodist Hymnal*, 626, stanza 1.
67. Ibid., 617, stanza 2.
68. Compare the image of a "fountain filled with blood drawn from

Emmanuel's veins," penned in the eighteenth century by another British hymn writer, William Cowper. See *The United Methodist Hymnal*, 622, stanza 1.

69. Ibid., 617, stanza 5.
70. Ibid., 629 (refrain). Copyright permission obtained, Archdiocese of Philadelphia, 1977. All rights reserved.
71. For a full exposition of the theology expressed in this phrase, see the book by James F. White, *Sacraments as God's Self-Giving, Sacramental Practice and Faith* (Nashville: Abingdon, 1983). In this book, one finds White's most complete expression of sacramental theology. As the hymnody we have reviewed demonstrates, his language is typical of sacramental theology in the latter half of the twentieth century. His work also served to shape that theology.
72. *The United Methodist Hymnal*, 629, stanza one.
73. Ibid., 629, stanzas two through four.
74. Ibid., 629, stanza five.
75. Hoyt L. Hickman, "Word and Table: The Process of Liturgical Revision in the UMC," 123-24.
76. Ibid., 124.
77. Hoyt L. Hickman, Volume Editor, *The Worship Resources of the United Methodist Hymnal. Introduction to the General Services, Psalter, and Other Acts of Worship*, (Nashville: Abingdon Press, 1989), 64-65.
78. *The Book of Hymns*, 830.
79. *The United Methodist Hymnal*, 26-31.
80. John Wesley, "The Duty of Constant Communion," *The Works of John Wesley, Volume 3, Sermons III, 71-114*. Edited by Albert C. Outler (Nashville: Abingdon Press, 1986), 437.
81. http://www.eskimo.com/~lhowell/bcp1662/communion/index.html Accessed November 16, 2004.
82. In light of this long process of theological and liturgical correction, it is worth noting that James White campaigned successfully for the inclusion of Charles Wesley's hymn "Victim Divine" in the recently published *The Faith We Sing* edited by Hoyt Hickman. (Nashville: Abingdon Press, 2000), 2259. Inclusion of the imagery presented in this hymn moves against the trend of the last half-century.
83. Smith, 282.

4. The Meals of Jesus: Justifying an Open Table on Wesleyan Grounds

1. Dwight W. Vogel uses this phrase "depth dynamic" in his liturgical theology. See "The Depth Dynamic of Christian Worship: A Trinitarian Perspective," *Worship* 76:4 (July 2002), 313-24. In his usage, "depth dynamic" refers to the theological affirmations that lie deep "beneath ques-

tions of style, rubrics, text, and symbolic action." According to Vogel, "these dynamics are 'deep' because they are beneath what we see and hear and read and do, although their presence is manifested there. They are 'dynamic' because they are vital and interactive. They do not 'stay put' but manifest an interactive energy in which no one facet can be understood apart from another" (pp. 315-16). Such a depth dynamic is foundational to the pattern of doctrinal and liturgical development that I am describing with my phrase "theological trajectory."

As these phrases suggest, faithfulness to a tradition does not mean that churches must do everything exactly as their forebears did, that, for instance, they must speak in the same language or use the same rites and ordo. Faithfulness is more broadly conceived as a commitment to their prevailing theological views and liturgical practices. Such a rendering of tradition will inevitably draw the reaction of more conservative Christians. Such reactions, though sometimes exasperating, are a necessary part of the traditioning process.

2. John Wesley, "The New Birth" in *The Works of John Wesley, Volume 2, Sermons II 34-70*, Albert C. Outler, editor (Nashville: Abingdon Press, 1985), 196.

3. See the argument expressed in *This Holy Mystery*, 15.

4. Philip Schaff, *What is Church History, A Vindication of the Idea of Historical Development* (1846) in *Reformed and Catholic: Selected Historical Writings of Philip Schaff*, edited by Charles Yrigoyen, Jr. and George M. Bricker (Pittsburgh: The Pickwick Press, 1979), 114.

5. John Henry Newman, *An Essay on the Development of Christian Doctrine* (London: Basil Montagu Pickering, 1878), 97.

6. See, for instance, Richard Hooker, *Ecclesiastical Polity, The Fifth Book*, Ronald Bayne, editor (New York: Macmillan and Company, Limited, 1902), chapters 19-21, pp. 68-93.

7. In 1784, the newly formed American Church inserted Article XXIII, now titled "Of the Rulers of the United States of America." Wesley had omitted Anglican Article XXXVII, "Of the Civil Magistrates." See *Book of Discipline, 2000*, paragraph 103. For details on the development of this Article in the Methodist Episcopal Church, see *Doctrinal Standards in the Wesleyan Tradition*, by Thomas C. Oden (Grand Rapids, Mich.: Francis Asbury Press, 1988), 125-26.

8. *The Works of John Wesley, Volume 18, Journals and Diaries I* (1735-1738), 249, *Journal* entry for May 24, 1738.

9. Mark W. Stamm, *Sacraments and Discipleship, Understanding Baptism and the Lord's Supper in a United Methodist Context* (Nashville: Discipleship Resources, 2001), 33-39. See also *Baptism and Initiation in United Methodism: Toward an Evangelical and Catholic Synthesis* (Th.D. dissertation, Boston University, 1995), 356-403. Daniel T. Benedict, Jr. offers such a proposal in his book *Come to the Waters: Baptism and Our Ministry of Welcoming Seekers and Making Disciples* (Nashville: Discipleship Resources, 1996).

10. For more information on the class system, read David Lowes Watson, *The Early Methodist Class Meeting: Its Origins and Significance*, foreword by Albert C. Outler (Nashville: Discipleship Resources, 1985, revised 1992).

11. *The Methodist Hymnal* (1905), 89 of The Ritual. See also *John Wesley's Prayer Book: The Sunday Service of the Methodists in North America* with introduction, notes and commentary by James F. White (Cleveland, Ohio: OSL Publications, 1991), 140-41.
    Compare the *Book of Common Prayer*, 1549, 1552, 1559, 1662, 1928. Methodist hymnals of 1935 and 1964 shortened the warrant, reading only the second half of Mark 10:14, "Let the children come to me, do not hinder them, for to such belongs the kingdom of God." See *The Book of Hymns*, 828. The warrant from Mark 10 is not included in either *The Book of Common Prayer* (1979), or *The United Methodist Hymnal* (1989), thus departing from a long-standing Anglo-Methodist tradition.

12. See the discussion by Aidan Kavanagh in his book *The Shape of Baptism: The Rite of Christian Initiation* (New York: Pueblo Publishing Company, 1978). Commenting on the Roman Catholic *Rite of Christian Initiation of Adults*, a modern renewal of the catechumenate, Kavanagh wrote, ". . . the document's purpose is less to give liturgical recipes than to shift the Church's initiatory polity from one conventional norm centering on infant baptism to the more traditional norm centering on adults. Nowhere does the document say this in so many words. If this is not the case, however, then the document not only makes no sense but is vain and fatuous." (p. 106).
    Citing Kavanagh in the context of this book about a sacramental exception raises an interesting semantic question: If the baptism of infants is not the norm for the church, should we then call it a sacramental exception? Because the baptism of children is such a long-standing practice, I cannot bring myself to call it an exception, although those committed to a *praxis* of believers' baptism might want to describe it using those terms, perhaps as an ecumenical gesture. Citing the long history of infant baptism, however, we might better call the baptism of children "co-normative" rather than reverting to the exception category.

13. Stamm, *Sacraments and Discipleship*, 38-39.

14. *The Treatise on the Apostolic Tradition of St. Hippolytus of Rome, Bishop and Martyr*, edited by Gregory Dix. Reissued with corrections preface and bibliography by Henry Chadwick (London: The Alban Press, 1992), xxi.4, p. 33.

15. *Tertullian's Homily on Baptism: The Text edited with an Introduction, Translation and Commentary by Ernest Evans* (London: S.P.C.K., 1964), 39.

16. Dietrich Bonhoeffer, *The Cost of Discipleship*, Revised and unabridged edition, containing material not previously translated. (New York: Macmillan Publishing, 1963), 261.

17. In his diary and journal, Wesley often referred to her by this name, "Miss Sophy."

18. *The Works of John Wesley, Volume 18, Journals and Diaries I (1735–1738)*,

edited by W. Reginald Ward and Richard Heitzenrater (Nashville: Abingdon Press, 1988), 473, Diary for February 15, 1737.

19. *Works*, Volume 18, 467. Manuscript Journal for January 25, 1737.

20. Ibid., Manuscript Journal for February 1 and 3, 1737.

21. Ibid., Manuscript Journal for February 26, 1737.

22. Ibid., Manuscript Journal for March 4, 1737.

23. Much has been made of Wesley's various misadventures with women, including his ill-advised marriage to Mary Vazeille many years later. It is likely that Wesley was indeed called to the celibate life. In that case, this story of his relationship with Sophia Hopkey illustrates the deep sacrifice and pain related to such a commitment. Even with that caveat, Wesley's handling of the case was incredibly clumsy.

24. *Works*, Volume 18, 488. Manuscript Journal for March 12, 1737.

25. Ibid., 188, Journal for August 11, 1737.

26. *The Book of Common Prayer, 1662.* See http://www.eskimo.com/ ~lhowell/bcp1662/communion/index.html Accessed November 16, 2004.

27. In modern circumstances, such a rubric might be used against a person who had publicly declared allegiance to the Ku Klux Klan. Conversely, it would not apply to a person who was struggling with tendencies toward racial prejudice but was not publicly justifying or even glorifying such sin. That is not to say that an unrepentant racist is justified in answering the call to communion. I mean to say that such sin becomes a matter for direct confrontation and possible excommunication primarily when it becomes a matter of public knowledge.

Even if the discipline of excommunication is rarely practiced, it is important that the church retain the possibility of exercising it. As with all human attempts at administering justice, some who deserve excommunication will avoid detection and the possibility exists that some will be unjustly accused. Excommunication exists only for the rehabilitation of the offender and the instruction of the faithful. Thus it should be done in the utmost humility and the possibility of restoration to full communion must exist. Here there must be no life sentence without possibility of parole. Issues related to excommunication will be discussed at some length in chapter 8.

28. *Works*, Volume 18, 547-48, 552. Manuscript Journal for August 16, 1737.

29. Ibid., Manuscript Journal for August 16, 1737. One finds here reference to an affidavit sworn by parishioner Margaret Burnside in August 1737 stating that on March 19, 1737 Wesley had reproved Mrs. Williamson for her insincerity.

30. Ibid., Journal for July 3, 1737.

31. In those days, for a single priest to court an eligible parishioner was not considered a breach of pastoral ethics. Nevertheless, the saga of John and Miss Sophy offers good reason to retain our current prohibition of such relationships.

32. *The Book of Common Prayer, 1662.* See http://www.eskimo.com/lhowell/ -bcp1662/baptism/index.html Accessed November 16, 2004.

33. *Works*, Volume 18, 190-91. Journal for August 16, 1737.
34. Ibid., Journal for September 2, 1737.
35. Ibid.
36. John Wesley, "The Duty of Constant Communion," 436-37.
37. Luke Tyerman, *The Life and Times of the Rev. John Wesley*, M.A. Volume I (New York: Harper and Brothers, Publishers, 1872), 168.
38. Whether Tyerman would agree or not, I would argue that the reforms of Vatican II represent a movement away from ritualism toward a deeper sacramental piety.
39. *The Works of John Wesley, Volume 20, Journals and Diaries III (1743–54)*. Ed. By W. Reginald Ward and Richard P. Heitzenrater. (Nashville: Abingdon, 1991), 305. Journal entry for September 30, 1749. My reading of Tyerman led me to this Journal entry. See Tyerman, *The Life and Times of the Rev. John Wesley, M.A.* Volume I, 151-52.
40. "The Scripture Way of Salvation," *The Works of John Wesley, Volume 2, Sermons II, 34-70*. Edited by Albert C. Outler (Nashville: Abingdon Press, 1985), 156-57.
41. Ibid., 166. In this text, Wesley called them "works of piety," which he defines as "public prayer, family prayer, and praying in our closet; receiving the Supper of the Lord; searching the Scriptures by hearing, reading, meditating; and using such a measure of fasting or abstinence as our bodily health allows."
42. I am grateful to Perkins student Doug Fox for pointing me to Wesley's Journal entry for June 27, 1740, in which Wesley describes Holy Communion as a "converting ordinance," that is, as an instrument God uses in bringing a sinner to faith in Jesus Christ.
43. *The Works of John Wesley, Volume 19*, 154-55, Journal entries for June 22 and June 23, 1740.
44. Ibid., 154, Journal entry for June 22, 1740.
45. Ibid., Journal entries for June 19 and June 22, 1740.
46. Ibid., Journal entry for June 24.
47. Ibid,, Journal entry for June 25.
48. Ibid., Journal entry for June 27.
49. Ibid.
50. Ibid.
51. Ibid.
52. Theodore H. Runyon, "The Importance of Experience for Faith," *Aldersgate Reconsidered*, edited by Randy L. Maddox (Nashville: Kingswood, 1990), 103-05.
53. *The Works of John Wesley, Volume 19*, 159, Journal entry for June 28.
54. John Wesley, "The Nature, Design, and General Rules of the United Societies in London, Bristol, Kingswood, and Newcastle-Upon-Tyne," *The Works of John Wesley, Volume 9, The Methodist Societies: History, Nature, and Design*, edited by Rupert E. Davies (Nashville: Abingdon Press, 1989), 70.

55. *The Works of John Wesley, Volume 9, The Methodist Societies: History, Nature, and Design,* 70-73.
56. Ibid, 70.

5. A PASSIONATE COMMITMENT AMONG METHODISTS

1. Lester Ruth, *A Little Heaven Below, Worship at Early Methodist Quarterly Meetings* (Nashville: Abingdon Press, 2000), 78-81, 163.
2. *Discipline,* 2000, paragraph 104, pages 76-82.
3. *Early Christian Fathers,* Richardson et. al., 175.
4. "The Didascalia of the Apostles" and "The Apostolic Constitutions" in *Springtime of the Liturgy,* ed. Lucien Deiss, 224.
5. See chapter 4. See also *The Book of Common Prayer, 1662.* http://www.eskimo.com/~lhowell/bcp1662/communion/index.html Accessed November 17, 2004.
   For another example, see John Calvin's "The Form of Church Prayers and Hymns with the Manner of Administering the Sacraments and Consecrating Marriage According to the Custom of the Ancient Church" in *Liturgies of the Western Church,* edited and introduced by Bard Thompson (Philadelphia: Fortress Press, 1961), 206.
6. Mark A. Noll, "Landmarkism, Landmark Baptists" in text found at http://MB-SOFT.com/believe/text/landmark.htm Accessed November 17, 2004.
   See also Old Landmarkism by J.R. Graves. http://www.pbministries.org/History/J.%20R.%20Graves/Old%20Landmarkism/old_landmarkism.htm Accessed November 17, 2004.
7. Waller, John Lightfoot, *Open Communion Shown to be Unscriptural and Deleterious* (Louisville: G.W. Robertson, 1859).
8. Ibid., 13.
9. Ibid., 18.
10. Ibid., 26.
11. Ibid., 59.
12. Ibid., 73-74.
13. Robert Hall, *On Terms of Communion; With a Particular View to the Case of the Baptists and Paedobaptists* (Boston: Wells and Lilly, 1816).
14. Ibid., iv.
15. Ibid., 13.
16. Ibid., 66.
17. Ibid., 96.
    Hall describes an odd kind of double language that remains at levels of contemporary church life. Christians proclaim the mutual recognition of baptism, and this is a significant ecumenical achievement. Nevertheless, these baptisms are not recognized as fully effective—that is, while a Catholic would consider a properly baptized United Methodist a fellow Christian, the major effect of that baptism, admission to Holy

Communion, is not offered. The baptism is recognized, but in a less-than-perfect manner. In like manner, in The United Methodist Church, gay and lesbian members are not excommunicated. Thus we insist that their baptism remains effective. Nevertheless, the church refuses to recognize the spiritual gifts for ordained ministry that may emerge from that baptism, thus setting aside Wesley's practice of discerning gifts and graces as the primary evidence of fitness for ministry. Again, their baptism is recognized, but in a less-than-perfect manner.

18. Ibid., 99.
19. Ibid., 38.
20. Ibid., 52-53.
21. Ibid., 72.
22. Samuel Worcester Whitney, *Open Communion, or, the Principles of Restricted Communion, Examined and Proved to be Unscriptural and False, In A Series of Letters to a Friend* (New York: M.W. Dodd, 1853).
23. Ibid., 30.
24. Ibid., 99-100.
25. Ibid., 78. Italics by Whitney.
26. Ibid., 81.
27. Ibid,, 114.
28. Ibid., 7.
29. Ibid., 106.
30. Review of *Open Communion* by S. W. Whitney. *Methodist Quarterly Review*, Vol. 7, No. 4 (1853), 617.
31. I have commented on representative sources. Other significant texts written by Baptists and others of a similar mindset include the following: G. H. (George Herbert) Orchard, *The History of Open Communion* (Nashville: South Western Publishing Company, 1857). He claimed that the Lord's Table was properly fenced from the beginning, since of the 120 disciples mentioned in the first chapter of Acts (who had been with Jesus from the beginning) only eleven of these communed with Jesus in the Upper Room (pp. 9-10). Particularly noticeable in his argument is the claim that those who opened the Table did so that they might have an easier life, avoiding censure and becoming more prosperous and acceptable (pp. 38-39). They practiced the open table as a way to avoid hardship and persecution.
J. B. Peat. *The Baptists Examined; or Common Sense on Baptism, Close Communion, and the Baptists.* Third Edition. (Chicago: Kenney and Sumner, 1869). My research assistant Tom Miles provides the following synopsis: "This is a very humorous book, written (presumably) by a Baptist, which purports to be an extended dialogue between a Methodist and a Presbyterian. Throughout the book the Presbyterian, who is depicted as a clear thinker, shares his wisdom with his Methodist friend. The Presbyterian, though he apparently remains a Presbyterian, can clearly see the hypocrisy of the pedobaptists, and with great wit and sympathy explains

to the Methodist what it is that the Baptists believe and their reasons for holding these beliefs. The Methodist invariably finds himself befuddled at the hypocrisy of pedobaptist churches such as his own, and always responds with something to the effect of 'Gee, I never realized we were so stupid. Of course we can't expect the Baptists to practice open communion.'"

Crammond Kennedy, *Close Communion or Open Communion? An Experience and an Argument* (New York: American News Company, 1868). The author grew up a Baptist under the closed communion arguments and became a Baptist preacher. Eventually he changed his ideas, moved by Jesus' command "Do this" and the fellowship he shared with other Christians (pp. 27-28).

Not all advocates of closed communion were Baptists. Some of the advocates were Campbellites. J. T. Pressley (sic., correct spelling is Pressly although the title lists the erroneous spelling), professor of the United Presbyterian Theological Seminary of Allegheny, Pennsylvania, presents an interesting case. In his book, *Close Communion: or, "Church fellowship"* (Cincinnati: William Scott, 1866), he argued for a communion open only to those who would subscribe to all of the principles expressed in the Westminster Standards.

32. Review of his Reply to "Evils of Infant Baptism" as it appeared in *Methodist Quarterly Review* 9:2 (April 1855), 304.

33. *Open Communion* 2nd edition (Philadelphia: Smith and Peters, 1858). His other titles are as follows:

     Baptism: Its Nature, Obligations, Modes, Subjects, and Benefits (Richmond, 1843).

     Experimental Religion: Embracing Justification, Regeneration, Sanctification, and the Witness of the Spirit (Richmond, 1854).

     Class Meetings (Richmond, 1855).

     Reply to "Evils of Infant Baptism" by Robert Boyle C. Howell, D.D. (Richmond, 1855).

     Recognition in Heaven (Richmond, 1856).

     Initial Life (Nashville: Southern Methodist Publishing House, 1885).

     A Reply to the "Problem of Methodism" (by Rev. J.M. Boland, D.D.) (Nashville: Publishing House of the Methodist Episcopal Church, South, 1889).

34. Review of *Open Communion. Methodist Quarterly Review* 12:4 (October 1858), 592.

35. Leonidas Rosser, *Open Communion*, 59. The Charles Wesley phrase is from the hymn, "Come, Sinners, to the Gospel Feast."

36. Along with the Church of England, Wesley believed that baptism placed a child in a regenerate state, but that this benefit was eventually lost through sin. See "The New Birth" in *The Words of John Wesley*, Volume 2, *Sermons II 34-70*, ed. Albert C. Outler (Nashville: Abingdon, 1985), 199-200.

     See also his *Journal* entry for May 24, 1738, in which he said, "I believe, till I was about ten years old I had not sinned away that 'washing of the Holy

Ghost' which was given me in baptism . . ." *The Works of John Wesley,* Volume 18, 242-43.

37. Rosser, 105-06.
38. Ibid., 237.
39. Ibid., 200.
40. Ibid., 27.
41. Ibid., 168.
42. Ibid., 169.
43. Ibid., 193.
44. Zachariah A. Parker, *The People's Hand-Book on Immersion, Infant Baptism, Close Communion and Plan of Salvation; or Justification by Water Versus Justification by Faith,* second edition (Nashville: Publishing House of the Methodist Episcopal Church, South, 1891).
45. See review of the first edition in *Methodist Quarterly Review* 22:1 (o.s.) 7:1 (n.s.) (January 1884), 139-40.
46. Parker, 52.
47. Peter Cartwright, *The Autobiography of Peter Cartwright,* Introduction by Charles L. Wallis (Nashville: Abingdon Press, 1984), 34.
48. Parker, 25-44.
49. Ibid., 32-34. Italics by Parker.
50. For instance, most scholars agree that the so-called Institution Narratives in the Gospels are not eyewitness accounts of the origins of the Eucharist. Rather, they reflect the developed practices of the faith communities that wrote them.
51. Ibid., 116-17.
52. Ibid., 133.
53. We have not, of course, exhausted the sources that discuss open communion and related issues.
   These occur in a variety of places, and they involve Methodists and other pedobaptists. One interesting text comes from eighteenth-century Scotland. The title of this pamphlet by Thomas Bennett is something of a dissertation in itself: *Terms of Communion Agreed Upon by the Scots Methodists: But Generally Known by the Specious Denomination of The Presbytery of Relief, Their Own Explanation of Said Terms, with Remarks Upon Both, In a letter From a Presbyterian to his Friend in Aberdeen. The Second Edition with the Addition of the 9th, 10th, and 11th Deductions and the Foot Note upon Deduction 5th* (Edinburgh, 1778). The Methodists, it seems, wanted to hold communion with all who held the essentials of the faith, but they did not specify these essentials. According to Bennett, however, the distinction itself is unbiblical (pp. 11-12). All that has been revealed in the Scriptures is essential, and Christians are to stay away from those who walk unsoundly (p. 12). This text is interesting in that it gives early evidence of a more open Methodist table, as well as a sharp critique of the practice from beyond Methodism. The Methodists were not, of course, advocating the communion of those who were not yet Christian.

Another interesting title comes from Rufus Anderson, an early nineteenth-century Congregationalist pastor in Salem, Massachusetts. *The Close Communion of the Baptists, in Principle and Practice, Proved to be Unscriptural, and of a Bad Tendency in the Church of God; in Seven Letters, Addressed to the Friends of Fundamental Truth, and of Practical Religion.* (Salem, MA: Joshua Cushing, 1805). Anderson was responding to a Baptist church planted in Salem in the year before he wrote this text (pp. 30-31). The argument is like many of the others we have noted in this chapter. According to the author, the Baptists and their insistence on baptism by immersion is the problem, yet he would be willing to grant them this practice if they would abandon their close communion practice (pp. 36-39). He appealed to the fellowship they shared at other times: "It is well known that Baptist ministers, in concurrence with their people, are in general willing to commune with their Paedobaptist brethren in the pulpit. And in words, as well as practice, they acknowledge our ministers to be ambassadors of Christ . . . My brethren of the close communion scheme, although you acknowledge them to be ambassadors of Christ, and invite them into your desk; yet you exclude them from your table!! Is this consistent? Is not baptism a prerequisite as much required for pulpit communion, as for table communion? It seems, therefore, that you give them some credit for their baptism" (pp. 23-24).

54. For further descriptions of the relationship of religious identity and piety, see the book by Linda J. Clark, Joanne Swenson, and Mark Stamm, *How We Seek God Together, Exploring Worship Style* (Bethesda, Maryland: The Alban Institute, 2001) and my article "Developing Congregational Style" in *Worship Matters, A United Methodist Guide to Ways to Worship*, Volume I, edited by E. Byron Anderson (Nashville: Discipleship Resources, 1999), 86-92.

55. According to the mission statement quoted on their Web site, "Reconciling Ministries Network is a national grassroots organization that exists to enable full participation of people of all sexual orientations and gender identities in the life of the United Methodist Church, both in policy and practice." http://www.rmnetwork.org Accessed November 17, 2004.

56. I am using pseudonyms for the names of the interview subjects and their congregations.

57. Stamm interview files, Houston interview #4.

58. Ibid.

59. Stamm interview files, Houston interview #2.

60. Stamm interview files, California interview #7.

61. Stamm interview files, California interviews #5 and #6.

62. Stamm interview files, California interview #10.

63. Stamm interview files, New Jersey interview #1.

64. Stamm interview files, Suburban Dallas interview #2.

65. Uncritical use of marketing language can have a similar deleterious effect on the conduct of evangelism.

66. Stamm interview files, Suburban Dallas interview #2.

67. Stamm interview files, Holy Pentecost Church interview #3.

68. Stamm interview files, Suburban Dallas interview #4.

69. Stamm interview files, California interview #2.

70. Stamm interview files, California interview #3.

71. Stamm interview files, New Jersey interview #3.

72. Stamm interview files, Suburban Dallas interview #1.

73. Stamm interview files, New Jersey interview #2.

74. Stamm interview files, Suburban Dallas interview #3.

75. Stamm interview files, California interview #1.

76. Stamm interview files, New Jersey interview #4.

77. Stamm interview files, Holy Pentecost Church interview #4.

78. Ibid.

79. Stamm interview files, New Jersey interview #1.

80. Eamon Duffy, *The Stripping of the Altars, Traditional Religion in England 1400–1580* (New Haven and London: Yale University Press, 1992), 94.

81. Stamm interview files, Holy Pentecost interview #3.

82. Stamm interview files, Houston interview #2.

83. Stamm interview files, Houston interview #2.

84. Stamm interview files, Houston interview #3.

85. Ibid.

86. Ibid.

87. Stamm interview files, California interview #3.

88. For an excellent discussion of this concept of religious affections see the book by Don E. Saliers, *The Soul in Paraphrase, Prayer and the Religious Affections* (Akron, Ohio: OSL Publications, 1991).

89. The chancel rail at St. Luke's is placed at the end of a long, narrow nave. Three steps above the rail one comes to a split chancel with pulpit and lectern. Choir space is arranged behind these. The high altar stands on the back wall. In an earlier day, the celebrant would have offered the Eucharistic Prayer at that high altar, with his back to the people. The insights brought forth by the Liturgical Movement and Vatican II have influenced pastors to bring the altar-table closer to the congregation and to face them across it. In many cases, St. Luke's being one of them, portable altar-tables are now used for the Great Thanksgiving. St. Luke's retains the high altar as sacred prayer space.

90. Stamm interview files, California interview #3.

91. Stamm interview files, New Jersey interview #5.

92. Stamm interview files, Houston interview #5.

93. Stamm interview files, California interview #9.

94. Stamm interview files, Suburban Dallas interview #5.

95. Advertising campaigns for United States military service have used the call to adventure and ordeal as an enticement. In like manner, advertising for some high-end products challenges people to spend more that they may

acquire something of higher value. Regardless of what we may think of military service and such products, they indicate that it is possible to make high demands in a culturally relevant manner.

96. Stamm interview files, California interview #6.

97. For a discussion of the issues related to celiac disease, a debilitating condition caused by a severe allergic reaction to wheat gluten, see the article by Wanda Zemler-Cizewski, "The Eucharist and the Consequences of Celiac Disease: A Question of Access to Holy Communion," *Worship* 74:3 (May 2000), 237-47.

98. Stamm interview files, Suburban Dallas interview #5.

99. Stamm interview files, Suburban Dallas interview #1.

100. Stamm interview files, Suburban Dallas interview #1.

101. Stamm interview files, California interview #3.

102. Stamm interview files, California interview #7.

103. Stamm interview files, California interview #2.

104. Ibid.

105. Ibid.

106. Young children (sometimes even infants) are admitted to communion in most United Methodist congregations. This practice, which I support, has emerged in relatively recent times. I discuss some of the theological implications of communing children in the following article: "Christian Initiation on Two Tracks: Reflections on Liturgical Piety and Practice Among United Methodist Evangelicals," *Worship* 77:4 (July 2003): 308-25.

107. Stamm interview files, Suburban Dallas interview #2.

108. The early drafts of *By Water and the Spirit* called the church to eliminate confirmation, both the term and the practice. When many protested this move, the framers of the document insisted that confirmation was a relatively recent practice in the church. Those claims are both correct and incorrect. On an official level, they are correct. Although the Church of England practiced it, John Wesley did not include confirmation in *The Sunday Service*. See *John Wesley's Prayer Book: The Sunday Service of the Methodists in North America* with introduction, notes, and commentary by James F. White (Cleveland: OSL Publications, 1991).

The Methodist Church did not use the term in its official ritual until *The Book of Worship* of 1964. *The Book of Worship for Church and Home* (Nashville: The Methodist Publishing House, 1964), 12-14. Testimonies like that by Mr. Sachs, however, indicate that the practice of confirmation, and its name, existed on the local church level long before 1964.

109. Stamm interview files, California interview # 7.

110. Ibid.

111. Ibid.

112. Stamm interview files, California interview #7.

113. As I reflect on Carlton's story about Hattie, I am reminded of the analysis that Joanne Swenson, my colleague on the Boston University Music, Worship,

and Religious Identity Project, made of the Community United Methodist Church in Byfield, Massachusetts. After spending a year observing that small rural United Methodist congregation, she described their experience of God by drawing on images from a meeting of their Nurturing Committee. At that meeting, women sat around a kitchen table preparing greeting cards for church members and friends, some of whom were experiencing celebrations and some times of difficulty. Pregnant at the time of the meeting, Joanne felt their concern with particular poignancy. As the committee members moved through their agenda in a casual and less than businesslike manner, much more like a coffee klatch than a formal meeting, their children kept running in and out of the kitchen through a screen door that led to the back porch and beyond. As Joanne saw it, their images of God and church were reflected in that meeting. God's church was like that house with the swinging screen door, where all persons are welcomed unconditionally. Such perceptions abound in Methodist congregations, and they are ritualized in the invitation to the Lord's Table. Clark, Swenson, and Stamm, *How We Seek God Together*, 29-42.

114. Stamm interview files, Holy Pentecost Interview #4.
115. Ibid.
116. Ibid.
117. Stamm interview files, New Jersey interview #3.
118. Ibid.
119. Ibid.
120. Ibid.
121. When those who were invited first made their excuses, the servants were told to go and "bring in the poor, the crippled, the blind, and the lame" (Luke 14:21b). To use the language of the contemporary church growth movement, those in greatest need were Jesus' "target audience."
122. See "The Order for the Administration of The Sacrament of the Lord's Supper or Holy Communion" in *The Book of Worship for Church and Home* (Nashville: The Methodist Publishing House, 1964), 19.
 The phrase, of course, originates with Thomas Cranmer and *The Book of Common Prayer* (1549) and has been a part of the English speaking liturgical tradition since that time. http://www.justus.anglican.org/resources/bcp/1549/Communion_1549.htm Accessed November 17, 2004.
123. Stamm interview files, New Jersey interview #5.
124. *Discipline, 2000*, paragraph 161, p. 101.
125. Ibid.
126. Stamm interview files, New Jersey interview #5.
127. Ibid.

6. OPEN TABLE AND THE SUFFERING OF JESUS

1. *The Book of Hymns*, 830, p. 15.
2. In "A Service of Word and Table IV" (1989) the prayer of oblation has been

moved to the position immediately following the Words of Institution, the place it held in *The Book of Common Prayer* 1549. We should not, however, speak of this move as if it were the correction of an error. See *The Worship Resources of the United Methodist Hymnal, Introduction to the General Services, Psalter, and Other Acts of Worship*, ed. Hoyt L. Hickman (Nashville: Abingdon Press, 1989), 80.

In Cranmer's 1552 rite, the oblation was moved to the position following communion (the position it held for Methodists through the 1966 text). It had been moved for a clear theological purpose, to avoid connecting the communion elements themselves with the language of sacrifice and offering. Sacrificial language that had to do with the church's offering was spoken after communion, making it clear that the church was not offering Christ's body and blood as a new propitiatory sacrifice. The acceptable sacrifice was one of thanksgiving and discipleship ("our souls and bodies").

3. *The Book of Hymns*, 830, p. 17.
4. *The United Methodist Hymnal*, 9.
5. Ibid., 10.
6. Ibid.
7. Compare *The Book of Hymns*, #830-17.
8. *The United Methodist Hymnal*, 11, 15. Since one speaks the words of delivery while holding either bread or chalice, and not a hymnal, it is likely that servers will speak these words from memory or, as it were, from the heart. The liturgical writer who believes that his or her *text* will decisively shape the words of delivery may be overly optimistic.
9. James F. White, "Word and Table I Commentary," 1:41 through 1:42.
10. Ibid.
11. Robert Brian Peiffer, *How Contemporary Liturgies Evolve: The Revision of United Methodist Liturgical Texts (1968–1988)* (Unpublished Ph. D. dissertation, University of Notre Dame, 1993), 210-11; 268.
12. *United Methodist Hymnal*, 30. Compare to *The Book of Hymns*, #830, p. 15. The form in *The United Methodist Hymnal* has been sanitized from the version endorsed by John Wesley in 1784. In Wesley's version, the final sentence reads "Grant us therefore, gracious Lord, so to eat the flesh of thy dear Son Jesus Christ, and to drink his blood, that our sinful bodies may be made clean by his body, and our souls washed through his most precious blood, and that we may evermore dwell in him, and he in us." Note the increased sacramental realism in Wesley's text—the language about eating flesh and drinking blood. This language is far more graphic than the phrase "so to partake of this Sacrament..." found in "Word and Table IV." See *John Wesley's Prayer Book: The Sunday Service of the Methodists in North America*, with introduction, notes, and commentary by James F. White (Cleveland: O.S.L. Publications, 1991), 135. The version in *The Book of Common Prayer* (1979) Rite II is more like Wesley's version. The original version (1548) was as follows:

"We do not presume to come to this thy Table (O merciful Lord) trusting in our own righteousness, but in thy manifold and great mercies. We be not worthy so much as to gather up the crumbs under thy Table. But thou art the same Lord, whose property is always to have mercy: Grant us therefore, gracious Lord, so to eat the Flesh of thy dear Son Jesus Christ, and to drink his Blood, in these holy Mysteries, that we may continually dwell in him, and he in us, that our sinful bodies may be made clean by his Body, and our souls washed through his most precious Blood. Amen."
http://www.justus.anglican.org/resources/bcp/Communion_1548.htm Accessed November 18, 2004.

13. *The Hymnal 1982* (New York: The Church Hymnal Corporation, 1985), S-157 through S-166.

14. *Prayers We Have in Common*, International Consultation on English Texts. Second Revised Edition. (Philadelphia: Fortress Press, 1975), 17. The classic text is as follows:
O Lamb of God, that takest away the sins of the world, have mercy upon us.
O Lamb of God, that takest away the sins of the world, have mercy upon us.
O Lamb of God, that takest away the sins of the world, grant us thy peace.
The Book of Common Prayer, 1979, 337. *The United Methodist Hymnal*, 30-31.

15. Betty Pulkingham, "Jesus, Lamb of God," copyright © 1974 in *Fresh Sounds*, compiled by Betty Pulkingham and Jeanne Harper (Grand Rapids, Mich.: William B. Eerdmans Publishing Company, 1976, 41.

16. James F. White, *Sacraments as God's Self-Giving* (Nashville: Abingdon, 1983).

17. Edward Schillebeeckx, *Christ the Sacrament of the Encounter with God* (Kansas City, Missouri: Sheed Andrews and McMeel, 1963), 44.

18. Stamm, *Sacraments and Discipleship*, 92-95.

19. *The United Methodist Hymnal*, 34.

20. "Ignatius to the Smyrnaeans," trans. Lightfoot and Harmer, *Apostolic Fathers* (1891 translation), 2:1-3:1. http://www.earlychristianwritings.com/text/ignatius-smyrnaeans-lightfoot.html Accessed November 18, 2004.

21. Ibid, 6:2.

22. *The United Methodist Hymnal*, 880.

23. *The Book of Common Prayer* (1552).
http://justus.anglican.org/resources/bcp/1552/Communion_1552.htm Accessed December 15, 2004.

24. John Calvin, *The Form of Church Prayers*, Jasper and Cuming. *Prayers of the Eucharist*, 216.

25. See, for instance, Gordon W. Lathrop, *Holy Ground, A Liturgical Cosmology* (Minneapolis: Fortress Press, 2003), 139, 142.

26. Eugene LaVerdiere, *The Eucharist in the New Testament and the Early Church* (Collegeville, Minn.: The Liturgical Press, 1996), 48-50.

27. Lathrop, *Holy Ground*, 30-38.

28. Raymond E. Brown, *The Death of the Messiah, From Gethsemane to the*

Grave, A Commentary on the Passion Narratives in the Four Gospels, Volume One (New York: Doubleday, 1994), 170.

29. John Thornburg, unpublished reflection in conversation with the author, September 2002.
30. Eamon Duffy, *The Stripping of the Altars, Traditional Religion in England 1400–1580* (New Haven, Conn.: Yale University Press, 1992), 389.
31. *Book of Common Prayer* 1552. Compare *United Methodist Hymnal,* 28.
32. *Book of Common Prayer* 1552. Compare *United Methodist Hymnal,* 29.
33. *The United Methodist Hymnal,* 10.
34. Ibid.
35. Although the 1745 collection of *Hymns on the Lord's Supper* contains the most original and creative Wesleyan reflections on the Eucharist, these hymns have found surprisingly little usage in United Methodist circles. The inclusion of "Victim Divine" in *The Faith We Sing* makes it the third of the 166 *Hymns on the Lord's Supper* in official United Methodist hymnals. "O Thou Who This Mysterious Bread" (*UMH* 613) and "O the Depth of Love Divine" (*UMH,* 627) are the others.
36. According to Hoyt Hickman, White had previously urged its inclusion in the 1989 hymnal and the committee was willing to do so but they could not find a suitable hymn tune.
37. The full five stanzas are found in *The Faith We Sing,* (Nashville: Abingdon Press), 2259. Some relatively minor changes have been made for the sake of inclusion.
38. J. Ernest Rattenbury, *The Eucharistic Hymns of John and Charles Wesley.* American edition, Timothy J. Crouch, O.S.L., editor (Akron, Ohio: OSL Publications, 1990, 1996), 189, #116, stanzas 1, 2, 4.
39. Ibid., 191, #122, stanza 3.
40. Ibid., 191, #124, stanza 3.
41. Ibid., 193, #131, stanza 1.
42. See also Matthew 26:31, 56, 58, and 27:55. See also Luke 23:49.
43. Rattenbury, *Eucharistic Hymns,* 193, #131, stanza 2.
44. Ibid, 193, #131, stanza 3.
45. Ibid., 193, #131, stanza 4.
46. Ibid., 196, #141, stanzas 1, 4-8.

7. FORMATION AS A MEANS OF GRACE

1. See Stamm, *Sacraments and Discipleship,* 33-39.
2. "The Nature, Design, and General Rules of the United Societies in London, Bristol, Kingswood, and Newcastle upon Tyne (1743)" in *The Works of John Wesley,* Volume 9, *The Methodist Societies: History, Nature, and Design,* edited by Rupert E. Davies (Nashville: Abingdon Press, 1989), 69.
3. Ibid., 70.
4. Ibid., 70-1.

5. Ibid., 71.

As the note by Rupert P. Davies indicates, however, the proscription of "costly apparel" is biblical, based on First Peter 3:3. The remainder of Wesley's prohibition is an extrapolation upon that verse from First Peter.

6. Ibid., 72.

7. Ibid.

8. Ibid., 72-3.

9. Ibid., 73.

10. Ibid.

11. "A Short History of the People Called Methodists" in *The Works of John Wesley*. Volume 9, 484-85.

12. Ignatius of Antioch, *To the Ephesians* in *Early Christian Fathers*, edited by Cyril C. Richardson (New York: Macmillan Publishing Company, 1970), 93.

13. I discuss this dynamic in *Sacraments and Discipleship*, 117-22. The well-known claim of Stanley Hauerwas and William Willimon that Christians are "resident aliens" expresses a similar insight. *Resident Aliens, Life in the Christian Colony* (Nashville: Abingdon Press, 1989).

14. Aidan Kavanagh, *The Shape of Baptism: The Rite of Christian Initiation* (New York: Pueblo Publishing Company, 1978), 186.

15. Stamm, *Sacraments and Discipleship*, 35-36.

16. *Rite of Christian Initiation of Adults, Study Edition* (Chicago: Liturgy Training Publications, 1988), 14.

17. Stamm interview files, New Jersey interview #2.

18. Stamm interview files, California interview #7.

19. *The United Methodist Hymnal*, 26.

20. For a United Methodist position, see Daniel T. Benedict, Jr., *Come to the Waters, Baptism and Our Ministry of Welcoming Seekers and Making Disciples* (Nashville: Discipleship Resources, 1996).

For the Episcopal Church pattern, see *The Catechumenal Process, Adult Initiation and Formation for Christian Life and Ministry* (New York: The Church Hymnal Corporation, 1990).

21. *Rite of Christian Initiation of Adults*, paragraph 116, pages 59-61.

22. "The General Rules," in *Works of John Wesley*, Volume 9, 73.

23. Lester Ruth, *A Little Heaven Below, Worship at Early Methodist Quarterly Meetings* (Nashville: Kingswood Books, 2000), 114. For further discussion of issues related to slaveholding and manumission requirements among early Methodists, see also pages 110, 126, 170.

24. For instance, some churches continue to arrive at differing conclusions on the matter of just war and the just use of lethal force. *The Apostolic Tradition* insisted that soldiers can join the church, but only if they refuse to take the military oath and do not serve as an executioner. See *The Apostolic Tradition*, Dix, ed., 26. Although the United Methodist Church opposes war and seeks peaceful resolution of conflict, church members may serve in the mil-

itary. Pastors are called to counsel members who are considering military service, presenting them with possible alternatives. *Discipline 2000*, paragraph 164.G and 331.1.l.

25. Smith, *From Symposium to Eucharist*, 173-217. Smith insists that the Christian Eucharist is a development of the ancient symposium pattern, a set of conventions governing banquets and related issues like invitations and after-dinner conversations. According to Smith, the arguments in First Corinthians are best understood against the background of the symposium.

26. I am indebted to Kenneth Hein's book *Eucharist and Excommunication, A Study in Early Christian Doctrine and Discipline* (Frankfurt, Germany: Herbert Lang Bern and Peter Lang Frankfurt, 1973) for showing me the relationship of these passages to the topic of excommunication.

27. Ibid., 281.

28. Ibid., 302.

29. Ibid., 384.

30. http://justus.anglican.org/resources/bcp/1549/Communion_1549.htm Accessed November 18, 2004.

31. Bard Thompson, *Liturgies of the Western Church*, 206.

32. See other examples in Thompson: Martin Luther (p. 116), Ulrich Zwingli (p. 153), *BCP* 1549 (p. 249), John Knox (p. 301), *The Westminster Directory* (p. 368).

33. Dietrich Bonhoeffer, *The Cost of Discipleship*, revised and unabridged edition containing material not previously translated (New York: Collier Books, Macmillan Publishing Company, 1963, first published in 1937), 47.

34. Ibid. 326-28.

35. Ibid., 328.

36. Laurence Hull Stookey, *Baptism, Christ's Act in the Church* (Nashville: Abingdon Press, 1982), 80-81.

37. *The United Methodist Hymnal*, 7.

38. Scott J. Jones, *United Methodist Doctrine, The Extreme Center* (Nashville: Abingdon Press, 2002), 41.

39. *Services for the Ordering of Ministry in The United Methodist Church*, prepared by the General Board of Discipleship and the General Board of Higher Education and Ministry in collaboration with the Council of Bishops, Adopted by the 2004 General Conference, 20-22. http://www.gbod.org/worship/ default.asp?act=reader&item_id=11789. Accessed December 15, 2004.

40. Jones, *United Methodist Doctrine*, 294.

41. *Psalter Hymnal* (Grand Rapids: CRC Publications, 1987), 964.

42. Ibid.

43. Ibid., 988.

44. *Psalter Hymnal Handbook* (Grand Rapids, Mich.: GRC Publications, 1988), 847.

45. Ibid., 988.
46. Ibid., 989.
47. Ibid., 990-91.
48. *Discipline*, 2000, paragraphs 2701-2719.
49. Ibid., paragraph 165.C.
50. Ibid., paragraph 161.G.
51. Stamm, *Sacraments and Discipleship*, 42.

8. OPEN TABLE AND HOSPITALITY

1. Rattenbury, *Eucharistic Hymns*, hymn 101, 185-86.
2. Colman McCarthy, "An Easter Celebrator," *The Washington Post*, 19 April 1987, Section D, 7.
3. We knew Mike from that day until he died from lung cancer in 1999, still a resident of the Scott House. He preached at First Church on several occasions and some persons remained in correspondence with him. For further information on his life and death, see the following article: Colman McCarthy, "Michael Kirwan Dies; Catholic Worker for Washington's Poor," *The Washington Post*, 13 November 1999, Metro Section, page B07.
4. Sheila Durkin Dierks and Patricia Powers Ladley, *Catholic Worker Houses* (Kansas City, MO: Sheed and Ward, 1988), 1-11.
5. Jim Forest, *Love is the Measure, A Biography of Dorothy Day* (New York: Paulist Press, 1986), 2-3.
6. Ibid., 89.
7. Keith F. Pecklers, *The Unread Vision, the Liturgical Movement in the United States of America, 1926–1955* (Collegeville, Minn.: The Liturgical Press, 1998), 104-113.
8. In the marriage liturgies of the Eastern Orthodox tradition, the bride and groom are given crowns as part of the ceremony. Why so? It is not, as some narcissistic moderns might presume, that the occasion of their wedding makes them king and queen for a day. Hardly. The nuptial crowns evoke the crowns given to martyrs (see Revelation 4:4-10, see also 7:9-17). They point to the sacrifices one must make in hospitably receiving a spouse and the children that are likely to follow. Mark Searle and Kenneth W. Stevenson, *Documents of the Marriage Liturgy* (Collegeville, Minn.: The Liturgical Press, 1992), 68-69, 268.
9. This list of characteristics is my own summary of Asperger Syndrome, based on my readings and interaction with AS itself. It is that of a concerned layperson. For a more scientific description of AS, see the O.A.S.I.S. (Online Asperger Syndrome Information and Support) Web site.
http://www.udel.edu/bkirby/asperger/ Accessed November 22, 2004.
Other important sources are the following:
Patricia Romanowski Bashe and Barbara L. Kirby, *The OASIS Guide to Asperger Syndrome, Advice, Support, Insight, and Inspiration* (New York: Crown Publishers, 2001).

Rebekah Heinrichs, *Perfect Targets: Asperger Syndrome and Bullying, Practical Solutions for Surviving the Social World* (Shawnee Mission, Kansas: Autism Asperger Publishing Company, 2003).

10. One can find a brilliant attempt at expressing such understanding in Mark Haddon's novel, *The Curious Incident of the Dog in the Night-Time* (New York: Doubleday, 2003). Haddon tells the story from the perspective of a child with AS. Haddon resists the AS label, however, saying that he prefers the term "odd." He said, "In the old days you were allowed to be odd...Too many people now who would have been odd find themselves with a label and getting sucked into some kind of system." See review by David Noonan published in *Newsweek*, September 8, 2003. Accessed September 2, 2004 from http://www.bridges4kids.org.
    The church should be the place where the odd ones are welcomed.

11. Patricia Romanowski Bashe and Barbara L. Kirby, *The OASIS Guide to Asperger Syndrome, Advice, Support, Insight, and Inspiration* (New York: Crown Publishers, 2001), 431-35.

12. "The grace of our Lord Jesus Christ, the love of God, and the communion of the Holy Spirit be with you." Compare with *Mil Voces Para Celebrar, Himnario Metodista* (Nashville: The United Methodist Publishing House, 1996), 17.

13. Jeff Painter, "A Former Homosexual Testifies to the Gospel of the Grace of God," *Good News* 16:1 (July–August 1982): 30, 47-49. James S. Robb, "Showing Homosexuals a Way Out . . . They can change, says Russ McCraw," *Good News* 17:3 (November-December 1983): 18-23.

14. Another relevant article is "Healing for the Homosexual," by Rick Grant, *Good News* 19:1 (July-August 1985): 10-16. Grant's is less of a testimonial article than the other two mentioned above. He noted the importance of accepting Christ as a factor in the "healing" of a homosexual (pp. 14-15). Yet he also acknowledged the necessity of accountability structures as part of the healing process.

15. *Discipline*, 2000, paragraph 161.G.

16. Ibid., paragraphs 304.3, 806.9.

17. Ibid., 188.

18. Ibid., 216.1. This vow and the others listed in *The Discipline* come from The United Methodist Service of the Baptismal Covenant, *The United Methodist Hymnal*, 34.

19. James S. Robb, "Bishop Dies of AIDS; Gay Activity Denied," *Good News* 21:1 (July-August 1987): 41.

20. Ibid., 41-42.

21. James V. Heidinger II, "Bishop Crutchfield, AIDS and Methodism," *Good News* 21:1 (July-August, 1987): 6.

22. Robb, 42.

23. See the discussion in my article "What is an Order? Reflections on the

Vocation of Elders and Deacons," *Quarterly Review* 24:4 (Winter 2004), 337-49.

24. See a discussion of these issues in *Becoming Gay, the Journey to Self-Acceptance* by Richard A. Isay, M.D. (New York: Henry Holt and Company, 1996), 3-9.

25. Richard B. Hays insists that the church's preoccupation with homosexuality has caused it to avoid much weightier issues such as the war of aggression in Iraq. See "A Season of Repentance: An Open Letter to United Methodists," *The Christian Century* 121:17 (August 24, 2004):8-9.

9. A GENEROUS READING OF THE FINAL RUBRIC

1. Gordon Lathrop, *Holy Things, A Liturgical Theology* (Minneapolis: Fortress Press, 1993), 33-36, 64-66, etc.

2. *The United Methodist Hymnal*, 39, 43, 49, compare 53. See also *The United Methodist Book of Worship*, 94, 99, 102, 105, and 110, compare 114.

3. *This Holy Mystery*, 15.

4. Ibid. *By Water and the Spirit, A United Methodist Understanding of Baptism*, in *The Book of Resolutions of the United Methodist Church* (Nashville: The United Methodist Publishing House, 2000), 814.

5. See the Service of Holy Communion in *The Book of Common Prayer*, 1549. http://justus.anglican.org/resources/bcp/1549/BCP_1549.htm Accessed September 28, 2004. The registration rubric continued in *The Book of Common Prayer* 1662 and was a key dynamic in the Sophie Hopkey fiasco (see chapter 4). To compare versions of *The Book of Common Prayer* see the immensely helpful Web site http://justus.anglican.org/resources/bcp/ Accessed September 28, 2004.

6. *The United Methodist Book of Worship*, 374.

7. *The United Methodist Hymnal*, 36.

8. Stamm interview files, Houston interview #5.

9. Stamm interview files, California interview #3.

10. *The United Methodist Hymnal*, 39.

11. See the Roman Catholic *Rite of Christian Initiation of Adults*. For a United Methodist adaptation of the catechumenate, see the book by Daniel T. Benedict, Jr., *Come to the Waters, Baptism and Our Ministry of Welcoming Seekers and Making Disciples* (Nashville: Discipleship Resources, 1996). Note my discussion of this topic in *Sacraments and Discipleship*, 33-43.

12. Portions of this list first appeared in my paper "The Challenge of the Open Table for the Reform of United Methodist Sacramental Life: Practices and Prospects," *Proceedings, North American Academy of Liturgy Annual Meeting*, Manhattan, New York (January 3-6, 2004), 135-36.

Index